THE NEW HANDSHAKE

THE NEW HANDSHAKE

Sales Meets Social Media

JOAN C. CURTIS AND BARBARA GIAMANCO

 PRAEGER

AN IMPRINT OF ABC-CLIO, LLC
Santa Barbara, California • Denver, Colorado • Oxford, England

Library of Congress Cataloging-in-Publication Data

Curtis, Joan C., 1950–
   The new handshake : sales meets social media / Joan C. Curtis and Barbara Giamanco.
    p. cm.
   Includes bibliographical references and index.
   ISBN 978–0–313–38271–0 (hbk. : alk. paper) — ISBN 978–0–313–38272–7 (ebook)
  1. Selling.   2. Social media.   3. Internet marketing.   4. Target marketing.
I. Giamanco, Barbara.   II. Title.
HF5438.25.C87   2010
658.8′72—dc22   2010011354

ISBN: 978–0–313–38271–0
EISBN: 978–0–313–38272–7

14 13 12 11 10   1 2 3 4 5

This book is also available on the World Wide Web as an eBook.
Visit www.abc-clio.com for details.

Praeger
An Imprint of ABC-CLIO, LLC

ABC-CLIO, LLC
130 Cremona Drive, P.O. Box 1911
Santa Barbara, California 93116-1911

This book is printed on acid-free paper ∞

Manufactured in the United States of America

Contents

Acknowledgments   vii

Introduction   ix

PART ONE: THE EVOLUTION OF SELLING AND BUYERS   1

Chapter 1: The Evolution of Sales   3

Chapter 2: The Evolution of Buyers and Online Communication   13

Chapter 3: The Wild, Wild West of Social Media   21

Chapter 4: What Are You Waiting For?   29

Chapter 5: Consultative Selling: Make New Friends but Keep the Old   43

Chapter 6: What Does Your Social Media Customer Look Like?   53

Chapter 7: Developing the Corporate Mindset   63

Chapter 8: Charting Your Course: The Three P's: Purpose, Plan, People   73

PART TWO: SOCIAL MEDIA OUTLETS—WHAT WORKS BEST WHEN AND HOW TO BEGIN   87

Chapter 9: Sales Meets Facebook   89

Chapter 10: Sales Meets LinkedIn   97

Chapter 11: Sales Meets Twitter 109

Chapter 12: You Digg It, I'm Delicious, We All StumbleUpon 119

Chapter 13: The Blogosphere 127

Chapter 14: Netiquette 141

PART THREE: DEVELOPING A SOCIAL MEDIA SALES STRATEGY 155

Chapter 15: The First 15 Days of the 30-Day Social Media Sales
Challenge: What You Need to Do to Get Started Now 157

Chapter 16: Seeing the Finish Line: Meeting the 30-Day Social Media
Sales Challenge 171

Postscript: Accessibility and Customer Service—When Technology
Fails Us 181

Appendix: Resource Guide 183

Notes 187

Index 195

Acknowledgments

I would like to dedicate my part of this book to my mom, Isabelle O'Neal. She is a woman who has never stopped learning. She taught me the value of embracing everything new and not shying away from nor fearing risk. My mom never met a "gadget" she didn't love, whether it was a computer, a hand-held device, or a bread maker. Even in her most senior years, she sends me e-mails regularly. She embodies everything we talk about in *The New Handshake*. Rather than let her mind atrophy, she is willing to take the risk and try something new and different.

I would also like to thank my writing partner, Barb Giamanco. Barb worked hard on this project and shared much of her knowledge of sales. She never shied from a task and she delivered the goods whenever asked. Together we made a formidable team. —J.C.

* * *

I will begin by acknowledging my writing partner in crime, Joan Curtis. Without Joan's book experience, writing guidance, and steady prodding to hit our deadlines, seeing my name on the cover of a book might never have happened. What was the flash of an initial idea is now a reality. Thanks, Joan!

Capturing the concepts buzzing around in my head and transforming them into words that made business sense was not always easy. To R. Mark Moore, I say "thank you, thank you, thank you for all the hours you spent listening to me talk it out!" I appreciate your patience, your calming support when I felt out of my league as a writer, and your technical guidance and contributions to our project.

Finally, I want to acknowledge my mother, Arlene. My obsessive love of reading and quest for knowledge is her fault! She believed that learning continued long past graduation day, and I am so glad that she instilled that passion in me. Sadly, Mom passed away earlier this year and will never read our book, but I know that she is proud of me for turning a longstanding personal goal into a physical reality. —B.G.

Introduction

Mark Cuban, billionaire entrepreneur and chairman of HDNet Television, says, "In the Internet age, executives have to learn how to shape information about themselves and their companies, or the Internet will do it for them, and it won't be pretty."[1]

According to Scoble and Israel in *Naked Conversations*, we are facing a revolution in the way businesses and customers communicate.[2] The authors make a compelling case for how the blogosphere has changed the way businesses talk to one another, their customers, their partners, their vendors, their employees, their investors, and the media. We will discuss the evolution of the blog and the impact of blogging on sales in Chapter 13. Today's businesses face an even greater challenge than the blog, and that is the power of social media. The sales and marketing components of business feel the impact of this revolution more intensely than any other sector. A new trend in the way companies are doing business is emerging. Companies must move quickly to adapt to this next generation of sales, currently being dubbed Sales 2.0®.[3] According to Axel Schultze, chief executive officer of Xeesm.com, "Whatever sales approach used to work doesn't work anymore. Scripts and canned speeches about features and benefits fall on deaf ears. Sales need to be visible, proactively engaged and patient."[4] Will you be ready to respond to the pace of change?

The New Handshake offers an alternative to the traditional sales approach and provides the tools and strategies for doing so. The premise of *The New*

Handshake is that in the midst of this communication revolution sales must adopt a new approach that incorporates social media. When we overturn the old business practices, what emerges is something one person called "smarketing." Sales and marketing no longer work as two separate entities. Instead, they work in tandem. According to Anneke Seley, author of *Sales 2.0*, we are experiencing a complete corporate cultural overhaul in which the lines of sales and marketing are becoming more and more blurry. This is the essence of *The New Handshake: Sales Meets Social Media*. Seley and Holloway made a great case for the transition from Sales 1.0 to Sales 2.0 in their book, and they discussed the need for corporate readiness before such a move can happen. They introduced a wider use of the telephone and the Web for sales functions. These steps paved the way for the next major step in the process: the social media. In an October 23, 2009 blog post titled "What Is Social Selling," Axel Schultze said "social selling is a sales technique that leverages social media, to get and maintain a 360 degree picture of the clients and their influencer on an ongoing basis. It allows salespeople to manage and maintain five times as many active customers compared to traditional techniques."[5]

In any organization, sales keep the engine humming. Without sales, company operations will grind slowly to a halt and eventually stop completely. *The New Handshake* represents an emergence of a sales approach that blends consultative selling and relationship selling with the use of technology and social media tools. By consultative selling we mean selling that consults with customers to uncover customer needs. By relationship selling we mean creating a strong relationship before pushing products onto customers. Relationship selling characterizes business-to-business (B2B) selling. In the past, sales pushed products onto customers under the assumption that the company knew more about what was good for them than they did. The move toward more consultative selling emerged in the late 1970s. Combining consultative selling with the tools of the social media creates a new evolution in sales that began with Sales 2.0. That evolution in sales is driven by a new set of buyers. Most people now refer to an evolution in buying versus an evolution in sales. As buyers change the way they purchase, sales must respond with practices that meet those buying needs.

As with any major change, people tend to overreact. The overreaction takes two forms: they toss out everything that smacks of the past or they ignore the new trends and label them as passing fads. For companies to succeed in this new sales environment, however, business leaders must recognize that it will require much more than simply updating existing customer relationship management (CRM) systems. Slapping new technology onto outdated processes and mindsets simply gets you more of the same lackluster results. As Seley and Holloway point out, Sales 2.0 requires a cultural shift.

Fifty years ago a salesperson probably had five customer interactions a week. That same salesperson 10 years ago increased individual customer interactions to 50 or more. Today, with the introduction of the social media, a salesperson could interact with a customer 50 times a day—and some people might consider that a conservative number. We now have communication tools that are flexible enough for immediate response and interaction. According to Shirky in *Here Comes Everybody,* "we are in the middle of a remarkable increase in our ability to share, to cooperate with one another and to take collective action, all outside the framework of traditional institutions and organizations."[6] There is no reason to believe that these communication tools cannot be used to generate sales.

How have people selected products to buy over the centuries? The most effective means for buying has always been by word-of-mouth. Imagine Person A has 12,000 followers on Twitter. Imagine that person finding your product so valuable he Tweets about it to his 12,000 followers. Now, imagine Person B reads that Tweet and decides to "ReTweet" it to her 8,000 followers. Person C sees Person B's Tweet and Tweets about your product to his 10,000 followers and so on. This is word-of-mouth at its best. These thousands of people got exposure to your product, and it cost you nothing! Word-of-mouth and engagement have always been the most effective ways to sell products. Today, the social media offer tools that mimic word of mouth on steroids. What an opportunity for sales! Before you get too excited, though, we must examine the best way to employ these tools. Much depends on your product, your customer, and your orientation to Sales 2.0.

President Barack Obama did more than make history as the first African-American president. He showed us how to combine the old handshake with the social media. He created a *new handshake* in the world of politics. The Obama presidential team integrated social media with all forms of media to achieve success. They recognized that the old-fashioned form of politics would not put Barack Obama in the White House. They also recognized the potential of the social media. Taking a huge risk, they enlisted the help of experts in the new world of social communication. There they created an army of supporters with over 13 million people on an e-mail list as well as 5 million people connected as friends on social network sites, including 3 million on Facebook alone.[7] Barack Obama traveled the country, shook hands, made speeches, and cultivated donors. Combining these tried-and-true methods with the new methods of communication, his team built a following never before seen on the political scene. John McCain called his opponent a rock star. Obama became a rock star because his communication methods produced crowds of rock-star proportions. He recognized the need to combine the old handshake with the new handshake, and he did so with a strategy.

The Obama team did not just say, "Hey, we need to start using social media." Instead, they decided what they wanted from the social networks and how they would communicate within those networks. They recognized that people getting excited online was not enough to win a national election. The results of the 2008 Obama campaign shifted the communication dynamic for all political campaigns in the future. Obama created an evolution in political interaction the way *The New Handshake* will do for sales. The lessons learned from the Obama campaign are lessons we can apply within the realm of sales.

David Plouffe, Obama's chief campaign manager, described the strategy his team used as follows:

1. Be consistent in everything you do. Your core message must stay the same. Use the *power of the people* to deliver your messages.
2. Repetition in all kinds of media outlets creates power for your brand, but you must *maintain control of your brand*.
3. Diversify your media strategy to get to your audience. Find your audience and determine the best way to reach it. Incorporate the communication tools that touch your audience. The Obama team used conventional advertising, texting, Facebook, MySpace, and e-mail Listserves. *Use every tool out there that will help you reach your audience.* Recognize that some people never read newspapers and others never see Facebook.
4. Do not be afraid to innovate and take some risks.
5. Learn the profile of your current customers. Empower them to keep you informed about what works and what does not work.
6. Be *authentic!*
7. Embrace the new technology as it emerges but do not let the new technology take you away from your task. Plouffe, said, "Technology must meet your core objectives."

The New Handshake will show companies and salespeople how to adopt what the Obama team learned. We will help you design a more proactive, creative approach to reaching new customer markets and to creating sales opportunities where none existed before. *The New Handshake* will demonstrate how innovative uses of the social media will create a word-of-mouth form of selling that will erase geographical boundaries. Social media have allowed people to go back to building communities on a much larger scale, making the world smaller in the process. This new emergence of sales will include a change in the way people approach the sales process. Sales 2.0 salespeople will recognize that the *new handshake* combines a consultative selling approach with the effective use of the right social media tools to support the process. This book presents a strategic approach to social media and the tools to create a Social Media Sales Strategy.

Consultative selling is not new, but often salespeople prefer to take orders and make accidental sales rather than reach out proactively, especially during a prosperous, growth economy. This book will demonstrate how progressive companies embrace consultative selling in both the good and bad economic times and how the integration of the right social media makes that happen. The companies we highlight will demonstrate how technology with the proper orientation and training produces results. This book will help you determine the *purpose* for employing the social media within your organization and the *plan* for doing so, and guide you to support the *people* who will implement the technology. *The New Handshake* includes more than tooting the newest, whiz bang technology; it means reaching out in a way that makes sense to your business and finding the tool that best fits your needs and the people you serve.

WHY READ THIS BOOK?

The New Handshake aims to do more than make a case for Sales 2.0 and the use of social media. You can read many excellent books that tell you it is time to jump on the social media train. In fact, a plethora of books enter the market each year dealing with the impact of the Internet on the way we communicate. Many discuss the challenges presented by today's information overflow. Research and statistics agree that communication is exploding in ways never before imagined. People are hungry for information about how to keep up with the changes. An area most affected by these changes is the manner in which we market our products and services to potential buyers. We will discuss how the buyer and seller relationship has changed and how the relationship between sales and marketing has changed. Furthermore, we intend to give you a road map for developing a Social Media Sales Strategy that focuses on relationships by using a cacophony of tools, including online blogging, social bookmarking, and social networks. This is what you can get from reading this book:

1. A clear understanding of the impact the social media are having on communication in the marketplace.
2. Examples of how companies adjusted to these communication changes and are in the process of adapting strategies within their cultures.
3. A road map for creating a Social Media Sales Strategy for your company.

4. A step-by-step description the major social media players, including LinkedIn, Facebook, and Twitter, with an indication of which works best depending on your sales focus (B2B or B2C).
5. A primer for using social bookmarking, social aggregators, and other add-ons in the realm of social media.
6. Guidelines for entering the social media without offending.
7. A new and wider understanding of the power of these communication tools in your industry.
8. A 30-day Social Media Sales plan, given your company culture and its social media readiness, for implementing change within your organization.

Essentially *The New Handshake* takes what has always worked in solid effective sales and adapts those skills and strategies to the new playing field—online, social communication outlets.

Chapters 1 through 6 explain the power of the communication revolution and how that has sparked an evolution in sales. If we look around over the last 30 years, nothing has changed as drastically as the way we communicate. Our refrigerators have evolved to sub-zero, our washing machines look more high tech, and our microwaves function much as they have for the last 30 years. Think back just 10 years and look at the vast changes in the way we communicate. Dial-up Internet services are obsolete. Fax machines are dying. Handheld devices no longer serve merely as telephones. The explosive changes in communication continue to astound us. To stay ahead of the game, we must be ever diligent. In these first chapters we will explore how other companies are responding to these changes; we will show the pros and cons for revamping, redefining, and integrating your sales and marketing strategy. We will encourage you to dispel your fears and the barriers that prevent you from taking the risk of embarking on a social media strategy. These chapters will give you an historical perspective of sales and buying behavior. We will make a case for moving forward by looking back at what has worked in the past. Combining what we know works with the new tools that today's technology offer will propel you into the next generation of sales and marketing.

Chapters 7 and 8 exemplify what you must do to take a practical look at your own company, its culture, goals, and customers. This analysis enables you to examine the social media tools that fit best. We will illustrate the use of social media and sales with examples from companies currently experimenting with the new handshake. You can adapt what they have done to your organization.

Chapters 9 through 12 introduce you to the major social media players. You will meet Facebook, LinkedIn, and Twitter, and you will get clear-cut examples on how to set up your profile and begin putting each application to work for you. In Chapter 12 you will learn about Digg, Delicious, and StumbleUpon as well as other bookmarking and aggregating resources to help you accelerate your sales processes. By the time you finish these chapters, you will have the basic information you need to launch your sales operation into the world of social media.

Chapter 13 tells you everything you need to know about blogging and how blogging fits within a Social Media Sales Strategy.

Chapter 14 answers your questions about what is appropriate and what is not within the social media platforms. Whether you are communicating on Twitter, Facebook, or LinkedIn, you will quickly discover the unwritten rules of engagement. This chapter will help you avoid stepping on landmines.

Chapters 15 and 16 challenge you to launch your own Social Media Sales Strategy. Using an example from a typical medium-sized business from the point of view of a sales rep, we will walk you through a step-by-step 30-day Social Media Sales Challenge. By the time you finish Chapter 16 you will be ready to design and implement a sales strategy for your organization. You will be ready to take that all-important step into the realm of social communication.

Part One

THE EVOLUTION OF SELLING AND BUYERS

Chapter 1

The Evolution of Sales

What prompts you to purchase a product? What does it take for you to hit the purchase button on your computer? The psychology of sales has mystified companies for centuries. Before we take a look at how the social media have turned sales upside down, it helps to examine the evolution of the machine that currently drives the worldwide, billion-dollar sales industry.

A sale, simply defined, means the transfer of goods for cash or credit. How that transfer occurs has continued to evolve since the day when the vendors showcased their wares in the market square or rolled their carts into the next prairie town. When you offer something "for sale," you are letting people know that you have something available for purchase. Transactional sales characterized early sales methods, and marketing was limited to the local geography. Buyers did not have many choices. Today's buyers face an infinite number of choices available to them due to the explosion of the world of all things digital. "The foundation of the entire shift in sales is in the consumer education process," said Axel Schultze, chief executive officer (CEO) of Xeesm.[1] If your business strategy does not reflect an alignment with this changing world, you may find your salespeople locked out.

THE EARLY DAYS

The late nineteenth century and early twentieth century gave birth to sales as we know it today. In *Birth of a Salesman*, Walter Friedman traced the history of sales beginning as far back as the snake oil salesmen and the 1916 World Salesmanship Congress through salesmanship in the twenty-first century.[2]

By the early part of the twentieth century, people like President Woodrow Wilson, Henry Ford, and others recognized the need to "professionalize" sales. Speeches to the World Salesmanship Congress emphasized that salesmen could transform America. They held it within their hands to, as Wilson said, "make the world more comfortable and more happy and convert them to the principles of America."[3] This congress expressed a desire to embrace a new era in salesmanship where specific principles would guide sales. No longer would salesmen conduct business with informal handshakes and slaps on the back. In 1916 a new handshake was emerging, and this handshake would grip the sales process for decades. What emerged was a science of selling that Friedman tells us paralleled the science of mass production. The free-for-all selling approach was reined in and systematized, and because the heart of that system remains intact, any attempt even today to turn sales upside down and inside out gets strong opposition. In 1916 the emphasis was to rein in the salesmen. Today, in the world of Sales 2.0, the focus is on letting the salesmen loose. Understandably, there's resistance. Why change something that has worked for decades?

The approach of *The New Handshake* is not to shed all the old ways, but to expand and grow by keeping what works and slowly eliminating what no longer works. We propose branching out from the traditional field of selling into more inbound selling using not just the telephone but also the social media. The Salesmanship Congress of 1916 sparked a *revolution* in sales. It was a time of tossing out the old and ushering in the new. *The New Handshake* sparks an *evolution* in sales—slow analysis and adjustment to the communication revolution and to the changes in buying behavior without tossing out practices we know are successful. So, what do we keep and what do we change?

Beginning with Mark Twain's efforts to sell the memoirs of Ulysses S. Grant, two important contributions to sales as we know it emerged. First, Twain understood one of the most critical elements in the psychology of sales: People buy from people that they know, like, and trust. He enlisted veterans from the Civil War to canvas the country and advocate for the book. To evoke a powerful connection with potential buyers, the veterans wore their Grand Army of the Republic badges. Twain shrewdly understood sales psychology, and he knew that for sales to succeed he needed to implement a consistent and well-monitored strategy centered on a highly talented sales team. In those early days, Twain rejected the free-for-all nature of sales. He understood the importance of hiring the right talent, and he took his time patiently recruiting reputable salespeople. For months, he and his nephew, Charles Webster, looked for just the right people to do the selling.

Building a team of talented salespeople in 1884 is not so different from building a team today. You carefully assess the skills and strengths needed to do the job. You look for the people who best demonstrate their ability to communicate and present your product or service. As in Twain's day, people are at the heart of the sale. Social media does not replace people; instead, it is all about people. Jim Collins stressed in his best-selling book, *Good to Great*, the importance of getting the best people on the ship and having the courage to toss those that do not fit overboard. Even with careful recruiting efforts, Twain was concerned that his sales team would not present the memoirs in their best light. He understood the importance of training his Civil War veteran sales team in order to achieve his sales goals. Each canvasser received a 37-page manual on how to present Grant's book to the customer, all the way down to the smallest detail. Once he hired the team and trained them, he ordered them to go out and drum up sales.

Later in 1887, Friedman describes how John Henry Patterson, National Cash Register Company (NCR) founder, created the first integrated system to monitor and train company salesmen. His methodology is still largely in use today, and it is the primary foundation upon which most sales training is based. Patterson had a charismatic, but controlling, winner-take-all personality, which drove him to systemize unique sales techniques that pushed his company sales over the top and marginalized his competitors. He expected his salesmen to dress a certain way and to follow his exact instructions as to what should be said during the sales call. Patterson's specific instructions and sales expectations became the NCR Primer, the sales bible of its time.

Patterson introduced an early version of account call planning. He knew that when salespeople thought through the typical questions or objections that might arise during the meeting, they could overcome objections immediately. That led him to design rebuttals that addressed buying indecision or outright rejection. Patterson gave birth to sales motivational training that included the training methodology of "role play." In Patterson's day, company salesmen lived great distances from the company and one another. As a result, Patterson organized sales conferences in which all NCR salesmen could bond, network, share success stories, and practice the sales techniques that Patterson mandated. Patterson assigned his sales teams territories and challenged them to exceed quotas to achieve higher commissions. Patterson's approach put the salesman on the frontline in the driver's seat.

While Henry Ford cut prices to increase the demand for his product, Patterson increased product demand with salesmanship.[4] He demonstrated that with a proper sales strategy, profits can soar. Furthermore, Patterson created a selling system that would live long after he and the NCR had perished. Thanks to Patterson we still talk about sales territories, quotas, and commission rates. Patterson's success in using an organized approach to the sales process ultimately sparked the World Salesmanship Congress. Once people like Ford saw that a systemized sales approach could deliver increases in sales and profits, they jumped on the ship next to the most notable business and political leaders of the time.

In 1936 Dale Carnegie emerged with his own ideas about sales. He placed great emphasis on the power of influence. His words continue to affect the way we market our products today. In his widely successful book, *How to Win Friends and Influence People*[5] Carnegie presented four major selling points:

1. The seller of the product is the *expert* and knows what the buyer needs.
2. The seller must influence, convince, and persuade the buyer to buy the product. The seller does this through pitching his information according to the buyer's needs.
3. The seller is in a better position than the buyer to see what is missing and to fill that gap.
4. If the seller does his job, the buyer will be ready to buy in the seller's timeframe.

Carnegie's advice in 1937 resonated with salesmen who were recovering from the Great Depression. His inspiring book gave new life to the people pounding the streets. He talked about how the most successful of us can overcome our challenges by sheer will and mindset. Even though his strategies appear dated today, he introduced the concept of the salesman pulling a product through the market rather than pushing it. His 12 steps to win influence may seem manipulative to the modern reader, but they clearly paved the way for the method of "solution selling" often used today. Carnegie's text encourages salespeople to discover what their customers want instead of thinking about what they, as sellers, want—to close a sale. Amazingly, Carnegie's book remains one of the top-selling sales books today. In other words, new salespeople still read his book and benefit from the basic principles.

As we look at the evolution of sales, it is startling that very little has changed in the mind of the typical salesperson in the typical American business over the past 50 to 100 years. Nigel Edelshain, who coined the term Sales 2.0 and is one of today's pioneers in the evolution of sales, began his career as an engineer. He moved into sales when the company he worked for gave him a choice to either sell or find another job. In the late 1990s, Edelshain began reading all he could about sales and was stunned to realize that Patterson's model of quotas and territories still existed. "I couldn't believe we were still using practices that began more than a century ago,"[6] he said.

Indeed, most organizations still employ a selling system very similar to Patterson's. While the way that a buyer approaches the purchase of a product or service has changed significantly, many salespeople still hang their sales hat on Dale Carnegie's belief that the seller, not the buyer, is in charge of the purchasing cycle. Companies are still trying to understand the pull versus the push approach. Essentially, businesses are still struggling with the psychology of sales. Most still do not know what it takes for a consumer to push that purchase button.

SALES 2.0 IN THE TWENTY-FIRST CENTURY

What does Sales 2.0 mean? To answer that question we first need to clarify the definition of Web 2.0. According to Tom Funk in his book, *Web 2.0 and Beyond,* John Battelle and Tim O'Reilly coined the term Web 2.0[7] and gave the idea a very broad definition. Funk, on the other hand, put it more simply: Web 2.0 transforms the Internet from the hands of the Web designers and techies into the hands of the people.[8] Web 2.0 includes everything from the social media outlets like YouTube, Facebook, and MySpace to the blogosphere. With increased bandwidth, always-on connections, higher speeds, and user-friendly applications, more and more people can access, participate, and interact on the Web. The Web 2.0 infrastructure enabled the creation of the technology that opened the floodgates. As we will talk about in Chapter 3, Web 2.0 emerged as a result of the wild abandon and ultimate crash of the first iteration of the Internet, which we now know as the "dot com" era.

How does Web 2.0 affect Sales 2.0? Just like Web 2.0, which puts the Internet in the hands of the people, Sales 2.0 puts the buying process in the hands of the customer. Edelshain told us he struggled with how most companies approached the sales process. He could not understand how organizations could invest so much money in something that had so little accountability. As an engineer he put it this way, "If I was a production manager who produced widgets, and if I threw 80 percent of my widgets in the trash every day, I wouldn't last long in my job." When we talk about sales, he explained, that is exactly what we are doing. Statistics show that 80 percent of leads from marketing fall down when they get to sales. "There was no logic to sales," he said, adding that he coined the term Sales 2.0 as a way of thinking about catapulting sales to the next level. "And, Web 2.0 technology will take us there."[9]

According to Anneke Seley and Brent Holloway, authors of *Sales 2.0: Improve Business Results Using Innovated Sales Practices and Technology,* the first book that dealt with this topic, "Sales 2.0 is not just about the Internet and the advances of Web 2.0. Technology will facilitate the Sales.2.0 movement—which centers on measurable customer-centered sales process, strong and aligned relationships, and the strategic application of sales resources for maximum profitability. It is a method that is measurable and enabled by technology."[10] This definition allows us to look at Sales 2.0 in a broad way.

Instead of applying Sales 2.0 to one form of technology or another, the essence of Sales 2.0 is to explore sales processes in search of efficiency and then find the technology that will complement that.

The New Handshake embraces both Edelshain's and Seley's definition. So, when you resist Sales 2.0 by claiming that the technology will change before you can implement a new program, remember that Sales 2.0 is more about a mindset change or a cultural change than a technology. Your goal is to embrace the technology that will help create efficiency and effectiveness in your sales operation. It is time for sales organizations to move away from a nineteenth-century sales approach that no longer works when courting the twenty-first-century buyer.

Seley goes on to explain the power of how Sales 2.0 works. "If you know what steps are necessary to get from point to point in the sales process and you notice that you are getting bogged down in one of those places, that's when you look at technology to help free you," she said. "For example, if you are having trouble making connections with people—you constantly get voice-mail and can't talk to the person, look to the technology tools that will enable you to get past this roadblock."[11]

Port and Marshall, in their book titled *Contrarian*, contend that the typical unenlightened salesman still uses the same tried-and-true methods he has used for the past 50-plus years.[12] These methods include cold calling to generate leads or prospecting by calling a certain number of people each day to generate potential clients. The unenlightened salesman uses scripted presentations assuming that all the clients have the same needs and wants. He goes into a potential sales meeting with the idea that his job is to "present the product or service, explain the features and benefits, handle any customer objections, and then close the sale."[13]

We are not saying that cold calling is dead—although some of the pioneers in Sales 2.0 believe it is no longer as viable a method as it was in the past—but *The New Handshake* suggests that embracing social media tools can make the initial contact with a potential buyer easier and more successful. Tom Canning of Connectize.com explained it this way, "Did we toss out the telephone when computers took over?" He said we will continue to use cold calling depending on the purpose and the nature of the contact. Cold calling, however, which used to be a backbone method in sales, will become less prominent. Rather than pick up the telephone and call someone we have never contacted, we will pick up the telephone and call someone with whom we have had an established relationship via Twitter or LinkedIn.[14] Trish Bertuzzi, CEO of The Bridge Group Inc., wrote in her blog post, *Cold Calling 2.0*, "There is no such thing as cold calling any longer." She contends that there is enough information at our disposal that we know everything we ever wanted to know about our buyers, "except, perhaps, what they had for lunch."[15]

Sales 2.0 challenges us to shed dated methods that came directly from Patterson's NCR Primer, written more than a century ago. Patterson's ideas turned the sales process around in his time, but many of his philosophies have no place in today's changed world of business. When you conjure up an image of a salesperson, what comes to mind? Is he a fast-talking (scripted) person whose eyes shift? Does she act as though she is listening to you, but she turns everything you say around to her advantage? Unfortunately, some of these stereotypes still exist. Joan recently attended a conference titled, "We Sell Success." When she entered the room, she felt the heaviness of unreality. On the stage stood a man talking too loudly from the microphone. He did not ask those in the audience what they wanted; he told them what he had to sell. The next speaker enthralled the audience with her knowledge and experience in an attempt to win them without understanding how they might define a win. By the fourth speaker, Joan had had enough and left.

Whether we are selling success or selling widgets, sales professionals must understand that the customer, not the seller, rules the buying process. Today's buyer wants honesty, transparency, and the ability to create trusted relationships with providers. In 2010 we are still in the push mode with old-fashioned selling techniques. If we simply put a different name on what we have already done or try to wrap what we have always done around the newest technology, we will not succeed in Sales 2.0 or whatever comes next. *The New Handshake* embodies much more than that. It truly means reaching out with a very different approach.

In the 1970s best-selling author Linda Richardson coined the term consultative selling. What Richardson meant was completely contrary to the salesperson-in-the-driver's-seat mentality of Peterson and Carnegie. Instead, she saw consultative selling as a way to uncover a customer's unique needs and to tailor the sales dialogue around those needs. Richardson created a sales model that equipped the sales professional with skills and strategies to achieve revenue goals while building strong client relationships. The emphasis became customer needs. We will talk more about consultative sales and how it applies to online communication in Chapter 5.

Sales 2.0 turns the stereotypical ideas of the past upside down and inside out. In fact, Port and Marshall make that the primary premise of their book. They contend that what worked in the past no longer works, and hence the *contrarian approach*. *The New Handshake* puts a slightly different spin on the contrarian approach by applying the brakes before tossing away the old methods. We say, "Hold on!" Not everything needs to be tossed into the proverbial trash. Let us leverage the best of what consultative selling offers. Let us keep the techniques we use today to build deep customer relationships while using new technology to create loyalty and retention. Let us listen to what Anneke Seley described as the most efficient and effective methods to reach this new modern buyer.

A number of years ago, Joan had a positive experience with a traditional salesman who understood the value of relationship. She and her husband decided they had too much life insurance and needed to eliminate a policy. On her husband's advice, she paid a visit to their life-insurance agent with the clear intention of streamlining their policies. The agent invited her to sit down in his cluttered office. He listened attentively to her concerns and shared alternatives and information about the policies. An hour later she left the office having signed up for a new policy! She would have never character-ized this interaction as sleazy or even fraught with pushy salesmanship. The insurance agent convinced her to purchase a new policy by paying attention to her concerns and showing her that he had her best interests in mind. Port and Marshall would say that the insurance agent used the *contrarian approach* to sell her insurance.

According to Port and Marshall, the contrarian approach includes the following:

1. **The customer is in the driver's seat**. Rather than you finding the customer through cold calling and other forms of "networking," customers find you. Port and Marshall write, "Sales professionals must find a way to build relationships and be there when the customer is ready to buy."[16] *The New Handshake* not only supports putting the customer in the driver's seat, but we believe they are already there! Tools like Twitter help salespeople locate potential cus-tomers that they otherwise might never have found. Does this mean the salespeople are driving the sale? No, it means that customers will find you, but you, too, will uncover potential prospects and customers when you put yourself out there and participate in marketplace.

2. **Customers decide how you will communicate with them**. Today's customer can either opt-in to or opt-out of your message with just a click of a mouse. Even though customers will decide if they want to communicate with you, you can attract them into the conversation with skillful use of blogging and micro-blogging. As Tom Canning shared in our interview with him, the essence of Sales 2.0 is collabo-ration. Axel Schultze talks about "social selling." By that he means instead of the traditional telesales "which are seen as interruptions, social selling is all about relationships."[17]

3. **The number of choices available to customers and their access to those choices is unprecedented**. In fact, Daniel Pink in *A Whole New Mind* asserts that today's customer has so many high-quality and economic choices that it is hard to distinguish one product from another. He contends that story, relationship, and design will win the purchase, not quality and economy.[18]

4. **Customers expect a relevant and valuable offer tailored to them.**
   Generic marketing and broadcast marketing will no longer work.
   This point emphasizes the need to bring sales into the marketing
   process sooner. Instead of the traditional marketing approach of
   going out and creating leads and then passing those leads to sales,
   The New Handshake asserts that sales and marketing join forces
   to acquire new customers and create engagement and loyalty.
   Salespeople become the "brand within a brand" and the frontlines
   of customer communication. When a customer talks to Anne at
   Zappos, he is not communicating with Zappos. That customer is
   communicating with Anne. Companies must release their salespeople from the restrictions of the past and enable this kind of
   branding and customer relationship-building.

5. **Dale Carnegie believed that the salesman decided when the customer should buy, but today's buyer decides when she will buy.**
   Today's buyer will not fall prey to heavy-handed sales techniques.
   "Buy today or miss this great opportunity" or "One day left on this
   offer." Today's savvy buyer knows that bargains and deals are always
   available. Push too hard and she will go elsewhere to find what she
   wants when she wants it. Early Internet sales practices incorporated
   these kinds of tactics because at the time they worked. Today's shoppers recognize these gimmicks and wonder why some sellers still
   insist on using this outdated model. If you create a "squeeze" page
   that screams with paragraph after paragraph about why this product is for you without knowing who might be reading, you are using
   the new technology in the old way. You might get one or two buyers,
   but this method goes against everything we are learning about the
   new buyer.

6. **The modern buyer carries what Port and Marshall call a "big
   megaphone."** If you do not treat the customer with respect, if you
   do not live up to your end of the bargain, if the customer feels
   slighted in any way, beware. Word of mouth has become world of
   mouth, and unhappy customers will not hesitate to tell the world.

How does all this affect the evolution of sales? The sales teams that travel
across the country by air and by car must still cope with negative stereotypes.
Whether they are selling on Twitter or face to face, they must contend with
negative views of salespeople. To build the kind of relationships necessary to
sell to the new buyer, salespeople must work hard to create loyalty and trust.
They must put the needs of the buyer before their sales quotas. At this unprecedented time in history, new technologies enable salespeople to listen,
observe, share, connect, and collaborate with customers and prospective

buyers. Adapted into a cohesive sales process, these technologies increase value while driving down the costs associated with the lifecycle of the sale. As Anneke Seley discovered in her inbound sales consulting business, Phoneworks, the old method of putting salesmen on the streets costs too much. It is not only costly, it is inefficient.

Furthermore, as soon as someone thinks you are trying to sell them something, that person shuts down. You cannot fake the know, like, and trust factor that Patterson tried to teach his sales professionals with canned scripts. Online, if your customer smells a sale, senses sleaze, imagines the stereotypical salesperson, you will not only lose a sale, but with the simple push of the delete button you will have tarnished your brand and alienated a potential customer. What is worse, your sleazy approach might provoke negative buzz all over the Web.

The Razorfish Social Influence Marketing Survey tells us that brands lack a significant credibility in the digital world. Why? Branding practitioners and marketers ignored the primary ingredient necessary to sell online: trust. In-your-face, push advertising no longer works either online or offline. The Razorfish report states, "It's no use devoting significant marketing efforts to this space unless you've already figured out how to serve as a trusted brand. The social platforms require a new marketing language—one that must not be overlooked."[19]

For sales to revamp and reach out with a new handshake, reps must do what the Joan's insurance agent did so naturally; namely, to tread softly along the dangerous and narrow path to relationship-building, particularly along the streets of the World Wide Web. When we analyze what worked in the past to discover what will work in the future, we come up with the same answer. That answer lies in what everyone on the social networks is talking about today—*building a strong relationship first*. Listen and learn what your customers want before you tell them about what you have to sell. Reach out to your customers in new ways and they will reach back. Throughout this book we will share examples of how companies created a brand around their people. Great salespeople have always known that success begins with the development of a trusted relationship. *The New Handshake* extends Sales 2.0 methodology to attract the new buyers of the twenty-first century.

In Chapter 2, we explore how the evolution of new buying behavior and online communication combine to drive changes in the sales process.

Chapter 2

The Evolution of Buyers
and Online Communication

THE EVOLUTION OF THE NEW BUYER

What caused the fundamental shift in a sales process that until recently was largely seller driven to one that is now customer driven? The answer is simple: a new type of buyer. Today's buyer wants and expects something quite different than the buyer in Patterson's day. Tom Canning went so far as to say that we are not experiencing an evolution in selling so much as an evolution in buying. Anneke Seley corroborated this bold statement when she said that sales processes have changed because buyers have changed. For sales organizations to adapt to the needs of this new buyer, they need to understand the three critical ways in which buying behavior has changed.

1. **The Internet gives buyers easy, almost instantaneous access to information.** Today's buyer is far more educated about the purchasing options available to them. Think about the last time you decided to purchase a car. You probably visited showrooms, talked to the salespeople, sat in various cars, and took test drives. You were at the mercy of what you learned from each showroom salesperson you encountered. There was no easy way to compare pricing of the same car in another state. Today, before even entering a physical showroom, you sit down at your computer to do your homework. You select the cars you like, examine the features you want, and

compare costs. You may even purchase your car online. When new buyers arrive at the sales showroom, they are armed with information. This is an informed consumer who is no longer at the mercy of the seller. The new buyer is the expert. Tom Canning said, "The buyers know more about our products than we do. Through the Web they can learn all they need to know before making a decision to buy. It's the super informed buyer versus the uninformed salesperson. Sales 2.0 and the technology tools out there provide salespeople with similar information. When salespeople participate, we level the playing field."[1]

2. **Buyers buy from one another.** These buyers do not just buy from companies; they buy from people they meet online. eBay revolutionized this form of buying. Combine Craig's List with eBay and you double the number of buyers buying from one another. Add in social networks and you further increase the opportunities for buyer-to-buyer purchases. Some companies see this type of buying as a threat. Amazon saw it as an opportunity. Amazon created a community that lets customers purchase from each other. Customers can select new products that are purchased directly from Amazon or they may choose to buy used and nearly new items from other customers. When a customer visits Amazon.com, they instantly become a buyer or a seller or both.

3. **Customers provide data to customers.** When Mom decides to buy a toy for her child, what does she do first? In the past, she might have browsed catalogs or visited the local toy store to compare options. While there, she might have selected something the salesman recommended based on his knowledge, because she had little else to go on. Like our car buyer, parents today seek out product information before making a purchase. For example, a dad who wants to purchase a videogame for his son runs a quick Google search on the game title. He studies and compares the prices and features. He locates nearby retail locations. So far, this process resembles the purchase of a car. But now Dad will also compare survey information and reviews about the game submitted by other parents. Was the game safe? How did the manufacturer deal with difficulties? What other games might be out there that offer the same features for a better price?

The success of a Social Media Sales Strategy hinges on the way that salespeople approach this new buying process. Tom Canning of Connectize.com suggests that when salespeople go on LinkedIn and enter the conversation, they establish themselves as an "expert" in something. The people they are conversing with may not be buyers at that moment. Later, when these same people are ready to purchase, they turn to the salesperson, whose name has become familiar to them. Canning said, "They recall that this person knew something about this product or service. They remember reading her responses to the LinkedIn questions or reading her blogs. They might make a direct inquiry to that person. These salespeople become the helpful people we used to encounter on the sales floor of Home Depot. They are the Sales 2.0 'blue shirts' whom you encounter at Best Buy. That's how we're seeing salespeople responding to the new buyer."[2]

Kathy Tito, of CallCenterServices.com, uses LinkedIn extensively. She said one year ago she shied away from the platform. She saw it as a place for people to market themselves. Once she entered the space, she recognized the power it offered her and her company. "I've connected with the people I knew over the last 20 years in this field," she explained. "Through them, I connect with others and so on. I post my blog, and I answer questions. We get 70 percent of the hits to our Web site from my LinkedIn profile."[3]

BUSINESS TO BUSINESS (B2B) OR BUSINESS TO CUSTOMER (B2C)

Another distinction in sales today is the difference between business-to-business (B2B) selling and business-to-consumer (B2C) selling. If you sell B2B, you might think that the buying behavior we have described above does not apply to you. Although sales approaches differ for companies who sell B2B, the buying behavior remains largely the same. In fact, we contend that the buying process has larger implications for B2B sellers than for those selling in the consumer space. Clara Shih, author of *Facebook Era*, suggests that the higher the price of the item and the higher its complexity, the more important relationships and trust become. She adds that companies that sell directly to consumers (B2C) use more marketing and neutral advertising than customized niche selling indicative online.[4] This contention leads to the belief that B2C businesses are less likely to use online tools for sales than B2B when, in fact, the opposite is true. Amazon uses Twitter to promote the Amazon Daily Deal. Barack Obama used Facebook to build a community that would ultimately elect him to the White House. Whether you sell to business or to the consumer directly, a sound social media strategy will help you reach your objectives. Shih adds, "Why would a company use a person-to-person tool like Facebook for selling to an organization? The important thing to keep in mind is that individuals are at the heart of any organization. Purchase decisions are made by individual people, not entire companies."[5]

Josh Bernoff and Charlene Li, authors of *Groundswell*, add, "Businesspeople are people, too. There is no such thing as a social network for businesses or a business commenting on a blog. Businesses do not interact. People do."[6] As companies design their social media strategy they must keep people at the heart of their plan. In Chapter 8, we will talk about how companies need to tap their "people" power. The top-producing salesperson with a winning personality becomes your strongest asset on LinkedIn. The quiet product development engineer who sits at her computer most of the day can become your best blogger. Once companies recognize the power of the people within their organizations and take the risk to unleash that power, they will experience the magic of the social media.

CallCenterServices.com's Tito, whose business is solely B2B, helps companies design and implement their social media presence. She recently worked with a company that sells software to launch a business Facebook page, and in just a few short months the company began seeing positive responses from that effort. "We call it Web design," she added. "The question is not whether we should be doing this, but how to do it. Why not participate in a free platform that creates visibility and branding? The question we should be asking is *why not*,"[7] she continued.

Marc Perramond, of B2B seller InsideView, talks about salespeople who brand themselves. "With B2B, individual sales reps can brand themselves with tools like Twitter and LinkedIn,"[8] he said. Razorfish data confirms this belief and shows that buyers trust those closest to them before making buying decisions.[9] B2C buyers are less likely to pay attention to someone they do not know online. For them, recommendations from family members and friends hold more weight. Interestingly, however, the data also show that brands require increasing transparency. People are less likely to pay attention to corporate blogging or to anonymous peer reviews. The research confirms what we already know about B2B buying behavior—the sales cycle is built on relationship and trust. Even in the B2C world, salespeople can emerge as the trusted "spokesperson" for products or services. With time, they become the trusted "friend" whose advice the buyer listens to.

Furthermore, they create loyalty by remaining engaged with buyers after the sale via social networks. Salespeople are now even more accountable for their part in the buyer's decision. If your neighbor steered you in the wrong direction, you let that neighbor know. It has been said that when someone has a poor shopping experience, that person will likely tell at least 10 people. That same phenomenon holds true on social networks with one huge twist. Today's unhappy buyer does not tell just 10 people; they shout it to the world with the click of a button.

This is why companies need to establish a "listening post" to stay abreast of conversations taking place about them. When a savvy salesperson sees an unhappy buyer, she jumps on it and in more cases than not, the buyer does a complete about face. Making things right quickly strengthens customer loyalty.

Heather Lalley, in an Associated Press article on September 2, 2009, talked about savvy salesperson, Alecia Dantico, whom buyers know because she regularly sends them a virtual tin of Garrett popcorn. Dantico understands the power of community and has created a loyal group of followers one virtual tin at a time.

THE EVOLUTION OF COMMUNICATION ONLINE

The transformation from a sales process to a buying process did not happen in a vacuum. It happened because the methods that people use to communicate and relate to one another changed drastically with the widespread use of the World Wide Web. Naturally the way we decide to buy products changed along with all of our other major interactions. This idea fits with what Clay Shirky said in *Here Comes Everybody*, in which he talked about the sociological changes that the social media have created. He said, "The centrality of group effort to human life means that anything that changes the way groups function will have profound ramifications for everything from commerce and government to media and religion."[10]

When we look at communication of all types, we see an evolution in how we relate to one another. Salespeople previously had fewer choices, namely face-to-face, telephone, or written letter. They often wondered about the best time to use each of these media. Clearly, when they wanted to make a strong impact, such as close a sale, they chose a face-to-face interaction. If there was not a relationship in place, the first interaction was generally through a phone call or through a more impersonal business letter designed to secure the face-to-face meeting. In the early days, salesmen just dropped by the store. After years of struggle, that is, where they sent letters when they should have called or where they called when they should have communicated face-to-face, they finally figured it out.

Today, however, salespeople have many more choices, and the sheer number adds to the confusion around what to do when. As Joan points out in her book, *Managing Sticky Situations at Work*, a letter no longer seems impersonal. In an e-mail-centric world, we notice the letter or handwritten note that crosses our desk because we receive so few of them. We appreciate the time it took for someone to put a letter in an envelope and attach a stamp. These things suggest something more significant has changed. The telephone call, which used to be thought more impersonal, has become an "interaction."

Indeed, we have reached a new crossroads in communication where we must determine the medium for our message not based on convenience alone but based on purpose and intent.[11] Seley and Holloway advise that the customer determines the best method to use. They say that many field sales reps believe that customers will not purchase high-priced products without face time. In their book *Sales 2.0*, the authors contend that this belief may have disappeared with the typewriter. Indeed some customers still want face time, but many more than we ever imagined will purchase on the telephone. The authors conclude, "Sales 2.0 principles emphasize communicating with customers using the medium of their preference."[12]

What compels a salesperson to write on someone's Facebook wall or to send a message through LinkedIn? Is it better to send a direct message through Twitter or to shoot off an e-mail? As the choices grow exponentially, the need to have a purpose, intent, and strategy intensifies. People are streamlining their social media participation, according to the Razorfish research, which found that 40 percent of the people they surveyed belong to one or two social networks. Razorfish concludes, "This suggests people are choosing to concentrate their networks instead of spreading themselves too thinly and as people chose to go where everybody else goes, preferred online communities are emerging."[13]

Indeed, friends form groups and communicate online solely to create relationships. Li and Bernoff said that the drive to interact and be social is a natural state that touches all of us and embodies the need to connect.[14] In fact, many people will tell you they prefer to interact online than to talk on the telephone or face-to-face. Even though we are basically social beings and interacting with one another is a fundamental part of our existence, the speed, efficiency, and somewhat anonymity of online communication make it our method of choice. More and more people are joining Facebook, with more than 400 million users at this writing. The majority of Facebook users, however, do not have multitudes of friends. Shih tells us that most people prefer no more than 120 friends. Furthermore, she points out that even if you have 120 friends you probably only interact on a regular basis with 10 or 15 of them.[15] This means that as a people, we still maintain close, personal interactions. Yet, we enjoy the opportunity to relate to great numbers. In later chapters we will introduce the quality-plus-quantity-equals-access phenomenon to help you augment your lead-generation efforts.

Perhaps you are like one of Joan's clients who said, "Isn't Facebook basically a social place? Won't my staff waste too much time on those sites rather than doing their jobs?" In truth, Facebook and MySpace began as social sites. MySpace won the attention of teens who love texting and online interaction. Do you remember the days when you spent hours talking to your best friend on the telephone even though your best friend lived two houses away? Today's teens enjoy the same kind of intense interaction with one another, but they do it through MySpace and their cell phones.

Facebook began as a way for college students to create that same sense of community on campus. When freshmen entered college campuses, they had few friends or connections. Their intense desire to connect with one another was met by Facebook—spearheaded, by the way, by a college student on a college campus. When they graduated, they continued the relationships that began in college. Imagine how this kind of deep relationship building can grow. From teen on MySpace to college graduate on Facebook to young professional on LinkedIn, what we have is a generation that has grown up digital and is very comfortable interacting in the online space.

The thought of employees wasting time on social sites worries most companies, and rightly so. Razorfish tells us that most social network users admit to at least six hours a week on the social media sites.[16] Trish Bertuzzi balked at the thought of one hour a day on the social media. "That's five hours a week that they could be spending following up on leads,"[17] she said. On the flip side, investing those five hours a week wisely can shorten the sales cycle through better prospecting and lead generation. Time, then, is something the organization must figure out based on its purpose and plan and then monitor and control it.

Bernoff and Li tell us that the Gen Y'ers use the social media in much greater numbers than their older counterparts. What is the significance of this statistic? These young people will be tomorrow's buyers. Companies that jump on the bandwagon and reach out to the new buyer with the *new handshake* will position themselves to respond to their customers in the way their customers demand. Each day brings new opportunities. Instead of fearing and doubting the social media, we must learn how to embrace it.

THE SOCIAL MEDIA TIPPING POINT

Best-selling author Malcolm Gladwell described the *tipping point* in his delightful book of the same name. He took incident after incident and demonstrated how small events combined at the right time and in the right way to cause an explosion of interest. Gladwell described three types of personalities that help spark a tipping point; namely, the Connectors, the Mavens, and the Salesmen.[18] The Connectors connect with other people naturally. They are the people who invariably say, "You ought to meet so-and-so." They seem to know everyone. The Mavens are the people who know everything. They carry around a wealth of information. Whenever you want to know trivia or vital statistics, ask a Maven. The Salesmen are the persuaders. They convince and persuade you toward action. According to Gladwell, there must be a convergence of Mavens, Connectors, and Salesmen for the tipping point to occur.

The example in Gladwell's book that best illustrates the tipping point occurred with the rebirth of Hush Puppy shoes. Hush Puppies, the popular, geeky, suede-looking shoes that our grandfathers wore, nearly died out by the early 1990s. Something happened, however, in 1994 that triggered a renewed interest in the brand. Someone bought a pair of Hush Puppy shoes in a small shop somewhere in Manhattan. That sale sparked another sale. Soon people were searching the stores throughout Manhattan for Hush Puppy shoes. By the fall of 1995 things began to explode. Designers showcased Hush Puppies in their collections. Gladwell wrote, "By 1995, the company sold 430,000 pairs of the classic Hush Puppies, and the next year it sold four times that, and the year after that still more, until Hush Puppies were once again a staple of the wardrobe of the young American male."[19]

When Gladwell wrote the *Tipping Point* in 2000, MySpace and Facebook were hardly more than daydreams in the minds of creative teens. We might argue that the social media today, from Facebook to Twitter, are in the midst of their own tipping point, exploding in ways we cannot yet predict. What gives us even greater pause is that the social media are also the instruments that will spark tomorrow's tipping points. A Connector on Facebook comments about the great shoes he bought at a little shop in Manhattan. Imagine the lightening speed that would result from that comment. Gladwell's theories about how little things can make a big difference have not changed; they have intensified. Today, the tipping point is the social media made up of a world of Connectors and Mavens. *The New Handshake* invites the Salesmen to the party.

In Chapter 3 we will discuss the wild, wild West of the social media and what that means as you begin thinking about a new selling strategy.

Chapter 3

The Wild, Wild West of Social Media

THE RUSH FOR GOLD

In early 1995, Cornell undergraduates Stephan Paternot and Todd Krizelman stumbled upon a primitive chat room on the university's network and quickly became hooked. Recognizing the potential for developing something more powerful, they soon launched a social community—theGlobe.com—that garnered 44,000 visits within the first month of going live on the Web. Paternot and Krizelman stunned the financial world in 1998 when on Friday, November 13, theGlobe.com issued its IPO and by day's end set a record for achieving a 606 percent increase over the initial share price. Thus launched the new economy.[1]

METEORIC RISE AND SPECTACULAR FALL

The six years from 1995 through 2001 is typically defined as the period of investment and speculation in Internet firms. During this wild period many factors combined to cause the infamous dot-com bubble, which would soon burst with devastating results. Internet usage in 1995 marked the beginning of a major surge in growth, causing companies to recognize the opportunity the Internet presented for selling their products and services. This recognition resulted in the birthing of a multitude of Internet start-ups by the mid to late 1990s, theGlobe.com among them. Soon these companies came to be known as "dot-coms," in reference to the .com in many Web addresses.

When the bubble burst in 2001, many people saw this plunge as a signal that the hype and promise of the World Wide Web had reached its conclusion. The outlandish behavior and excessive spending of many an overnight dot-com millionaire fueled that belief. Among them was Stephan Paternot, CEO of theGlobe.com. He was publicly lampooned for his behavior and dubbed "the CEO in the plastic pants" after being shown in a piece videotaped by CNN during a night on the town. Dancing on a nightclub table wearing shiny leather pants, he had the audacity to make the outrageous statement, "Got the girl. Got the money. Now I'm ready to live a disgusting, frivolous life."[2] As these young, 20-something dot-com millionaires literally sprung up overnight, the media and the public stepped back to scrutinize them with a more critical and discerning eye.

The meteoric rise and fall of the one-time darlings of Wall Street was as much due to the dubious financial promises of quick returns on investment made by these dot-com gunslingers as by the static nature of the dialogue between company and consumer in this early iteration of the Web. In fact, there was no "conversation" with the customer. Companies did as they pleased with little or no concern about buying patterns or consumer need. They cared neither for investment returns nor for consumer response. These early days mimicked the infant stages of the gold rush when the dream of "striking it rich quick" so overpowered conventional business wisdom that traditional questions regarding what the consumer wants or who will actually purchase your product got lost in the shuffle.

In this wild, Wild West of Web 1.0, these so-called Internet darlings eluded the standards of business practice and accountability that plagued their brick-and-mortar counterparts. People with more money than sense tossed insane amounts of capital at CEOs who exhibited giddy exuberance during investment presentations that were often more glitz than substance. Holding shares in a company, which never recorded a profit, became the gold of the 1990's rush.

What did all these early forays into the wild, Wild West of technology produce besides a bunch of bankrupt millionaires? For one thing, it created an army of online buyers whose buying behaviors continue to shape today's online marketplace. These consumers of yesteryear gave today's consumers three things of lasting value:

1. **Convenience.** As the world became increasingly hectic and fast paced, the Internet now offered shoppers an alternative. Although the early online buying experience was clunky at best, the Internet exposed shoppers to the convenience of buying what they needed from the comfort of their homes without having to waste time running from place to place to make purchases in traditional ways.

2. **Cost savings.** The Internet took the idea of coupon clipping to a whole new level. Beyond the savings of time and money invested in tanking up the car or stacking the calendar with sales presentations from hungry vendors, the Internet opened the door for the buyer to peruse information about the vast array of available product options before making a selection. As we pointed out in the last chapter, this approach empowered the buyers and ultimately gave them more confidence that they were securing the best deal. What we did not talk about in Chapter 2 was how this added buyer information affected the marketplace. With more people searching for the lowest price, the best quality for economy, sellers had to adjust to keep up with the competition. Suddenly, the buyer instead of the seller was driving product and pricing decisions.

3. **Choice.** Internet-empowered buyers accessed information like never before. Instead of spending inordinate amounts of time comparing and contrasting the pros and cons of similar products and services either by moving from store to store or by listening to endless presentations by salespeople with their own agendas, these buyers now surfed the Web at their leisure. With more time to search, consumers learned how to uncover many more choices than those at their neighborhood outlets. The Patterson model of a field rep coming to your door or into your boardroom and demonstrating the product in a manner he or she chooses was fading as fast as last year's rotary phones.

The wild, Wild West of the Internet produced a new kind of consumer who would demand a more powerful place in the sales scheme of things. In other words, the Web created a giant monster in the form of a savvy consumer. This giant remained quietly in the background during the 1990s because in this early phase of the Internet, the information was still a one-way communication channel between the seller and the buyer. Consumers were still at the mercy of what the seller presented to them. That dynamic would begin to change significantly with the advent of Web 2.0.

ENTER WEB 2.0

Eric Knorr, executive editor of *InfoWorld*, first used the term in front of a large audience in the December 2003 special issue of the business IT magazine *CIO*. Later, as we pointed out in Chapter 1, most people credit Battelle and O'Reilly with coining the term at an O'Reilly Media conference brainstorming session in 2004. There, Dale Dougherty and Craig Cline also used the term, which shortly became notable. Dale Dougherty, Web pioneer and

O'Reilly vice president, noted during the conference that "far from having 'crashed,' the Web was more important than ever, with exciting new applications and sites popping up with surprising regularity."[3]

ENTER SOCIAL MEDIA

Social media tools define the next-generation Internet that supports social interactions and connections with people as well as collaboration and sharing and the creation of user-generated content. For those companies leading the way in the world of Web 2.0, the ability to harness the "collective intelligence" emerges as a central principle. Although Web 2.0 can be thought of as the engine driving the car, the social media tools make that driving experience so much more pleasurable. Much that has been written about Web 2.0 and Sales 2.0 downplays the social media because of the ongoing debate about how much impact those tools will have in these evolving and ever-changing environments. What we do know is they have an impact.

The New Handshake proposes that social media will become part of the inside sales strategy for most companies. By inside sales, we mean selling within the confines of your organization. Seley and Holloway provide an excellent analysis of the launch of one of the first "inside" sales organizations when they discuss OracleDirect, which they term "the Ivy League of Inside Sales."[4] To better understand what inside sales or inbound selling means, we turn to a blog post written by Matt Bertuzzi. He defined the phenomenon as "most or many of the following activities: cultivating prospective buyers; conveying the features, advantages or benefits of a product or service; and if appropriate closing a sale." He went on to say that the difference between inside sales and field selling is the seller relies on phone and Web-based technologies.[5]

THE ORACLEDIRECT STORY

According to Anneke Seley, who pioneered the inside sales operation at Oracle in the 1980s, OracleDirect paved the way for a new kind of selling. In her book, *Sales 2.0*, she highlights the growth of telesales and Web selling at Oracle that began more than 20 years ago. Looking at what happened at Oracle, we can learn some lessons before we embark on a Social Media Sales Strategy. As Trish Bertuzzi said, "Before companies launch Sales 2.0, they should ask themselves have they launched Sales 1.5."[6] In other words, if your business is still entrenched in the old selling techniques, jumping immediately into Sales 2.0 might prove disastrous. In the 1980s there were no pioneers. Oracle had to chart the course through the dangerous terrain of the wild, Wild West without a map or compass. Let us look at the OracleDirect Story and see what we can learn from that experience.

The first obstacle Seley and her team encountered was resistance from the established field sales team. To counter this resistance, Seley explained, they began slowly with a pilot rollout in an area where the field reps were most accepting. "The pilot program became a standard process for regional (and global) implementation at Oracle and has become a best-practices methodology in Sales 2.0 companies."[7] Seley reported that in its first year OracleDirect contributed $6 million in incremental revenue.

Initially the OracleDirect sales teams focused on orders under $50,000. The contention at the time was that no one would execute a purchase of more than $50,000 without a personal face-to-face visit. In the early years, OracleDirect completed most of the orders under $50,000. Later, however, the company noticed fluidity in this number. In reality, some customers preferred to make all purchases virtually and others preferred a face-to-face interaction even for smaller purchases. The lesson learned was the same lesson David Plouffe talked about when designing the communication strategy for the 2008 Obama campaign. *We must communicate with customers in their preferred mode.* We must have systems in place to enable a variety of communication channels. To implement this kind of flexibility in communication, Seley explained, Oracle created team selling: "OracleDirect reps and field reps share territory and determine together—on a deal-by-deal basis—who will manage each opportunity."[8] In other words, if the customer wants to deal by telephone, the size of the order is irrelevant; the OracleDirect sales rep will deal with that customer. Team selling also helped reduced the conflict between field salespeople and inside salespeople.

In addition to overcoming the resistance on the part of established field reps, Oracle had to deal with issues that arose between sales and marketing. For the new sales operation to work, Seley explained that sales and marketing had to become integrated and aligned. This alignment included strong financial rewards for achieving goals that match both marketing goals as well as the goals of the new sales operation. Because most field sales reps complain that marketing does not send qualified leads, and marketing complains that the sales reps do not follow up on the leads they send, OracleDirect provided an opportunity to bridge this divide. Using the telephone and the Web, OracleDirect worked in partnership with marketing to track the source of the incoming leads and to assign those leads a rating. "The integration of marketing and sales, supported by performance goals and compensation are critical components to a Sales 2.0 company,"[9] Seley said.

Developing a cultural mindset for the changes in sales proved critical for Oracle. In addition to overcoming the resistance of field reps, OracleDirect had to demonstrate that it could sell complicated technological applications by telephone. While experimenting with telesales, another important lesson emerged. The sales team experienced more success with telephone and Web sales with customers who had already purchased. They found less success with initial sales, particularly with non-technical buyers. As a result, Oracle-Direct created a business sales strategy to expand long-term relationships with Oracle applications customers after the initial purchase.

Another interesting component of the early OracleDirect experience was incorporating a career path from OracleDirect to field selling. This career path gave credence to the skill of the field rep who could teach the OracleDirect sales rep important skills. The team included two to three face-to-face visits for inside sales reps per year. " . . . the Inside Sales team keeps relationships with customers and field reps strong by supplementing their primarily telephone and Web-based communication with occasional face-to-face visits."[10]

Finally, OracleDirect recognized the need to stay on top of the technology world. They recognized that technology changes, and those changes bring new and exciting methods for different kinds of communication. Over the years the sales teams have added applications, including Webinars, online Solutions Factory, Instant Messaging (IM), and Web Diagrammer. Seley quotes Norm Gennaro, vice president of Sales Consulting for OracleDirect, "IM is a huge part of our lives today, and I can't imagine a sales call without it."[11]

As we move along the continuum of the communication revolution sparked by the explosion in technology, we might say that the social media have become a huge part of our daily existence. Many sales reps are experimenting with it now and learning that it, too, will become so much a part of our lives that we will not be able to imagine a sales call without it. Kathy Tito described the social media as stealthy, saying, "These tools seem to have snuck up on us and taken over. Before you know what has happened, you can't manage without them."[12]

Today, OracleDirect has an active blog designed to recruit new sales reps. It has a Facebook page that includes a discussion board for customers to freely converse about products. If you log onto OracleDirect's recruitment blog, you can follow the company on Twitter. The company created a YouTube video that shows life in the world of an OracleDirect sales rep. OracleDirect is currently using the social media to attract talent to the sales team and to orient customers to OracleDirect buying. Next year's usage of the social media for OracleDirect might include a Social Media Sales Strategy that mirrors the Sales 2.0 strategy the company pioneered.

Those companies that embrace the principles of community, collaboration, authenticity, transparency, connectedness, and immediacy realize that they can no longer just talk at their customers and prospects. Instead, they must engage customers and prospects in a dialogue and create relationships that go far beyond the "tactical" transactional sales approach we have become used to. Savvy adopters of Web 2.0 principles recognize that increasingly sophisticated and networked users demand something more: enter Sales 2.0 and a very new consumer with new demands on the sales force.

What can we take away from the OracleDirect experience as we consider the integration of social media into the sales process?

- Understand that there will be resistance, especially among seasoned sales professionals.
- Pay attention to the cultural mindset and make change gradually.
- Incorporate the old with the new.
- Throw away your assumptions about the way you think buyers buy and instead respond to the way buyers actually buy.

Authors Levine, Locke, Searls, and Weinberger in their 2000 publication of *The Cluetrain Manifesto* accurately predicted the stunning transformation that turned the world of communication upside down. They were perhaps the first to define the concept of an online global conversation. They said, "The Net is a real place where people can go to learn, to talk to each other, and to do business together. It is a bazaar where customers look for wares, vendors spread goods for display, and people gather around topics that interest them. It is a conversation."[13]

The wild, Wild West of the Internet produced a frenzy of activity. The most notable result from this frenzy was the creation of a new consumer who demanded convenience, cost savings, and choice through the new outlets. Web 2.0 not only gave these new consumers a voice by providing opportunities to interact with the seller and with each other, but it also set the stage for a revolution in communication via social networking tools. In less than a decade this emergence of communication evolved, and from it a revolution occurred in the way people interact and purchase online, producing what Nigel Edelshain foresaw when he coined the term Sales 2.0. *The New Handshake* takes us even further along the path of change and into the realm of social media. Joyce Stoer Cordi, a leading management consultant, wrote that "actual customer research I led last year (2008) found that these sources (online research and social media tools) are used by nearly 90 percent of executives in the information gathering phase of a purchase decision."[14] If executives are informing their purchases via the social media, what does that tell you about purchase patterns?

As the wild, Wild West of the social media unfolds, some companies grab their prospecting tools and rush to the nearest social media site. Others wait and wait, wondering where the nougats lie and how to uncover them. Chapter 4 explores what might be holding you back and dispels the myths that stymie many companies from taking that all-important first step.

Chapter 4

What Are You Waiting For?

IT IS TIME TO GET ON BOARD

The explosion of social media into mainstream consciousness has seemingly come out of nowhere. As we showed in Chapter 3, the social media groundswell has been building for some time—like a bubble about to burst, and it is fair to say that the buzz right now is deafening. The question is if you can hear it, and, if you can, what you intend to do to get onboard.

While there is a growing familiarity with tools like LinkedIn, Facebook, Twitter, blogs, and YouTube, companies large and small still wonder about the business reasons for using social media. They often ask:

- Why should we care?
- Where do we start?
- How can we manage the information?

Why Should We Care?

Whether you understand it or not, you need to realize that your potential buyers are surfing the Net, reading blogs, participating in forums and group discussions, asking for product and services referrals from their social networks, and joining online communities. Even if you wanted to "opt out," choosing instead to use outdated approaches to sales and marketing, your potential customers—and your savvy competitors—are most definitely online. Your prospects are tuned in to what they want, what is available, where to purchase, and how much to spend. The bigger the sale, the more educated the buyer. As we have seen from the experience with OracleDirect, these experienced buyers are opting to purchase using all kinds of tools.

With 66 percent of the 40 million LinkedIn users deemed "key decision maker," with 400-plus million people on Facebook and growing an average of 5 million new users each week, with 41 percent of these users over the age of 35, and with millions more conversing over Twitter, you cannot ignore the opportunity. What salesperson in her right mind would turn her back on the chance to showcase her product or service to such a large audience? The name of the game then is visibility. If you are not participating online, you are missing huge opportunities to reach an audience you would otherwise not be able to connect with in an easy and cost-effective way. As Tom Canning said, "Any salesperson who is not Tweeting or not blogging is really missing out."[1] He added that customers know more about sellers than ever before.

Kathy Tito reminded us that the question is not should we participate, but why should we not? Part of what you need to do is examine how your buyers are interacting on the Web. It is not a question of whether they are interacting; it is how they are interacting. B2B sales operations understand their customers. They profile clients regarding demographics, product needs, and buying patterns. It is time to explore Internet use as well.

Where Do We Start?

Though the buzz around social media has clearly been heating up for some time, in many organizations there remains strong resistance to using online tools such as blogs, wikis, and social networking sites to achieve business results. Policymakers and gatekeepers fear what they do not yet understand. Rather than embrace the opportunity, they erect barriers in front of their employees and suggest that social tools like LinkedIn, Twitter, Facebook, and blogging will fade into history as fads. As we pointed out in Chapter 3, this kind of close-minded thinking is contrary to the level of authenticity necessary for a successful Sales 2.0 strategy that incorporates social media. The first place you must start is with your own company, its culture, and its tolerance for openness.

As we explained at the outset of this book by quoting Mark Cuban, "In the Internet age, executives have to learn how to shape information about themselves and their companies, or the Internet will do it for them, and it won't be pretty." Indeed, it will not be pretty because if you are not in the conversation, you have no way to respond. Being proactive and not reactive enables you to take charge of how the world portrays your company.

To complicate matters, in a sales organization revenue and margin reign supreme. These values often conflict with the core value of social media—the importance of authentic, transparent interactions. Today's economic situation has created a sales pressure cooker that consists of impatient managers, nervous marketing reps, fearful legal departments, paranoid human resources personnel, and rigid training. First, management hinders their rep's ability to take the time to build an online presence given the manager's impatient, short-sighted focus on closing the deal now. Axel Schultz said, "There is a bias among upper management that these approaches take too long and sales are needed now."[2] Second, marketing professionals complain that sales reps will compromise the brand unless managed closely, thus insinuating that sales reps can not be trusted to accurately communicate the message. Third, the legal department focuses on mitigating risk rather than facilitating innovation. Fourth, human resource managers concern themselves with compliance and avoiding lawsuits rather than using creative means to source new talent. Fifth, training groups believe that only they, as subject matter experts, can create employee learning and development programs. *Too many conflicting agendas keep companies routed in outdated modes of operation that no longer appeal to the twenty-first-century buyer.*

Yesterday's competitive advantage is just that. No matter how much companies want to cling to what they have always done, their success will depend on their ability to embrace this changing world. The downturn of the economy in 2008 may be the crack in the armor to stimulate companies to move out of their boxes. In fact, Anneke Seley's June 24, 2009 blog post, "Transforming a Sales Organization: A True Sales 2.0 Story," talks about a multimedia company that is launching a Sales 2.0 strategy. "They are doing it because they have no choice," Seley said. "They saw their profits decline and then disappear."[3]

Given such urgency, where do you start? You start by objectively looking at yourself and what your company stands for. You start by turning your eyes away from the bells and whistles of the new media and toward your own policies, procedures, and cultural barriers that restrict creativity—your own sales pressure cooker. In fact, you decide if getting on the bandwagon is worth the risk of change. If your answer is yes, *The New Handshake* will give you the tools to kickstart the process.

How Can We Manage the Information?

Viewed by many organizations as merely social applications rather than business applications that can drive specific results (i.e., sales), the social media are offhandedly dismissed. When we combine the cultural bias that exists inside companies today with outdated mindsets powered by the old-fashioned sales practices that have existed for almost a century, we can easily understand why many companies move too slowly to adopt this new way of building relationships with their buyers. Many companies give the social networks a backward glance—meaning, they instruct their marketing and sales-people to "manage" it. They want to control the information going out and monitor the information coming it. Three fears cause them to limit employee access to social networks. They fear that employees cannot communicate the company message; they fear employees might air dirty laundry; and they fear employees might waste time "talking to their friends."

To exemplify these fears Seley told us about a comment that arose during the 2009 Sales 2.0 annual conference. An executive from Microsoft said, "My salespeople are spending all day on Facebook and not doing their job." Seley replied, "It's not Facebook that's the problem. If people aren't doing their job, they should be fired."[4] Organizations can control the abuses of Facebook as much as they can control the abuses of online surfing. People must be held accountable for doing their jobs. If people are not doing their jobs, Seley points out, it is not the fault of the tool.

Contrast these typical concerns with a new sales perspective whereby sales teams have the ability to demonstrate the capabilities of your products and services before meeting your buyers, to expand your reach beyond local borders to touch new prospects, and to create business partnerships that broaden your capabilities in order to increase sales revenue. The question is not how you can control the information but *how you can create enough trust in your organization to let go of the information.*

Today's savvy companies and salespeople understand this new world of social media and networking. They know that the old "hop on a plane" model of selling no longer makes sense. *The New Handshake* challenges sales to meet social media head on. It challenges you to create a more targeted form of sell-ing that is Web based and includes social networking. This form of selling encompasses a model whereby sellers embrace the idea that they can attract, interact, and close business with buyers online. The new handshake approach, when done within the framework of a supportive company culture, leads to higher sales velocity, volume, and profits.

SALES MEETS SOCIAL MEDIA

In previous chapters we looked at how Web 2.0 evolved and its relationship to Sales 2.0. Taking this analysis one step further, let us examine how Sales 2.0 has evolved into the realm of the social media. The Internet has gotten an upgrade so to speak and thereby changed the way buyers source information, make decisions, communicate with suppliers, and buy products and services. As Canning and others suggest, any sales organization choosing not to integrate social media into their sales strategy will become less and less relevant. Social media provide sales professionals with the opportunity to listen and to influence through their participation in sites like LinkedIn, Twitter, and Facebook. They can establish a reputation as a trusted advisor known for anticipating upcoming trends by aggregating information relevant to their industry using RSS feeds, news readers, and bookmarking tools (see Chapter 12).

By harnessing the power of the people, they can anticipate and solve problems in ways that the competition could only dream of. In a video by Thrive America, for example, Jason Prance was asked how Thrive America could become even more visible beyond its blog and video content development. Prance suggested that the company develop a podcast linked to its RSS feed on iTunes.[5] His response illustrates that no matter what you are doing, more opportunities exist. The question is: how willing is your company to take advantage of what waits at your fingertips?

A perfect example of this kind of innovation with sales and the social media comes from a highly traditional company, Procter & Gamble (P&G). The authors of *Groundswell* describe how P&G captured the attention of young girls aged 6 to 11 in order to sell a most difficult product—tampons.[6] The company recognized that there are some issues young girls do not wish to talk about, hear about, or see anything in connection with. The authors told us that Bob Arnold, who found himself in charge of marketing feminine care products to this population, came up with an innovative solution. He spearheaded a blog called beinggirl.com, and this blog did not talk about feminine products and instead talked about everything it meant to be a young girl in this day and age. With the help of a psychologist, Dr. Iris Prager, who answered the girl's questions, the blog created a community of girls talking about everything from boyfriends to their first periods. At the end of each response, Dr. Iris signed off with the name of the product.

According to Bernoff and Li, what P&G did was create a relationship with its target market. With the subtle sales message in each signature and a lot of sensitivity, the company not only created visibility for its brand of tampons, it also created trust. If Dr. Iris recommends a certain tampon through her subtle message, which one do you think the girls will purchase? In fact, *Groundswell* reported that the traffic on beinggirl.com in 2007 was up over 150 percent over the previous year. How do you think these numbers might translate into sales?[7]

If you are just getting your feet wet with regard to social media, you are most likely approaching it backwards, as most of us do. Companies typically approach the social computing world by looking first at the nifty, whiz-bang technologies available. It could be a Tweet here, a blog there, a LinkedIn profile, a Facebook fan page, or a few YouTube videos thrown up on the Web site. That is a mistake! The strategy we present in *The New Handshake* consists of a four-prong approach: People, Purpose, Plan, and Technology (PPPT):

People

P&G knew its market. The company understood that young girls congregate around the social media. *Who are your customers? Where are they likely to participate online?* Given how important creating a trusted relationship is in advance of the sale, you diminish your chance of success if you are not connecting with your target buyer in the right social group. In the past sales professionals asked, Whom are we selling to? Whom can we get to purchase our product? How can we land a meeting? Now, sales reps face different questions, namely: Who are our potential buyers? What kind of relationship can we create with them? How can we develop trust with our buyers? These questions will shape your Social Media Sales Strategy.

The people side of the equation also includes your employees. Your people comprise the social media movers and shakers of your company. Each brings something unique to the table and that unique skill set adds to your brand and helps deepen the relationship with your market.

Purpose

P&G had a purpose for its use of social media. The company could not reach its target market through traditional advertising. The girls refused to watch commercials about tampons, particularly in plain view of their brothers or fathers. Rather than dig the well deeper, P&G decided to dig in another place. The purpose was to win the respect and trust of the market first and sell products second. This shift in purpose enabled the company to meet a very tough marketing challenge. What is your purpose? Is it visibility? Is it to push your product onto your consumer? Is it to create a brand? As we will point out in later chapters, you will use different social media tools depending on your purpose. You may say your purpose is visibility and branding. If so, you will use the social tools that best enable you to accomplish both these goals. Even though P&G is in the business of selling its products, the company made sales a secondary, not a primary, purpose.

Plan

Now that you know who your people are and what your purpose is, you can start creating your Social Media Sales plan. Some companies begin small. They start with an internal blog to bring their employees onboard. People and purpose will drive your plan. How will you implement a social media strategy? Which parts of the organization will be involved? How will you engender support from the top? What policies and procedures need to change? Remember the lessons learned by OracleDirect when the company first introduced virtual selling. The new best practice for the introduction of any piece of a Sales 2.0 strategy is a pilot that fits the needs of your organization.

Technology

This last step is often the first step in many organizations. Those companies who have experienced success in the use of the social media know that technology comes last. When you know your market, your purpose, and your plan, then you are better positioned to choose a set of social media tools that align with your sales strategy. As new tools enter the market, you adjust if needed, just as we are seeing now with OracleDirect. Changing the company culture is the most challenging step; once that is done, the technology shifts come easy.

People buy from people that they know, like, and trust. They want to know that the company they choose is reliable, dependable, and will deliver what they say they will. This dictum has survived for thousands of years and is not likely to change any time soon. We will talk about the psychology of the know-like-and-trust factor in the next chapter and how that impacts your Social Media Sales Strategy. Companies heading down the path to adopt a social media strategy to drive business results, cannot just say, "We need a corporate wiki." Doing so would have as little effect as purchasing an update to their current CRM system (that no one is using effectively right now anyway) with fancy reporting and mobile extensions. A successful Social Media Sales Strategy requires much more.

Successfully integrating social media into your sales strategies and processes requires that you know what you expect to accomplish, who you are actually targeting, what you intend to say to them, how to utilize the right tools to achieve your objectives, how to execute your plan, in what ways you intend to measure your results, and finally repeating the cycle. It requires the right people, the right purpose, the right plan, the right technology, and the right accountability if you want to hit your sales targets. These components, by the way, are essential to sales success whether you use social media or not.

BLENDING THE APPROACH

You can accomplish big things when you blend social media into your sales approach. For example, you can reduce accidental sales because you and your sales team will more effectively contact, connect, communicate with, and convert a larger pool of the "right" buyers on a consistent basis. Furthermore, the persistent and consistent focus on activities drives sales conversion over and over again that ultimately leads to increased revenue. In other words, your reps will fill the pipeline with sales opportunities that have a greater likelihood of closing.

Unfortunately as we will talk about in later chapters, even in today's twenty-first century world of business, plenty of old-school salespeople still refuse to change the way they sell. They insist that the only way to close the deal is to meet people face to face. OracleDirect confronted this resistance when the company first introduced telesales. Today, seasoned field reps snub their noses at using LinkedIn or Twitter to develop credibility for what they have to offer, citing a sales presentation that delivers a list of features and benefits as the only way to sell. In reality, these seasoned reps are partially correct.

When we examine the new media, we must consider retaining what currently works while we add innovation. Chapter 5 looks at how to bring on the new tools without tossing out the tried-and-true sales methods of the past. This idea parallels the way Barack Obama led his campaign. He incorporated facets of the social media within a strategy that included stump speeches and traditional advertising. Indeed, we would be remiss if we tossed out face-to-face interactions. The blending of the old with the new creates opportunities for face-to-face selling as well as telephone selling and selling via the social media.

What the social media tools provide is a more efficient lead-generation process that looks something like this: The salesperson connects with contacts on LinkedIn, Facebook, Yahoo groups, blogs, and other social networking outlets. Those contacts generate many more leads than ever imagined because of the span of connections. Instead of cold-calling, they create warm leads through online tools. From those leads come the phone calls and the face-to-face meetings and, later, closed sales. The modern, savvy Sales 2.0 professionals need never make another cold call so long as they extend *the new handshake*. Seley and Holloway refer to this process as cold calling 2.0. Some sales professionals still rely on cold calls, but they are doing it less and less.

Another legacy we inherit from the old-school types is the refusal to admit that the entire world is not their ideal client. Essentially, they believe that everyone could buy from them. Although technically that may be true, you will get more sales traction by narrowing your focus. A colleague of Barb's once talked about "land and expand." To him, this meant owning a particular market space to make it easier to land the initial business. Once inside that market space, you can expand what you have to offer. This concept of land and expand goes one step further as we explore blending sales with social media. Indeed, the trust developed through the social media gives today's salespeople a "foot in the door." That funnel of trust could begin with simply reading a blog or following a discussion in a chat room and end with hitting the purchase button. The new mantra for Sales 2.0 is *patience*. Can today's modern, hard-driving business executives patiently work the system, patiently wait until the savvy consumer decides to hit the purchase button?

CREATE, MANAGE, AND PROMOTE YOUR BRAND

Companies fear losing control of their corporate brand, but as Joel Postman reminds us in his book, *SocialCorp*, consumers already control the company's brand.[8] Even if you are not participating in this new world of the Internet, a conversation already exists about your company. Choosing to ignore the conversation does not mean that it is not happening. It is like the child who covers his eyes and believes no one can see him. A recent blog post on Twitter discussed one company's inept response to negative buzz.[9] The company produces organic clothing. All was going well; in fact, too well. Increased orders pushed the company way behind with shipping the product. Several buyers Tweeted about their frustration. It did not take long for the negative Tweets to score big with Google. Yikes! Thus began that company's worst nightmare.

You might wonder how to prevent this kind of negative press. The answer to that question is you cannot prevent it. If this company had responded to the customers in a timely manner, they would not have engendered angry, frustrated customers. Forward-thinking companies understand how critical it is for them to be part of the dialogue. Adam Brown, Coca-Cola's director of social media, told Heather Lalley in a September 9, 2009 Associated Press article, "Having the world's most recognized brand, we feel like there's an obligation or responsibility when people are talking about us to respond."[10]

From a sales perspective, by using social media effectively, you can create a powerful impression of who you are, what you value, and your capabilities, expertise, service, and support without ever meeting your prospective buyer. Today's knowledge-driven buyers go online and ask their colleagues whom they should buy from. If you are not there—you lose! If you meet someone at an event and that person later looks up your LinkedIn profile and finds it terribly written or, worse still, not there, what does that say about you? Indeed, customers are much more leery of companies that are not participating than those that are.

Would you buy from someone who does not have a Web site or whose Web site looks as if it has not been updated? We recently called a publicist to explore her services. When we asked to see the publicist's Web site, we were told she did not have one. How in today's world can anyone profess to be a publicist without a presence on the Web? We did not call back. For B2B where the sales decision costs much more than B2C, a professional Web presence is as necessary today as a slick brochure was yesterday.

FILLING THE FUNNEL

As we have suggested, one effective use of social media is to create sales opportunities among buyers who may be unaware of a business need. In addition, the social media provide tools for your salesperson to create a compelling case for pushing that purchase button among buyers who may realize they have a need but are not yet fully motivated to act. Approached this way, Sales 2.0 influences the buyer's view of a potential solution: one that tilts the scale in favor of the solution provided by the seller.

The popular book, *The New Solution Selling* by Keith M. Eades, suggests that without pain there is no change. He goes on to say that, with the complex decisionmaking consistent with today's world, businesses need to holistically understand their buyers.[11] If there was ever an argument to be made for the use of social media as a component of a well-thought-out sales strategy, this is certainly it. Technology enables the hunting, gathering, and mining of data, which in turn propels salespeople to more clearly understand the challenges that their prospective buyers now face.

MEASURING THE ROI

Joel Postman advises that any well-run company must use hard and soft measures to gauge its effectiveness. By hard measures, he talks about revenue and lead generation, and by soft measures he talks about brand perception and engagement. He tells us that businesses must measure social media by those same standards.[12] The tools to measure the effects of social media on specific business results are in the early stages, but there are tools available for measuring site traffic and the behavior of visitors who land at your Web site door. Trish Bertuzzi reported that 70 percent of her company's Web site traffic came from her LinkedIn profile.

While the ability to measure tangible results when using social media continues to evolve, companies may now realize the substantial price savings of their initiatives. The most impressive results thus far come from Dell. In a blog post titled, "Dell Reaches $6.5m in sales via Twitter," we see the earliest measurable impact on sales. In that same post, Dell representative Richard Binhammer reported that the company's success stems from a number of things, including the company's willingness to brand with a face. The face of the Dell Outlet Twitter account is Stephanie. Stephanie is not all about selling; instead, she answers questions and participates in the conversation. Binhammer boiled down Dell's success on Twitter to three things: "Being there for people who are looking for our products, offering sales opportunities that are meaningful to our customers and interacting with people."[13]

Hubspot grew out of the need for small businesses to put these new applications to work for them. The idea being that these businesses need help

FEDERAL APPLIANCE ACHIEVES HIGH ROI
WITH THE NEW HANDSHAKE MODEL

When Dale Underwood created Federal Appliance, he had no idea he was reaching out with a new handshake. What he did know was that the Internet had forever changed how businesses would find new customers. Furthermore, in his quest to drive more sales for his company, he discovered how to truly measure his marketing return on investment (ROI).

Now chief executive officer of Federal Appliance, LLC, Underwood began his career in information technology (IT) as a programmer. He moved from developing software to selling enterprise IT products and services. In 1998 he and a partner formed a value-added resale (VAR) business focused on providing IT equipment to large government and commercial accounts. "I enjoyed the VAR business, but we were working with the old handshake model." he explained, "That means we primarily used traditional outbound sales and marketing tactics like trade shows, cold calling, and on-site presentations."[14]

By 2004 Underwood noticed a significant change in the behavior of his customers. The self-service nature of the Internet coupled with increasingly rich content was empowering his customers to research the products he was selling. "As a VAR, it was becoming tougher to remain subject matter experts when customers were not only using the latest gear every day, but they began using the Internet to discuss their findings with peers," he said. "Potential customers moved quickly from needing VARs for access to technical information to being in complete control of their own research." Feeling the sand shift below his feet, Underwood realized it was time to try a different approach. In January 2005 he sold his interest in that business.

While others saw the new online world and its unlimited information as a threat, Underwood saw opportunity and decided to build a new, disruptive VAR business called Federal Appliance. By embracing the new handshake model and building on his past sales experience, he developed a way to engage new customers. "Customers were seeking information from online communities and blogs so we decided to use these new media as our core marketing strategy," he said. In addition to the primary Web site for Federal Appliance, Underwood created www.4equallogic.com to attract technical people in need of data storage equipment. His team created rich content that appealed to early market buyers. This content included project planning templates, configuration tips, and budgetary pricing via a third-party service called EchoQuote. Underwood designed the new site for Search Engine Optimization (SEO), and by the end of 2008 he noted that the blog was generating as many high-quality leads as the primary Web site.

Recognizing that traditional marketing efforts are hard to quantify, Underwood began analyzing the conversions made from his blog. Since each lead was tied to a specific product or service, he could easily measure the blog's effectiveness. "When someone reading our blog takes action, we not only capture the person's contact information, but we also capture the *dollar value* of what they requested." Figure 4.1 shows a one-year snapshot of the cost of using this new method as well as the marketing ROI in terms of marketing funnel lead value. From a pure marketing ROI perspective, for each $1 spent on new marketing methods, Federal Appliance returns $1,653 in potential revenue.

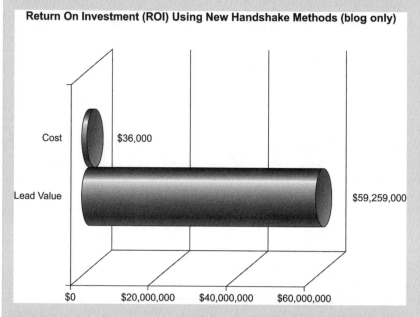

Return On Investment (ROI) Using New Handshake Methods (blog only)

Cost — $36,000

Lead Value — $59,259,000

$0 $20,000,000 $40,000,000 $60,000,000

FIGURE 4.1   One year snapshot of return on investment (ROI) using blogging

Federal Appliance saw the shift in buyer behavior early and made quick adjustments. By going against conventional wisdom and embracing new handshake methods, the company transformed itself into a top provider of data storage solutions with an extremely high marketing ROI.

understanding how to transform their static Web sites into a marketing machine. Furthermore, they needed a way to determine if the time and effort devoted to the social media affected the bottom line. "The easiest way to do this is to look at the source of your leads," said Rick Burns, marketing director of Hubspot.com. "Track them through the first visit to conversion and looking at this on a channel by channel basis. For example, if you got ten Twitter leads and ten from Google searches and 14 from LinkedIn, you can see where to focus your efforts."[15]

As Dale Underwood, CEO of Federal Appliance LLC, told us, "We found a way to measure marketing, and what we learned was that marketing has a much greater impact on the ROI than we ever imagined—probably 50 times!"[16] If you want to capture data that show how effective your Web site is or how productive your LinkedIn presence is, you can do it. The evolution of Sales 2.0 has happened, and its impact on today's marketplace is leaving a new footprint in the landscape. Seley and Holloway show us that telesales and Web-based selling positively affect the bottom line. The three companies they highlighted, OracleDirect, WebEx, and Genius.com, record impressive data. What makes us think that expanding into the world of social media will show us anything different?

Logic tells us that two-way, online communication with an emphasis on relationship building, coupled with the natural human desire to link with other human beings, will pay off. Clay Shirky in *Here Comes Everybody* writes, "Human beings are social creatures—not occasionally or by accident but always."[17] Canning said, "By Tweeting, I found Nigel Edelshain and the Sales 2.0 conference. We target salespeople. There's power behind this."[18] Can that power be measured? You decide.

Chapter 5

Consultative Selling: Make New Friends but Keep the Old

In our introduction we defined consultative selling as knowing what customers need and creating a dialogue around those needs. In this chapter we will take that concept and develop it in order to understand how the social media may enrich your current consultative selling efforts. We will also discuss the psychology of consultative selling and customer relations management (CRM) in relation to two-way communication, building engagement, and profiling online consumers. How can we integrate traditional selling with the new tools emerging? What do we keep and what do we toss? In other words, can we make new friends and keep the old?

Rick Burns of Hubspot told us that the most difficult part of this new world of sales is putting all the pieces together. Blending the old with the new and looking at what part works best for you and your business creates a lot of confusion. "It's like a big pile of Legos," he said.[1] He explained that Hubspot helps companies put the pieces together easily.

CUSTOMER RELATIONS MANAGEMENT (CRM)

If you work in sales, you know what consultative selling means and you likely use some form of CRM. In the 1970s best-selling author Linda Richardson coined the term consultative selling.[2] What Richardson meant was completely contrary to the salesman in the driver's seat mentality of Peterson and Carnegie that we discussed in Chapter 1. Instead, she saw consultative selling as a way to uncover customer needs and to base the sales dialogue around those needs.

Richardson created a sales model that equipped the sales professional with skills and strategies to achieve revenue goals while building strong client relationships. The emphasis became customer needs. Of course, the means by which to respond to those needs were face-to-face visits and long boardroom presentations. Sales professionals who adopted consultative selling developed campaigns that met the needs of their customers. In today's world of media choice, they are likely to choose a method to reach those customers in a manner the customer prefers.

CRM evolved as part of a consultative selling program. As a way to manage, track, and add value to each customer contact, CRM software systems emerged. These systems gave the salespeople a tool for keeping up with the needs and desires of their customers. It captured the science of sales with software designed to keep track of customer interactions. Unfortunately, the training and implementation of CRM systems left a lot to be desired. Many companies did not adequately train their sales forces to effectively use the systems. To the typical salesman trying to do his job, the system seemed cumbersome and useless. We do not wish to repeat the same mistakes with the introduction of the social media. With consultative selling and CRM, the tools for CRM became the driving force. The tail wagged the dog. In effect, the good idea presented by Richardson got lost in the implementation.

Today's market compels companies to develop a *social media strategy* in which the tools (technology) come after the concept, and those tools play a role in making the sales team's life easier, not more complicated. For that reason we created the four-pronged social media approach that was discussed in Chapter 4: People, Purpose, Plan, and, lastly, Technology. The three processes that Seley and Holloway developed in *Sales 2.0* for the initiation of a telesales and Web-based selling program mirror this approach. They, too, recognized the need for having the right people to implement the new process, a process that fits the objectives of the business, and the technology for implementation. Their three-prong approach matches our four-prong approach with the exception of the Planning phase.

For a social media strategy to work effectively, planning how to implement each tool takes a more prominent role than systems using more traditional technology—telephone and e-mail. Nonetheless, what we have learned from the early adopters of Sales 2.0 is that we cannot jump on board without understanding the People and Process. Technology serves to facilitate sales processes, not make them more cumbersome.

In a teleconference on creating talent using the groundswell, Josh Bernoff described something called the "Groundswell Approach-Avoidance Syndrome." He said if you suffer from any of the following symptoms, you are too focused on the tool and not focused enough on the strategy:

- You are obsessively interested in online applications such as blogs, Facebook, and Twitter. You worry yourself into a frenzied state because you do not understand how to use them.
- You are excessively excited when you hear about successful corporate applications. You know if they can do it, why can't you.
- You feel more and more nervous about answering your boss's questions about Web 2.0 strategy.
- You ask your teens, "Tell me more about this MySpace thing?" and you take notes on the responses.[3]

The *new* ultimate goal of sales is not closing the sale but building an enduring relationship. This enduring relationship leads to sales, but perhaps in the future. Although relationship-building is not a new concept, the importance of the relationships in today's online market takes on more prominence than ever. Harvey Mackay preached about building relationships in his well-known book, *Dig Your Well before You're Thirsty*.[4] At the time this book was being written, the concept of consultative selling was just emerging at full steam. Mackay encouraged salespeople to learn about the people they were selling to and to stay in close touch with them. He used examples of how he built his own successful career by never forgetting a birthday.

These small acts of kindness and remembrances created relationships that later turned into opportunities and sales. One of Mackay's top-10 truisms is that "a network replaces the weakness of the individual with the strength of the group."[5] Translating Harvey Mackay's principles into today's world of social media, we can only imagine the power of the group. Furthermore, the social media provide tools that make the kind of high touch that Mackay described in his book possible. Facebook not only alerts you to your "friend's" birthdays, it enables you to send personalized virtual gifts. What we must constantly remind ourselves when we embrace tools like Facebook is that the most important principle Mackay taught us is the power of the relationship, not merely the power of the network. Nigel Edelshain said that relationship is the biggest factor affecting social media. He added, "Why don't we use the tools in the social networks to promote referral based selling instead of cold calling."[6]

Clara Shih, in her book titled *The Facebook Era*, wrote, "More than ever sales reps must strive to maximize the lifetime value of their customer relationships versus maximizing the value of a single interaction."[7] Or, we might add a single sale. Today, CRM systems combined with the new online tools for selling offer the sales professional a way to keep track of her sales in a way that personalizes and deepens the relationship. Rick Burns talked about marketing with a "magnet instead of a sledge hammer."[8] He discussed using the social media tools to attract people to your Web site and then to convert them into buyers. "What you see now is people coming to your site with specific identifiable interests," he told us. "You can solve their problems as a salesperson. Instead of feature-focused, in-your-face selling with a sledge hammer, salespeople have an opportunity to come at selling in a more productive way for both sides."[9]

Burns said that in the past people thought of consultative as backing off and not being aggressive enough. "This is the wrong approach," he advised. "With social media, search engine optimization and other data, which we can help collect at Hubspot, the sales rep learns needs and can speed up the sales cycle. It builds up the perception of expertise and transparency."[10] Essentially, what Burns is talking about is building trust.

HOW THE COMMUNICATION REVOLUTION AFFECTS RELATIONSHIPS

Few people will argue with the notion that sales happen when someone knows, likes, and trusts you. Today's virtual world makes the ability to create this kind of trust more difficult. How can we create trust when we never meet someone face to face? How can we sell to someone we never eyeball? In what ways can relationships evolve from superficial to deep through the social media? Seley tells us that OracleDirect executives faced the same questions when they introduced telesales into the sales process. The company's initial response to these questions was to begin slowly and only with the smaller ticket items. Contrary to popular thought, customer preference carried more weight than the method of communication. Without realizing it, OracleDirect was moving into the communication revolution where everything we know about communication was challenged. Imagine the world of communication shifting sideways. OracleDirect discovered this shift and developed its Sales 2.0 program with sufficient flexibility to respond to customer preferences within the realm of a communication revolution.

Perhaps, contrary to another popular belief, we are learning that the relationship does not have to be that deep. Shih tells us that the social media are characterized by people with very few strong connections but with many more weak connections. Therefore, she makes the startling discovery that it is through *active use of those weak connections* and good use of the strong connections that relationships form.

To help us understand these relationships, we turned to two psychologists, Joseph Luft and Harrington Ingham, who developed a model of social interaction called the Johari Window in their book *On Human Interaction*.[11] What this model teaches us is that people interact with one another on the basis of four quadrants, as depicted in Figure 5.1.

The Johari Window

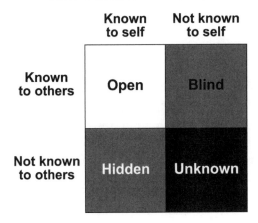

FIGURE 5.1   The four quadrants of the Johari Window

The Open Area

This area contains all the things we know about ourselves that we are willing to share with others. Examples of these kinds of things might be our love of animals or our propensity toward travel or our devotion to our family. When we look at companies and the social media, we read a lot about being authentic and transparent.What this means is that companies must strive to let go of the fears that prevent them from sharing and look for ways to open up. An excellent example of this phenomenon happened when the now famous blogger, Bob Lutz, began the blog for General Motors, called FastLane. When Lutz returned to General Motors at the end of 2004, he noticed bad signs for the company. The stock was plummeting. Customers expressed lackluster interest in the new product lines. Unable to get his message heard, Lutz decided to start a blog. Whether Lutz knew it or not, he was embarking on a strategy to widen the Open Area. He found a revolutionary way for the auto company to *communicate*. Although the blog could not solve all the problems GM faced, it opened the door to create a more trusting relationship between the company and the customer.

One of the biggest industry complaints about the social media is that it is too open. In the past salespeople held back information from their customers in order to allow them to go back to clients over and over. This tactic stretched out the sales process. After a while the consumer wondered why the salesperson did not share sooner. Clearly today's great salespeople recognize that everything is known already. Why hold back? Indeed, salespeople who share all their knowledge and expertise at the get-go have always been more successful.

The Blind Area

This area contains what others know about us, but what we do not know about ourselves. Some people call these our *blind spots*. Perhaps we tend to talk about ourselves a lot; perhaps we are overly indulgent with our children. All of us have blind spots that others see but that elude us. We are so close to ourselves, we cannot see our own strengths and weaknesses. Companies, too, are so close to their products and services they have no idea what others think of them. Marketers use focus groups to help uncover customer reactions to new products or to new ad campaigns.

What do companies do beyond the traditional focus groups to discover the blind spots that tell them what their customers think about their products and services? The social media provide a great place for opening the company's eyes to its blemishes. A good example of uncovering the Blind Area comes from *Naked Conversations*. When Microsoft hired Robert Scoble, they described him as someone who "lets his flaws hang on his sleeve. He's curious like a child and it's hard not to like and trust him." Being curious like a child enables you to open up to your Blind Area and win the trust of others. *Naked Conversations* goes on to say that the project at Microsoft that helped turn the company from one which kept everything hidden to a more open company was spearheaded by Scoble's blog. Blogs enable companies to learn what others think about them.

Online communities are another social media tool for uncovering blind spots. Some companies begin their own communities in order to learn what their customers are saying; others study and respond to existing communities. Essentially, opening the Blind Area means that you must *really hear* what is said about you or your product or service. If you do not hear it, it cannot move from the Blind Area into the Open Area. How does this work? One of the best examples of this phenomenon was discussed in *Groundswell*.[12] The producers of the CBS program, *Jericho*, recognized that they created a program that might attract a unique audience. Accordingly, they established an opportunity for an online community to form. That community immediately began talking about the storyline and the characters, providing excellent feedback to the show's creators. This community grew and flourished because the CBS team listened and responded to the flood of information they received.

When the network decided to cancel the program, a strong protest ensued. The community united and sent the producers 20 tons of peanuts because, according to the authors of *Groundswell*, the main character in the program frequently said, "Nuts." After having received more nuts than the mailroom could handle, CBS relented. They agreed to continue the program but enlisted the community to help increase the size of the audience. CBS used this online community to gauge its audience, to uncover blind spots, and to make changes. Too bad they forgot about the power of the community when they made the unilateral decision to cancel the show!

The Hidden Area

The things about us, our products, or our services that we do not want others to know constitute the Hidden Area. Obviously, the likelihood that we can keep things hidden decreases as online communication grows and expands. The challenge that the social media present is for companies to eradicate the fear that their customers might disappear if they know them too well and instead open themselves up for customer scrutiny. This represents a huge departure from the way most companies operate. Most prefer to keep information close to home. The strong worry that the company cannot release information without the lawyers looking at it first, without fine-tooth analysis of wording so as not to offend certain groups, without the marketing machine's approval to make sure everything fits the branding requirement, places restrictions at best and a sense of paranoia at worst on any social media strategy.

This view opposes the theory behind human relationships that Lutz and Ingham presented in the Johari Window. In contrast, instead of retreating into his Hidden Area or making excuses about a bad incident, Guy Stephens, a sales rep, used Twitter to build a relationship with an unhappy customer. In his blog post titled, "Confessions of a Corporate Tweeter,"[13] he tells us that he learned quickly that it is best to search what people are saying about his company. When he did this and found a negative comment, he immediately responded with the following Tweet: "Hi, I wrk 4 Carphone Warehouse. Sorry 2 hear u had a bad experience with us. Anything I can do 2 help?"

This response produced a dialogue and eventually enabled Stephens to resolve the customer's issue. Stephens used Twitter to stay in the conversation, and by so doing he built trust. He added that he sees Twitter as a mechanism to lead him to other deeper forms of communication, such as e-mail, telephone, and maybe face to face. In today's world of communication, keeping things hidden may be a notion of the past.

Remember the old adage, "Information is like sand. The harder you try to hold onto it, the more it slips through your hands." Finally, someone asked Josh Bernoff the following question in a recent teleconference on building talent through the social media: "How can we protect ourselves from unfounded negative aspersions on our company if we unleash the social media?" Bernoff responded that if you fear negative comments, you cannot unleash the social networks. He went on by simply asking, "Isn't it better to see the negative and have a platform of response? If you believe that people are only saying good things about your company, you are not living in the real world."

Releasing information from the Hidden Area shows your customers that you trust them. After all, whom do we tell our secrets to? Only those people we *trust*.

Nonetheless, we realize that some companies must protect their privacy. In those cases, you might opt for a more private network. It is possible to create private social networks without using public sites like Facebook and LinkedIn. Shih recommends exploring Ning. The closed networks offer more control and focused interaction among community members, but they lower engagement. She adds, "The value of social networking sites goes up exponentially with the number of members. It is precisely the reach, openness and transparency of public social networking sites that make them so compelling."[14] Our recommendation is to err on the side of openness. Take a deep breath, close your eyes, and let all that Hidden Area out.

The Unknown Area

The Johari Window contains a quadrant where we keep things that are deep in our subconscious minds that neither we nor others know. These things are left undiscovered until we unleash our creativity. Luft and Ingham tell us that once we listen to others and share openly—in other words, pay attention to our blind spots and release information from our Hidden Area,—we open the door to the Unknown Area. The social media provide opportunities to listen to our customers and to share and talk with them.

Bernoff and Li in *Groundswell* counsel us over and over that the challenge of the social media is not which tool to use but the discovery of ways to both *talk and listen* to customers. Talking and listening create a very large Open Area that helps us become authentic and transparent. Authenticity and transparency create trust. And trust, by the way, creates sales. That is why we strive for relationships. Probably the most successful woman entertainer of our time, Oprah Winfrey, delivered the commencement address at Wellesley College in 1997. Some rate this speech as the best speech of its kind ever. Why? "Authenticity oozes out of every paragraph of this speech," said Richard Green in an interview with *USA Weekend*.[15] The power of openness works not only for Oprah in commencement speeches, but can work for you if you are willing to let down the walls and welcome the multitudes.

This chapter dealt with the power of relationships and the effects of the communication revolution on the selling process. One kernel of knowledge that you might take away is that the communication revolution creates more and more openness. Less and less is private. The more we try to hold onto something, the quicker it will slip through our fingers. The social media are all about openness. Whether you choose to use Facebook or LinkedIn, you will have to make decisions on how much you are willing to share about yourself and your company. Indeed, the twenty-first century is not a time to crawl into your Hidden Area.

As companies begin developing social media packages they must determine where their customers are. In other words, are their customers using Facebook, LinkedIn, Twitter, or other networks, and how might they be using these tools? If your customers are not active users, what is the value of cultivating new customer relationships through the social media? In Chapter 6 we explore what the typical online user looks like and how he or she engages in the social media, and perhaps from that you will uncover the answer to that question: why be active when our customers aren't?

Chapter 6

What Does Your Social Media Customer Look Like?

We have emphasized in earlier chapters the importance of identifying your business purpose before embarking on a social media strategy. That purpose must include considering the ideal client you want to reach. According to Comscore.com, the social networking audience in 2008 grew by 25 percent worldwide.[1] Although amazing numbers of people are signing up on social media sites every day, what is most important is the understanding of what your "ideal customer" actually does when he logs on.

By utilizing social media you are looking for opportunities to leverage emerging trends, which you can then parlay into sales opportunities. To do that, you will need to understand the online buying behavior of your target buyers, the frequency of their social media usage, and the core tools that they are likely to use. The more you can learn about their online patterns, the better positioned you are to connect to them in the right social media communities and converse with them in ways they deem natural.

For example, Barb recently coached a client who was using Facebook, Twitter, and to a lesser degree LinkedIn. Though the client consistently and persistently used these social media tools, the sales results had not materialized. Delving into the question of "who is your ideal client?," Barb discovered that her client wanted to reach corporations, but she had focused her sales efforts primarily in Facebook. Though Facebook reports that more than 40 percent of its users are over the age of 35, LinkedIn is widely recognized as the social networking tool for business. Given LinkedIn's broader corporate appeal, Barb coached the client to revise her strategy. As you formulate your own strategy, you may discover that unlike this client, your typical customer is more likely to be active on Facebook. Given that situation, your sales approach will differ from the one you might use when approaching someone in the LinkedIn world.

Once you have defined your ideal clients and determined what their core social media communities are, you then need to determine what their online behavior looks like. You might find that your customers are primarily "watching" and not participating. Perhaps they are participating in discussions, but they prefer not to purchase products or services online. As you review the data that support how to reach and market to your ideal client online, you can create a strategy that specifically targets your customer and her preferences. B2B companies have a little easier time determining customer preferences than B2C because they have a narrower customer base. The challenge facing B2B, however, is most businesses move into new territories at a slower rate. In essence, what consumers did yesterday, businesses will do tomorrow. "When things change at the consumer level," Canning said, "within two years things change at the B2B level."[2]

PROFILING THE SOCIAL MEDIA CONSUMER

Forrester Research developed a tool to examine the social computing behaviors of the social media user. Forrester's Social Technographics[®3] profile tool classifies the participation of online consumers into six overlapping levels, giving us a more accurate picture of the types of online activity taking place. The six levels include Creators, Critics, Collectors, Joiners, Spectators, and Inactives.

Let us examine how Social Technographics work. If, for example, you are interested in the computing behavior of women aged 35 to 44, the data might reveal that the two top participation categories are Spectators and Critics. Once you learn this piece of information, you can then create a strategy that suits your online buyer. If, for instance, the use of customer reviews is a strategy that might bolster your sales, you would target Critics. Amazon pioneered the use of customer reviews to drive book sales. Spectators, on the other hand, do not actively participate. They watch and listen. Knowing you have a high percentage of your audience in this category, suggests a strategy that would focus on increasing visibility and promoting interest through interesting, useful content.

The numbers attributed to social media adoption and usage continue to rise significantly, as online users find new ways to connect, collaborate, and communicate in cyberspace. Forrester's Social Technographics profile tool, however, gives us a starting point from which to assess and identify how people are interacting with Web 2.0 services even if the daily data cannot keep up with the exploding numbers. Current research indicates that more people tend to join social networks than contribute or create blogs. These joiners listen to the conversation by sitting back and watching and by reading discussions and blog posts, but they will rarely comment or add to the discussion.

Human beings have a natural inclination to look before leaping. It is not surprising, then, that the percentage of people who will view and observe before they post and create is considerably higher. If you are new to social media, we recommend taking the time to observe the social norms of online participation in the communities you want to join. Chapter 14 examines this issue in greater detail.

Forrester's Social Technographics[4] profile tool also shows how age influences and predicts how people participate online. It is no surprise that younger users are more active online, but do not underestimate the significant rise in numbers among users aged 40 and above. You will want to engage the older demographic who currently holds more decision-making power as well as cultivate relationships with the younger user who will soon become more dominant as leaders in deciding which future products and services to buy. Though more online users today may be observing than are creating content, that phenomenon will continue to change over time as individuals and companies become more comfortable with the collaborative, everyone-has-a-voice nature of the social Web.

When *Groundswell* was written in 2007, 44 percent of the U.S. adults were inactive in the online world. One year later only 25 percent labeled themselves as inactive, according to a blog post called "The 2008 Social Technographics Data Reveal Rapid Adoption."[5] As the adoption phase speeds up, it is clear that the importance of social media for driving business results will gain more widespread recognition. That is one reason we do not recommend not participating even if the majority of your customers are Spectators or Inactives.

ENGAGING THE CUSTOMER

The mantra of this book is that people buy from people that they know, like, and trust. That phenomenon remains as true today as it did when Mark Twain sold door to door. Effective social networking provides the starting point that gives salespeople the ability to build trusting relationships that will create future sales opportunities. As you continue to craft your Social Media Sales Strategy by understanding the makeup of online users and their social media activity, you can ask some core questions to assess the success of your customer engagement process, namely:

- How do you want to connect with your potential buyers?
- What will you say when you are in front of them?
- What people resources are you willing to dedicate to monitoring the conversation?

- What specifically do you want your prospective buyers to do when you have captured their attention?
- What is your process for following up with your potential buyers once you have begun the conversation?
- How much information is too much information?

More than two-thirds of us are part of "member communities"[6] that include both social networks and blogs, according to Nielsen's online reports. The corporate adoption rate for utilizing social media to drive sales, create customer loyalty programs, and improve product and service offerings continues to rise as leaders recognize the tremendous power of using the social Web for business. That means that every day more and more of us are becoming part of the world of social media. As we look at engagement, therefore, *it is not so much a question of whether or not to engage, but how much.*

According to an editorial in *Selling Power Magazine*, Gerhard Gschwandtner said we must stop selling in the old way. He wrote, " . . . selling has fundamentally changed and pursuing the old tried-and-true tactics results in more of the same: high stress and lower sales."[7] He went on to discuss what he called the "conversation" economy and gave us action ideas that correspond with *the new handshake*: join the conversation; match your sales process with the way customers buy; replace pitching with collaboration; make buying easier; and create social networks that showcase your knowledge.

The social media offer a virtual smorgasbord of choices when it comes to the level of customer involvement you seek. For example, wikis are collaborative, online tools that enable employees or customers to design products or work together on teams. Joan is currently involved in an international wiki team to create a coaching/training initiative for people in the United Kingdom who have been "made redundant." That group posts comments, white papers, and webinar agendas on the wiki. Everyone on the worldwide team adds information and comments on the tools created. A second example for customer involvement might be through online communities that could galvanize the support function for your business—that is, customers helping themselves.

We have already discussed the power of the online community around *Jericho.* Dell, Zappos.com, Network Solutions, Comcast, Best Buy, eBay, and other companies incorporate idea exchanges into their strategy to get customers or employees involved with the creation or critique of new products and services. All these tools instill a sense of customer loyalty at a deeper level within the operations of the organization. One company executive said, "We want each person to be personally invested in our company, to feel a sense of accountability."[8]

We should not overlook the significance of active employee involvement in your customer acquisition, retention, and loyalty strategies. As Shih points out over and over, your employees are potential customers and referral partners who have networks. She sees employees as an excellent resource for creating and expanding involvement. For many B2B companies, developing a social media strategy to increase employee involvement is a great way to begin casting a wider net. For example, take a look at how the overall sales process to increase brand awareness and generate leads might include building referral networks with and through your employees. As you consider how you will engage the customer, also consider how you will leverage the social networks of your employees.

A decision-making model created in the 1970s provides an interesting and simple way for us to look at engagement and to create a strategy for how you want to engage and for what reasons. Tannenbaum and Schmidt introduced this model in 1973 and published it in the *Harvard Business Review*. It quickly won widespread use for helping leaders understand how and what to delegate. Companies may use the same model today to determine how much engagement they want with the social media. The T&S Model is based on a continuum of participation and authority, with the premise being that as leaders open themselves to greater participation, they give up authority. The two are mutually exclusive. As one goes up, the other comes down. Figure 6.1 shows how we have reworded and simplified the stages to adapt the T&S Model to social media decision-making.

The model begins in the *Tell* Mode, where you retain complete authority and allow for no participation. Information is simply broadcast out to the

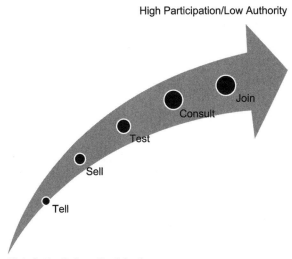

FIGURE 6.1 **The Tannenbaum and Schmidt (T&S) Leadership Model using our shortened terminology**

masses with no expectation of receiving feedback. Moving up the continuum to the *Sell* Mode, you give up some authority and add a small amount of participation. Here you share your decision by selling or persuading others to your point of view. You really are not looking for feedback, but you do care about what others think. The third stage, the *Test* Mode, moves toward the center of the continuum where you have made your decision, but others could persuade you to change your mind. You throw the idea out and listen to the responses. Once you have heard what people say, you might rethink your decision. This is the first place along the continuum where the decision might change. The fourth stage moves you into the *Consult* Mode. Here you have not made a decision, and instead you wish to consult with others and listen to their views before you decide what to do. Finally in the last stage, the *Join* Mode, you join with others to make the decision together. This is where you have the least authority and the most participation.

Several items of interest and importance exist with regard to customer engagement, the social media, and this model. First, companies must understand that if they have made a decision about something, they can never be in the Consult or Join modes. People feel betrayed if you act as if you want input to make a decision, but you have already made up your mind. Internal employee surveys often fall flat for this very reason. Most of us can recall a time when our bosses asked us what we thought about something, perhaps hiring a new team member. We shared our thoughts about why the individual was not a good fit for the position, only to learn later that the candidate had been offered the job before our bosses solicited our feedback in the first place.

That method is not a great way to build trust and rapport with others. Dell learned this lesson the hard way when its early online customer loyalty attempts looked like a tendency to defend rather than listen to what users were telling the company. As you strive to build community and credibility with your potential buyers, taking that approach will create a feeling of frustration and discontent among users in an online community. If, on the other hand, you have not made a decision and are willing to hear and respond to ideas, then either the Consult or Join mode works.

Second, it is important for everyone to understand the parameters, from those making the decision to the masses for which you are opening the participation doors. In other words, if you are in the Test Mode, you might say something like, "We are evaluating this new product. If you love it, we will take it to market; if you hate it, we will pull it back." If you are in the Sell Mode, you might say, "We have a new application that we are offering our customers. We hope you will find it as valuable to your work as we do."

Third, once you have unleashed the masses, it is hard to go back. Remember the example with CBS. The producers began in the Consult Mode by launching a powerful online community. When it came time to cancel the program, the company unwittingly moved into the Tell Mode. That caused a huge outcry. Had CBS continued in the Consult Mode, it might have posted the following message to the community: "We are concerned because the program *Jericho* does not have a large enough audience to justify continuing. This community has supported and helped us create and maintain this program. What ideas do you have that might help expand the audience or that might help make the program more attractive to our sponsors?" Such an approach might have saved the company from being inundated with peanuts.

WAYS TO ADAPT T&S MODEL TO YOUR COMPANY'S SOCIAL MEDIA STRATEGY

1. **Use the Tell and Sell Modes to create visibility.** Your blog posts and your Tweets simply tell readers about your product or service. You might also add information about the proper use of the product or service and you could include testimonials from others. The Tell and Sell Modes's purpose, then, is to create an understanding of the product or service, not to engage the customer in decision making.

2. **Use the Test Mode to discover new ways to operate, to try out new services, and to explore how services are being provided.** If you decide to use the Test Mode with the social media, you must remember that you have made the decision. You do not ask your readers to help you reach a decision. You ask them to react to what you have created or decided. If you listen to their reaction and respond to it, you begin engaging them. The most logical place for the Test Mode in the world of the social media is through blogging and online forums, which enable two-way communication. Some of the social networks are more conducive to Test Mode activity than others. For example, LinkedIn has a place for questions and answers where you could throw out a question related to a new product or service and gauge the response. You could also create a LinkedIn poll to gauge a simple response to a change in a product or service.

3. **Use the Consult Mode to enable you to really engage your customer.** The social media provide many opportunities for Consult Mode activity. If a large number of your customers are hooked into the social media—that is, your customers are actively involved by creating blog posts, they are responding to and bookmarking the content on the Web, or they are signing up on social media sites—you can engage them in many of the decisions that your company might face. The decision could be as small as how to package a new product or as large as what types of support services customers might enjoy. If you already have ideas and want to engage in a "multiple-choice"

type activity with the masses, you have moved back into the Test Mode. If, however, you really want the customers to come up with a plethora of ideas on their own, you are in the Consult Mode. Michael Dell used the Consult Mode when his company developed the Idea-Storm. This is a place where customers share ideas about what they like and what they do not like about Dell's products and services. The ideas are ranked by the customers, and the final decision about what ideas will be accepted lies with the company. When Kevin Rose founded the site Digg, he did so with the Consult Mode in mind. He wanted the masses of readers to rate online content. He delegated site moderation to the online community. Readers may either dig or bury articles. In an uproar in 2007 after the company made a uni-lateral decision (Tell Mode) to remove articles with a certain code in them, this is what Rose wrote on the company blog:

> after seeing hundreds of stories and reading thousands of com-ments, you've made it clear. You'd rather see Digg go down fight-ing than bow down to a bigger company. We hear you and effective immediately, we won't delete stories or comments con-taining the code and we'll deal with whatever consequences might be. If we lose, then what the hell, at least we died trying.[9]

This is an example of the power of the Consult Mode.

5. **Use the Join Mode when you want your customers to make decisions with you.** In the Join Mode, you no longer make the decision alone. Here you share decision-making with the customer in a completely collaborative manner. This level of participation becomes messier. How can masses of people make concrete decisions? The best exam-ple of the Join Mode and the social media is with Wikipedia. The founders of Wikipedia decided to "crowd-source" their online encyclo-pedia, with the idea being that many people have more information together than we each have separately. (By the way, this notion defines synergy—which says one and one equals three. When you take one of us and another of us and add it together you get more than two.) The Wikipedia experiment created a synergistic approach to an online encyclopedia. "Communities can build amazing things, but you have to be part of that community and you can't abuse them," said Jimmy Wales, founder of Wikipedia. Wales is talking about being completely in the Join Mode. On Wikipedia, anyone can edit or post to a page. The entire community works together on each post. What actually happens is that a very small percentage of people actually edit pages. In fact, the numbers suggest that 22 percent of

us use Wikipedia as a resource while just 6 percent contribute to a wiki once a month.[10] Furthermore, somehow in the messy world of the Join Mode, Wikipedia works. If someone posts inaccurate information, the community removes it. Today's numbers tell us that Wikipedia is the eighth most popular site on the Web.

What does all this mean with regard to the social media? It simply means that before you select the tool you might use, you must consider how much engagement you want and how that engagement fits with your overall company objectives.

In a recent digital conference on the social media, Aaron Kahlow, who is an online marketing guru, said, "The decision-making tree that illustrates how people choose to buy is changing before our eyes."[11] He went on to describe the following branches of that tree:

1. **Customers must find you.** That means through Google search engines. We saw how Dale Underwood launched blogging to help his high-niche customers find his company.
2. **Once they find you, they tend to lurk around you.** They read and study what you are all about. This is the look-before-you-leap syndrome and the Forrester definition of the Spectator user.
3. **After lurking awhile, they begin to participate.** This might involve posting on your blog or sending a message in your community forum or adding you among their Twitter followers. In Dale Underwood's case, he said, "We capture casual visitors to our Web site by giving them the option to find out pricing."[12]
4. **Once they start participating, you can begin to engage them.** They will become more engaged and committed to you. Here from a sales rep's point-of-view, you would either call or send an e-mail as a warm follow-up.
5. **Finally, they will purchase.**

In this chapter you learned a little more about what online users look like and how your customers are using the social media. You also learned how to determine the way you would like to involve your customers—that is, you can choose your mode of engagement, be it Tell, Sell, Test, Consult, or Join. Now, you are ready to take the big challenge—preparing your company to create a Social Media Sales Strategy. Chapter 7 will talk about developing the corporate mindset and assessing your company's readiness for moving into the realm of social media.

Chapter 7

Developing the Corporate Mindset

In the last two chapters, we reinforced the idea that building community, establishing relationships, and engaging prospects and customers result in sales success in this evolving social media world. Understanding what your potential clients actually do when they are online—create, sign-in, bookmark, critique, or watch—helps you determine what strategy you will use to develop your marketing message and conversational approach. As you think about how much engagement you want, you will need to ask yourself how that desire fits with your overall company objectives.

Understanding the various social media technologies is vitally important, but technology is merely an enabler and will do little unless the right social media align with the right people, purpose, and plan. Embarking down the social media path with the intent to increase short-term sales without having a clearly defined revenue plan will lead to lost money and time and serve only to frustrate your salespeople. In this chapter we will discuss some of the fears businesses face as well as what must be done to develop the corporate mindset to institute change.

The role of salespeople is the same as it has always been: to create a relationship with a buyer that ultimately leads to the sale of the service or product offered. With the advent of the social Web, significant changes in the behavior of today's buyer are causing many companies to scrap old sales processes that no longer work in this new world. Your prospects have moved to the online world of social communities, where their goal is to learn all they can about you and your product. As we noted in Chapter 2, they are reading about your products and services (and those of your competitors) on blogs and in forums. They are scanning YouTube videos, searching information on Facebook, viewing LinkedIn profiles, and reading reviews of your products and services from people who have already purchased from you.

A *New York Times* article stated that a survey by Opinion Research Corporation showed that "84 percent of Americans say online reviews influence their purchasing decisions."[1] Before salespeople even walk in the door, potential buyers have done their homework. Have you adjusted your sales process to align with this new model of buying behavior? Even if you think your company isn't ready for the social Web, ask yourself these two questions:

1. Can you afford not to catch up with the prospects that are already there?
2. What will happen if/when your competitor beats you to the social media finish line?

DEATH OF SALES 1.0

Willy Loman, the beaten-down traveling salesman made famous in Arthur Miller's 1949 classic, never fully accepted that to succeed in a changing world he had to change his approach. Unfortunately, he never did adjust and the ending proved very sad.

Sales organizations in many companies today are filled with Willy Loman types who refuse to change their sales approaches. Joan recently talked to a multimillion-dollar CEO who owns multiple large city radio stations. When she asked him what his sales teams have done to adjust to the changes in buying behavior, he responded, "I believe the social media and the mass media will combine. From where I sit, Twitter is a fad that will disappear." This kind of narrow response did not propel this man to success. He became successful by anticipating and responding to the trends. If he is not careful, he will watch the business he spent a lifetime creating disappear.

Narrow sales approaches continue to insist that the only way to close the deal is to meet someone face to face. Salespeople stubbornly refuse to admit when a sales opportunity has hit a dead end or, worse yet, never had any chance at all. As a result, sales opportunities are ignored, missed, or lost completely every single day because salespeople are using the same old tired sales techniques but expecting different results. These old-school sales types resist using online media as a way to build relationships because they believe them to be a waste of time or not a part of the sales process. Today's savvy professionals, on the other hand, understand this new world of social media and networking. They know that times have changed and that their approach to selling must change too.

FOCUS ON YOUR REVENUE STRATEGY

It is tempting when faced with slowing sales to slash budgets and search for the quick fix. In this challenging economy it is more important than ever to keep your primary focus on creating a revenue strategy that aligns with every aspect of your business. That focus requires patience and doing your homework. There is significant danger in selecting a technology to solve a problem that you have not clearly defined. Poor sales results can happen for many reasons. If you do not know the specific cause of the problem, how do you know what to fix? Do you throw money at a new marketing campaign, CRM system, or another sales training program? Should you adjust the compensation program or hold a contest? Do you jump into blogging, begin Tweeting away, or start a LinkedIn group? Do you move your people around, replace your sales management, or rearrange sales territories? These decisions come with significant risks and no guarantee that any of them will solve the underlying issues.

When Dale Underwood saw that what he provided to his customers was disappearing, he did not just pack up his tent and leave. Instead, he looked at what was happening among his buyers and he responded. He gambled that these new buyers would respond to a blog that addressed new questions. "What we realized through our research is that people want to know pricing information. They cannot get it from the manufacturer. We also realized that they want this pricing information early on," he said.[2] The gamble paid off.

According to the Aberdeen Group survey, while marketing budgets are being cut in response to the current economic downturn, the "best-in-class" companies are actually increasing their spending on social media marketing[3]. Best-in-class companies are those the Aberdeen Group measured with the highest return on marketing investment, the highest likelihood that customers would recommend their products or services, and the highest customer acquisition. If you want to be a best-in-class company, cutting the social media marketing budget is not the way!

The word-of-mouth marketing that the Aberdeen Group identified within the best-in class companies include the following:

- Viral marketing—messaging through e-mail, community marketing—fan groups, community networks, and discussion forums.
- Evangelist marketing—cultivating others to take a leadership role in speaking on behalf of your product or service.
- Influence marketing—communities or opinion leaders who will have an influence on others to purchase your products.
- Referral programs—online and offline tools that enable customers to refer their friends to you.[4]

Sales professionals can have an impact on each of these word-of-mouth marketing methods. In the world of Sales 2.0, sales organizations must continually monitor, evaluate, and augment their sales strategies with these new approaches and tools to drive specific objectives while they seek to balance the cost of selling with tangible sales results. Seley and Holloway illustrated this point with an example of a business that added just four sales development reps who incorporated Sales 2.0 strategies. They wrote, "After implementing sales development, this company produced $6.4 million in additional revenue, 25 percent more than with field sales alone, for an added cost of $607,500, resulting in an ROI of 1,053 percent."[5] Sales management, sales operations, marketing, human resources, customer service, and finance all need to work together as a team to focus on the one thing that matters most: driving revenue.

IT'S NOT ABOUT SELLING—IT'S ABOUT BUYING!

The philosophy of buying, not selling, may seem counterintuitive if you believe that online tools are a cheap way to market and sell what you have to offer to a large number of people. Nothing turns people off faster than a "slick Willy" who enters the scene and within minutes begins hawking his latest product or service. If this mirrors your approach, be prepared for a community smack down that will damage your reputation (see Chapter 14). Joel Comm in *Twitter Power* writes, "Gripping headlines and hard call-to-action on Twitter are more likely to drive people away than drive them to buy."[6] In Chapter 11 we will give you some tips for Tweeting to enable you to create a presence, a conversation, and a personality before you start tooting your product or service.

As sales professionals, we have traditionally been taught the following sales funnel: identify target opportunities, qualify leads, meet with potential customers, make presentations, write proposals, negotiate, and then *close the deal*. Old-school salespeople tended to walk in the door spewing out features and benefits without listening to what their prospects tried to tell them about what they needed. Mostly, these salespeople did not care. It was all about closing the sale. Much of this sales approach goes back to the early days of selling that we seem to have a hard time shedding. The blame for holding on to these practices also goes to management policies. Until businesses truly embrace Sales 2.0 and the social media by changing the way they reward salespeople, by changing their demands to close the sale, by changing the sales culture in the organization, salespeople will continue to cling to the old ways.

Now that buyers are more proactive in educating themselves about what to buy, the sales process has been transformed into a "buying process." It pushes the whole notion of solution selling up another notch. People do not want to be *sold to*. They want to build relationships with people that they trust to help them solve their business challenges. Axel Schultze, CEO of Xeesm.com, coined the term, "social selling." "Social selling is all about engaging with people early in the buying process," he said. "It's all about relationship."[7] Some of us have known this fact for a very long time. Others pretend they know it but act differently.

In some companies, the higher ups tell salespeople they desire a relationship with their customers, but they push those same salespeople toward closings. In an interview with marketing analyst Kyle van Hoften, he explained that upper management thinks in the short term, not the long term. "If an account manager has a choice to build up his Facebook page or to make cold calls that will result in an immediate sale, he chooses cold calling," van Hoften said. "Why? It's faster and it satisfies his boss."[8] The bosses of the world do not support the kinds of behaviors that create trust. They still fall into old selling habits that Michael Port and Elizabeth Marshall so aptly discounted in *Contrarian*. Why is it so hard to shed these beliefs? As you read what it takes to extend the new handshake, you might ask yourself what is holding you back. What are your fears? Can you risk lower short-term results for higher long-term rewards?

Imagine Tiger Woods when he first burst onto the professional golf circuit. Instead of sweeping the tour after his record-setting victory at the Masters in Augusta, Georgia, he stepped back, changed his swing, and ended up losing a number of tournaments. In fact, many sports commentators wrote him off. They said he was a "fad" that had been overrated. Hindsight saw those same commentators with egg on their faces. Tiger stepped back and decided to risk losing some tournaments in order to become unbeatable. How willing are you or your company to take those kind of risks? Extending the new handshake is not without risk.

Today's salespeople, who are willing to shoot for the long-term victory, can guide people through the new buying process. The new salesperson's role is to stay on top of trends, see into the future, and position herself as a well-educated navigator who is an open influencer instead of a convincer. A young sales rep recently told Joan that she saw her role as a "consultant," not as a salesperson. Anneke Seley agreed and said that some proactive salespeople are individually testing the power of the social media. She told us about an individual sales rep who developed a Slide Share on his LinkedIn profile, and whenever he updated his status box it went to all his connections. He leveraged these tools, and now a significant part of his pipeline and quarterly results come from LinkedIn. She pointed out, however, that "he's a lone salesperson experimenting with this. I see a lot of people balking at these new tools."[9]

IT'S TIME TO DEAL WITH THE PAIN

Chris Anderson, editor-in-chief of *Wired* magazine and author of the landmark book *The Long Tail*, reminds us that the Internet has transformed the buying process by offering up limitless choices. "In short, though we still obsess over hits, they are not quite the economic force they once were," he said. "Where are those fickle consumers going instead? No single place. They are scattered to the winds as markets fragment into a thousand niches."[10] Anderson suggests that competition for your potential buyer is fierce in this e-commerce environment. With more companies relying on the Internet for research and consumer recommendations to support their buying decisions, if you do not stand out, you will be locked out.

When it gets right down to it, sales has one job: *achieve revenue targets*. For many companies, this focus has been muddled by conflicting priorities, unclear expectations, and confusion over who does what. If the sales are not happening, does the sales manager or company president ride in on the white horse to save the day? If you say that nothing is more important than driving sales, but then constantly schedule lengthy meetings to discuss the state of the sales opportunity pipeline, what messages are you really sending? If the attitudes of your people are stuck in the traditional hop-on-a-plane-to-close-the-deal mentality, how far can you hope to get with the integration of social media?

Our interview with Kyle van Hoften suggested that he struggled as the director of marketing to convince the account managers of the value of the social media. He finally got their attention by showing them concrete examples. Later, when he became a consultant for that same company, he learned that the vice president was so sold on the power of LinkedIn that he only hired people with a certain number of connections. "It takes time to convince salespeople, but once they are convinced, they are sold," van Hoften told us.[11]

SOCIAL MEDIA ADOPTION OBSTACLES TO YOUR ORGANIZATION

One of the most common concerns we hear from corporate leaders is the fear that they will lose control of their corporate message and brand if they let loose the social media. Right now, many companies see the explosion of Web 2.0 technologies as more of a threat than as a business opportunity. They hide behind the perception that losing control or that customers complaining are bad things. As has been noted earlier, people are talking whether you choose to participate or not. Furthermore, control is just an illusion. Quoting authors Li and Bernoff in *Groundswell*, "The groundswell trend is not a flash in the pan. This is an important, irreversible, completely different way for people to relate to companies and to each other."[12]

This quote tells us precisely why your sales organization must take steps to adapt approaches to meet the needs of the new buying process that defines

RATE YOUR COMPANY'S SOCIAL MEDIA READINESS

For each question, rate your response from left to right, with the far left box indicating the highest level of agreement and the far right box indicating the highest level of disagreement.

1. Are your sales leaders prepared to adopt new sales communication approaches and tools?

Yes				No
5	4	3	2	1

2. Have you established sales communication guidelines and social usage policies?

Yes				No
5	4	3	2	1

3. Is your IT organization prepared to assist you in integrating the right social tools with your sales goals?

Yes				No
5	4	3	2	1

4. Do you use customer data, online surveys, and focus group feedback to update services, policies, and processes on the fly?

Yes				No
5	4	3	2	1

5. How well is your company "listening" to online conversations happening on the various social sites?

Yes				No
5	4	3	2	1

6. How ready is your sales team to respond to negative commentary?

Yes				No
5	4	3	2	1

7. Do your marketing VP and Sales VP meet jointly to collaborate on lead generation, branding, and the use of social media?

Yes				No
5	4	3	2	1

8. Does your company create collaborative opportunities for field reps and inside sales reps, including performance goals and compensation?

Yes				No
5	4	3	2	1

the social Web. You need to decide just how much you are willing to give in order to deepen the level of participation you have with your customers and prospects. If you hang onto control, you may only experience visibility. If you want to move further down the continuum, you will have to find a way to relinquish control and authority.

A July 29, 2009 article in the *New York Times* discussed ways small businesses are monitoring their online reputation. These businesses recognize that a negative comment on a blog or on a Twitter post could destroy them.[13] They cannot weather the storm like the big boys. They contend, however, that if they work at providing quality services and products, they can deal with these kinds of comments. Small businesses suggest taking the following steps:

1. Get on the social media sites and monitor what is being said about your company (Like Guy Stephens did). Search the sites like Twitter and set up Google Alerts to let you know when something is being said.

2. Respond to each negative comment. The best way to respond is through a private message. Do not get defensive and try and justify what happened. Instead, listen to what the customer says and inform. Many people are so surprised to hear from the company, they become quick converts.

3. If you are really angry by an online negative comment, step away and calm down before taking action. Jeff Diamond, owner of Farmstead Cheeses and Wines said, "The most important thing is not to argue with the customer. It's to listen to the customer and try to put yourself in their place."[14]

4. Do not write fake reviews. You will get caught, and when you do your credibility will be destroyed.

5. Look for patterns. If people are constantly complaining about something or praising something, pay attention.

SALES AND MARKETING

Although the focus of this book is on this new world of selling and the changes that sales must make in order to incorporate social media, we cannot dismiss the fine line between sales and marketing. In most organizations a love/hate relationship often exists between these two functions. Sales reps complain that marketing does not deliver qualified leads. They say there is a major difference between "quantity" and "quality." Salespeople become frustrated that marketing sends them a lot of leads, many of which are not qualified buyers. Marketing, on the other hand, pats itself on the back because it delivered on the numbers, thinking its job done and complains that sales do not follow up on the leads they provide.

These traditional forces are converging and thereby shrinking the distinction between marketing and sales, but much still needs to be done. Marketing, the longtime keeper of the corporate brand message, takes issue with salespeople who often butcher the corporate message that they worked so hard to craft. With the implementation of a social media strategy, it is more incumbent than ever for salespeople to communicate the corporate message in a consistent way. Marketing professionals fear that the use of social media to sell products and services will further intensify the misrepresentation of the brand. Business examples prove, however, that with the right homework in crafting a clear purpose and plan around your people, the social media can solidify and support the brand. The Aberdeen report quoted Emily Pelosi, director of marketing for Office Depot, "Social media adds value since it lets the customer determine how they want to interact with your brand. It also provides a platform for peer-to-peer sharing of information that allows your brand to reach new audiences."[15]

Marketing has always struggled to prove its worth to the financial side of the business. A social media strategy creates an opportunity for marketing professionals to take the lead in demonstrating how the social Web can drive specific, measurable sales results when implemented properly. This is not about maintaining tight-fisted control or positioning marketing as gatekeepers to innovative ways of thinking. There is, however, a leadership role for marketing by integrating social media into well thought out sales processes. Together, marketing and sales can participate, listen, and monitor the conversation, because to ignore the conversation may have far greater consequences.

Now that you have an idea of some of the issues that might get in your way, it is time to begin charting your strategy using the three P's: Purpose, Plan, and People.

Chapter 8

Charting Your Course:
The Three P's: Purpose, Plan, People

The last few chapters set the groundwork for developing your strategy. We have examined what selling tools worked in the past, paying close attention to consultative selling. We looked at the importance of relationship and a model to help you determine how much engagement you want when. Finally, we developed the questions you must ask to help you develop a corporate mindset for change. It is now time to chart your course by examining people, purpose, and plan.

FOCUS ON THE 3 P's: PURPOSE, PLAN, PEOPLE

We are living in an age that many innovation experts are calling "disruption." This much disruption shakes business leaders out of their comfort zones by forcing them to fundamentally rethink what they know, or thought they knew, about business. Not unlike the cultural shift from an agrarian society to an industrial one, we now face a transition unlike anything we have seen before. Unfortunately, some people and businesses will struggle with this disruption more than others.

As we have said from the outset, social media are here to stay. It is time for sales organizations to consider how this disruption alters the sales process and to find ways to devise strategies for addressing it. Buyers buy differently. The big question is how to capture the attention of your potential customers when they are overwhelmed with choices. We have already suggested that you rethink everything you knew about communicating. Now we are suggesting that you rethink everything you knew about selling. The primary objective is to *create value in a virtual world in the minds of people you have yet to meet.* Creating online relationships that will lead to closing sales requires three all-encompassing steps:

- Establishing a purpose and a plan for achieving your goals with people who are well trained to execute that plan.
- Choosing the right tool(s) to support your sales objectives.
- Investing in training to ensure that your salespeople use these tools consistently day in and day out.

Using social media to uncover opportunities, to research trends, to keep on top of competition, and to network changes the way we play the game. A social media strategy is not a quick fix for bigger sales problems, nor does it bring sales overnight. Like great offline selling, it takes time to build the relationships that lead to closing sales.

PURPOSE

As you begin the dialogue about your overall purpose for selling in this new world of the social Web, you must define who, why, and how you will leverage social media to increase sales. Before you can nail down the why and how, you must start with a clear definition of *who.* Who is your target audience? Hint: your market is not the entire world. Narrowing down the target audience often creates a challenge for sales organizations and their salespeople who naively want to sell to everyone. Granted, your product or service may be something that everyone could buy, but the danger in assuming the world is your customer means that your message lacks focus, clarity, and value to a majority of the people in the online world. What you talk about will not be relevant to each person. They will not read your blogs, and they will ignore your Tweets. Remember, people are overwhelmed with information as is. The goal is to craft your message in a way that strikes home with a particular target market.

When you narrow your focus, you penetrate and dominate your market niche quickly. The social media tools enable you to either speak to the entire world or to talk to specific groups within that world. On LinkedIn, for example, you can answer questions within categories that fit your market or you can answer questions haphazardly. The haphazard approach means more people will see your responses fewer times. To focus your answers within a certain category means the right people will notice you more often. You become an expert. Trish Bertuzzi described it this way, "I've used LinkedIn for years and years and I only network with people I know are in the tech or

B2B space I'm interested in. What's the use of networking with someone you can't help or can never help you?"[1]

She added that 70 percent of the hits on her company's Web site come from her LinkedIn profile primarily from the questions she answered. "When you answer a question, it resonates with someone and then that person goes to your site."[2] Once you have determined exactly whom your buyer is, you can learn more about what they are doing online. In Chapter 6, we talked about the six groups that made up the Social Technographics of online participants described in *Groundswell*. Understanding your online customer gives you a leg up on the "who" question. For example, does your ideal client tend to sign up but is not an active participant or does she tend to micro-blog but does not contribute to other blogs?

Next, you must consider the *why* of social media. What is it you hope a social media strategy will do? Do you wish to create visibility for your brand or do you wish to directly sell your products? As you examine your purpose, you need to return to thinking about the mode you wish to be in. If you are in the Tell Mode or the Sell Mode (see Chapter 6), you are looking at visibility or a push approach. These approaches limit the use of the social media. If you wish to move down the continuum to the Test, Consult, or Join Modes, your purpose changes from visibility to participation, which gives more leverage to social media. Your choices expand. As marketing consultant Kyle van Hoften said, "Facebook enables you to use the pull rather than the push approach to sales. You create trust. When people get to know you, they comment on what you're doing. Before long they begin asking you for more information."[3]

The final component deals with *how*. How do you intend to incorporate a social media strategy within the framework of your organization? Will it be a stepchild, led by a separate unit or will it become part of the culture of your organization? For most entrepreneurial businesses, it can become part of the culture. As we have seen with Dell and Procter & Gamble, however, even more entrenched companies have embraced the social media as part of their culture. Amazon exemplifies a pioneer company, never shrinking from anything new. Because online marketing and social media are part of the Amazon culture, the company responds and changes as new technology emerges. If you embrace the new handshake as part of your culture, you will be ready to respond to the inevitability of emerging new technology.

Here are some questions you might ask yourself to help you create your purpose:

1. Who is your target market?
2. What is your target market doing online?
3. How will the social media become part of your branding strategy or your image?

4. What is the primary purpose of a social media strategy within your organization?

5. What message do you want your salespeople to convey about your company, products, or services that can be channeled through social media word of mouth either by viral marketing, communities, evangelists, influencers, or referral?

6. How will you institutionalize the social media within your organization, and how will the salespeople disperse the information they learn from customers throughout the company?

PLAN

Now that you have considered your purpose, your next step is to address your plan. The plan will help guide your technology choice.

Some of the participants in our workshops have put up LinkedIn profiles and then waited for something to happen. They felt frustrated when no one contacted them. "LinkedIn really is useless," they tell us. These participants fail to realize that no one will reach out to them if they do not know that they exist. Success requires that your company and your salespeople manage and promote your brand using the social media tools. For example, promote your LinkedIn profile on your Web site, on your blog, in your newsletters, and in your e-mail signature line. Make it easy for people to find you on Twitter, Facebook and LinkedIn. Furthermore, like anything else, salespeople must work the social media. Trish Bertuzzi told us she spends time each day on LinkedIn, managing her groups, asking and answering questions, updating her profile, and publishing her blog posts.

To avoid wasted time and feelings of frustration and to ensure that your salespeople use social media effectively, you need to create a well-crafted Social Media Sales Plan. This plan encompasses sales, marketing, customer service, information technology (IT), legal, and human resources (HR) to discuss and decide on the overall approach. While you will need to create guidelines to help everyone adhere to any compliance regulations, to avoid potential legal problems, and to clearly communicate your expectations to all sales employees, we raise one caution: Do not let legal, HR, or IT quash what you want to accomplish. Though well meaning in their efforts, these groups tend to hinder innovation. Your goal is to create guidelines that you can monitor and update as needed. Following are some questions you might want to ask when getting started with your plan:

1. How will you actively monitor what is being said about your company or your competition through social media channels like blogs, online communities, and social networks?

2. What technology tools will you use every day to achieve your stated sales and marketing goals?
3. How does the Social Media Sales Plan align with the overall business strategy of your company?
4. What are the message, voice, brand, and overall platform that will support all of the activities, tasks, tools, decisions, and actions you will take?
5. What are you doing to align marketing and sales to create a team-like approach?
6. What support, guidance, and training are needed to successfully execute your Social Media Sales Plan?
7. How will you deal with the personal versus business information shared? How much is too much? How will you monitor the information?
8. How much freedom will you give salespeople for individual branding and what time guidelines will you incorporate so as not to become addicted to a particular social media tool?
9. What guidelines must you implement to ensure that your company information and message are consistent on the online profile of every person using social media?
10. Do your current sales processes and technology support your social media goals? If not, what will we need to do to fix those problems?
11. How will you respond to your customer preferences for different types of interaction, whether telephone, online, social media, or otherwise?
12. Will your salespeople need communication training, especially when it comes to writing and developing their profiles or creating daily blogs?
13. Will salespeople be responsible for blogging, micro-blogging, LinkedIn, or Facebook? What responsibilities fall under sales, marketing, or both? Who oversees what?
14. What mechanism will you need to put in place to ensure that sales management is not putting unrealistic pressure on the sales team to force the sales cycle before its time?
15. How willing are you to make the required financial commitment to train your people in the art of social media?
16. What specific sales results do you expect to achieve from your Social Media Sales Plan?
17. How will you measure those results?

Every company is different, and certainly you will need to answer all these questions and more. While it is important to take the time to think through your plan, we urge you not to get bogged down to the point where you never take the first step. You might choose to create a phased-in approach that allows your salespeople to start moving in a new direction and work out the kinks as you go along. We saw how OracleDirect slowly implemented Sales 2.0 strategies into its corporate culture. It is best to begin slowly with a pilot and tweak as you go in order to accommodate your unique products, services, and customers.

PEOPLE

Ultimately your salespeople will execute your Social Media Sales Plan, with sales management involved in monitoring and supporting the process. As we said earlier, using social media will not fix a broken sales process or solve the problem of having the wrong people in the wrong role. A fundamental question is whether or not you have the right people with the right skills to think like the new buyer and communicate with them on their terms.

In the new world of sales and social media, you can improve the current challenges that daunt sales organizations today, and those improvements will lead to an increased sales performance that is consistent and repeatable. As you consider the building blocks for your Social Media Sales Plan, examine some of the specific challenges that sales organizations typically face, including the following:

- Wrong people or poorly trained people in the sales role
- Poorly qualified leads
- Difficulty targeting new prospects
- Opportunities missed in current accounts
- Sales process not consistently repeated

Let us take a look at each of these areas from the standpoint of a social media solution.

Wrong People or Poorly Trained People in the Sales Role

In the classic business book, *Good to Great*, Jim Collins reminds us that it is first who, then what.[4] Of the executives surveyed for Collins's book, all believed in one powerful concept: You get the right people on your bus and they will figure out where to drive it. Often we see the reverse working in many organizations. We enact strategies and hire people (often the wrong people) to execute them. Here are some criteria you might wish to consider as you look at your sales team:

- What social media tools are people currently using? How many people do they have in their networks?

- How are people blending social media strategies with their current selling strategies?
- How responsive is your sales team to creativity and change?
- What successes have individual salespeople seen with consultative selling?
- What are your current customer retentions?

Poorly Qualified Leads

If you want to increase sales, start by looking at the first critical phases of the sales process: investigate and early qualify. A sales rep's ability to quickly identify, qualify, and focus on the right opportunities remains a big challenge in most sales organizations. What causes poorly qualified leads? Typical reasons include treating every sales prospect the same way, confusion about business priorities, inadequate training, poor time management skills, inconsistency in following the sales process, and having the wrong people in the role. Sales leaders know that money pours out the door when salespeople chase down phantom opportunities. The following example illustrates how much this problem costs.

Laura works for a medium-sized company that sells microchips. She operates with a $500,000 quota. After salary, commission, benefits, the cost for Laura is $120,000 annually. Assuming 2,400 hours of annual sales time, your cost per sales hour is $50. That does not sound so bad, does it? It would not be if Laura was actually *selling* 50 hours every week.

For an average company with a decent strategy and pretty good business alignment you might get five actual sales hours out of Laura each week. At five hours per week, Laura's $120,000 annual rate now costs you $500 per hour. That means you need to generate slightly more than $2,000 of revenue per hour if you hope to reach your annual target. To make matters worse, if Laura wastes those precious five hours on poorly qualified opportunities, the challenge of reaching your goal escalates. Why only five hours? Ask yourself how many meetings Laura must attend each week. How much administrative trivia or CRM and sales reporting must Laura do? How much time does Laura spend resolving customer issues when she is supposed to be selling? What about Laura's travel time, lunch hours, and breaks?

What can you do to significantly shrink wasted money and time on the front end of the sales process? We believe the answer lies in blending social networking tools like LinkedIn into a well-thought-out Social Media Sales Plan. The use of the telephone, e-mail, and face-to-face meetings do not go away, but *when you use social media to leverage your network*, secure introductions, and qualify opportunities, you speed up the sales cycle and increase the quality of your cost per sales hour.

Keep in mind that the use of social media will not "fix" a sales process that is broken, and social media will not help if your people are not right for the role or if they lack the proper training to do their job. Part of your Social Media Sales Plan is to make sure that the people you hire have expertise in both sales and social media.

Difficulty Targeting New Prospects

Usually when salespeople have difficulty targeting new prospects, they either do not understand who their target client is and they try to chase everyone or they have a network that is too small to do them much good. Without question, a professional network of trusted contacts leveraged correctly gives your company a competitive sales advantage. Your salespeople, as one of your most valuable assets, must dedicate time to keeping their networks up to date and then use those networks to achieve their sales goals.

LinkedIn provides a solution for online professional networking. With more than 60 percent of LinkedIn's 80 million users having high personal incomes and holding positions at the executive level or higher,[5] it is widely recognized as *the* professional networking tool. Effective use of LinkedIn allows you to move beyond geographic boundaries to reach a wider audience of potential customers whom you can convert to sales. Through LinkedIn you can shrink the sales cycles with better-qualified opportunities, which saves you money and time. In the next chapters we will compare LinkedIn with the other major tools, Facebook and Twitter. For now, let us examine the specific benefits of using LinkedIn as a solution for targeting new contacts:

- Extend your sales and marketing reach.
- Maximize time by focusing on the *right* opportunities.
- Leverage your network to secure introductions with target companies.

One of the most valuable elements of LinkedIn is the ability to create prospect lists using the Search application. We conducted a search of sales managers and sales vice presidents, and from this search we located 432 results. The key is to have a network that is rich enough to extract substantive data.

Quality plus quantity equals access. Most people wrestle with the question of how many contacts is too many. How can we have solid relationships with thousands or millions of people? We have talked about the importance of building a strong and extensive weak network in addition to your strong network. We contend that quality plus quantity equals access. In other words, both quality and quantity count. You may not have strong connections with everyone in your network, but the quality lies in making sure the people in your network are the right people who can open doors for you. As of this writing, for example, Barb has 542 contacts that give her access to a combined network total of 6.2 million people, and coincidentally just over 9,200 new people joined her network in the past two days.

To demonstrate the concept of quality plus quantity equals access, whenever Barb delivers workshops, she asks someone in the audience to shout the name of a company he or she wants to penetrate. Every single time someone mentioned a company, Barb produced someone from that company in her network. She demonstrated this point recently with a group of 60 CEOs. To say that these CEOs were blown away is an understatement. While writing this chapter, we experimented with this concept. Joan asked Barb whom she knew at Wells Fargo. She has a client that focuses on the banking industry and thought it would be interesting to test the theory in real time. She ran a quick search and entered the company name, Wells Fargo, on the LinkedIn search page. Within seconds she received a list of 70,939 names! Now that is the power of a network.

This search feature allows you to mine LinkedIn in multiple ways. You can search for People, Companies, Jobs, and Answers. Using this one function alone enables salespeople to fill the pipeline with prospects. Sales teams and salespeople can define their ideal targets and create a follow-up list. For example, Roger works for a company selling sales training programs and he wants to reach sales vice presidents in telecommunication companies within a 50-mile radius of his corporate headquarters. Using the additional LinkedIn's fields in the advanced search, Roger can filter his results to reach his intended buyer. Now that Roger has set up a targeted search, he can save it. Whenever anyone joins his network, his search is dynamically updated and he receives an e-mail to alert him to the new additions.

The search feature enables you to leverage your first- or second-line connections for an introduction, and it illustrates one of many ways to use LinkedIn to target new prospects. You will get the best results with a network that has both quality people and a good number of contacts for you to achieve access. If you only have 20 or so contacts and they are mediocre or haphazard at best, you cannot expect to achieve success on LinkedIn.

Opportunities Missed in Current Accounts

As we write this book, the economic times present what many people consider more challenges than opportunities. More than once we have heard business owners and salespeople tell us that they stopped connecting with their current customers because "they probably aren't going to buy anyway." Indeed, this assumption likely reflects the sentiment of a burned-out salesperson. What is even more disturbing is that it reflects a critical error in judgment about today's market. If salespeople believe they are making contacts just to close sales, they are not reaching out with the new handshake.

As we have said repeatedly, the social Web has changed the way your customers purchase products and services. If you are not visible to them, you risk losing sales opportunities. Buyers proactively educate themselves about what is available, thereby transforming the sales process into a buying process. When you are selling a product or service, whether you are the salesperson or the business owner, your job is to be visible, stay on top of trends, see into the future, and demonstrate to your customers that you are a well-educated navigator. In this economy more than ever, you must show your contacts that you are there for them—to help them get through the tough times.

It costs significantly less for a company to continue to cultivate sales relationships with people who have already purchased from them. Assuming you have done a great job delivering on your promise to customers, you now have an edge that is unmatched by your competition. If you or your salespeople have not talked to your current customers in a long time, now would be the time to get moving. Following are three tips to help you reconnect:

1. Evaluate your communication process with your current customers and create a strategy for re-engaging with them either through online discussions or online community groups. Look closely at how often your salespeople are touching current customers. You can monitor online networks like Twitter to determine the frequency with which your salespeople are posting to their communities. Hold account reviews with the entire team—sales, marketing, and customer service—to allow for brainstorming about how the business can add greater value to the customer relationship and to evaluate which online tools are working. Make sure that you formulate a plan for keeping your customer abreast of all that you have to offer. Buyers appreciate information about what is available. Use the online tools to help you stay in front of buyers. Do not worry if they are not ready to buy today. The goal is to make sure they think of you when they are ready to buy. You can use online article marketing to help inform buyers. Take a look at www.ezinearticles.com, www.submityourarticles.com, www.selfgrowth.com. These article banks enable you to inform customers without selling.

2. Use tools like LinkedIn or Facebook to expand your sales reach within an account. Who else in the company has a LinkedIn or Facebook profile? Are your salespeople telling you that their current contact has moved on to other things and they are not sure with

whom to talk? Use the LinkedIn Companies feature to search for new connections within the account. What forums are your customers participating in? Is there an opportunity for your salespeople to join and contribute to the discussion and at the same time remain visible with the account?

3. Create newsletters using e-mail marketing products like Constant Contact (www.constantcontact.com). Share relevant business content to keep your customers informed about industry trends, market opportunities, and the newest in what you have to offer. Reexamine the way Procter & Gamble used its community to help young girls with sticky adolescent issues and at the same time quietly added its branding information in each signature.

Savvy Communicator

How Well Do You Read NonVerbal Cues?

October 2009

In This Issue

Tips to Create a Powerful LinkedIn Profile

Sticky Situations and NonVerbal Cues

Managing Sticky Situations at Work

Favorite Links

Managing Sticky Situations At Work

Joan's blog--Say It Just Right

Total Communications Coaching

Greetings!

Maybe you answered that you don't read nonverbal cues very well. Most of us do not. We make assumptions and do not check them out. We often allow the nonverbal messages to go right over our heads.

In this issue we will look at the *power of the nonverbal message* when you say it just right. The lead article has an example of how understanding the nonverbal cues in a meeting could change the nature of your presentation.

We will also look at tips to create a *powerful LinkedIn profile*. How does your LinkedIn profile fit with your nonverbal message? That profile transmits all kinds of information about you. *Make sure it says what you want it to say.*

Feel free to forward this ezine to your friends and colleagues! And, we love it when you copy and share articles.

Join me on Facebook! or Follow me on Twitter!

FIGURE 8.1 An example of Joan's monthly e-zine using Constant Contact.
Source: Constant Contact

Your existing customer base is a gold mine of opportunity, a competitive advantage that is often overlooked. Stop randomly chasing new opportunities when "acres of diamonds" are sitting right in front of you.

Sales Process Not Consistently Repeated

Last year, we interviewed a top business coach and author, David Mason, who wrote *Marketing Your Small Business for Big Profits*. When asked what the key to revenue success was over the long haul, Dave said, "The key is always consistency and persistency. Basically, the idea is that the sales process is a science. If you faithfully follow a proven process every day—day in and day out—you will achieve success."[6] C. J. Hayden in her best-selling book, *Get Clients Now*, said it is not what you do so long as you do something consistently.[7] The same holds true of integrating and using social media as part of your sales plan.

Earlier we mentioned how people debunk LinkedIn, claiming it does nothing for them. That is exactly the wrong attitude. To achieve success in building a sales pipeline using the social media, salespeople must follow a daily process. Taking Dave Mason's advice, putting more time and effort into asking and answering questions, creating strategic status updates, making connections for others, sharing relevant business information, and creating rich prospect lists that are followed up on every day will eventually produce results.

When it gets right down to it, however, the key is patience. We hear people complain that they do not have time for this social media stuff. Our response: you cannot afford to not make the time. What could be more important for building a sales pipeline than utilizing technology in effective ways that lead to sales results? Ask yourself this question: how much time do your salespeople waste running around town to networking events that go nowhere or to one-on-one meetings that have no chance of producing a sale?

AVOID THE DOMINO'S DISASTER WITH A GOOD SOCIAL SALES MEDIA PLAN

In April 2009, two Domino's employees posted a YouTube video that showed the unsanitary preparation of pizza for delivery. Within days the YouTube video received more than 1 million views. References to the incident were in 5 of the 12 results on Google searches for Domino's, and Twitter was abuzz with comments.

Clearly, the two employees lost their jobs. What happened next, however, shows how companies are responding to online criticism. The company president, Patrick Doyle, created his own YouTube video. In it he apologized for the horrible behavior of the two employees and asked his loyal customers for their support. As one Domino's spokeperson said, it is like preparing every day for a safe drive home on Saturday night and then suddenly you get blindsided by a drunk driver. Nearly 1 million viewers watched Doyle's apology on YouTube. Without doubt, the company will have to do some back-pedaling and apologizing for quite some time. In reality, however, the CEO responded in the best possible way, quickly and with an online tool. Although some people criticize Doyle for waiting too long to respond—he had hoped it would all go away!—he finally did go directly to the people with the same tool used against the company. With honesty and transparency, he confronted the negative publicity.

How might Domino's have avoided this terrible incident? One option posed by TrainingTime blog is for better and consistent employee training. Companies that desire to create an online presence must bring their employees along with them within certain parameters. This is the *people* part of the Social Media Sales Plan. According to TrainingTime, "A great way to remind employees about how to act online when representing the company is through regular training."[8] Following are some general guidelines for social media:

- Use your real name and the company you represent. For salespeople we suggest developing your own brand, including your own photo.
- Speak for yourself, not for the company.
- Talk about the company as if you were talking within the office.
- Protect confidential and financial company information.

As you look at what happened to Domino's, you might shake your head and ask how training can teach people to act responsibly. Indeed, we cannot teach people not to break the law, but we can teach them what will happen if they do break the law. We can also be very clear on what breaking the law looks like. Let your employees know the consequences if they violate the social media guidelines. Give them clear and concrete examples of what constitutes a violation. Training may not be the full answer, but it is one very important piece in the puzzle.

This chapter outlined the key components for a Social Media Sales Plan by examining purpose, plan, and people in order to take the first step in charting your course. Once you know what your purpose is, know how to launch that purpose within your organization, and know the people who are responsible for making it happen, you can look at technology in the development of a Social Media Sales Plan. In this chapter you glimpsed how the power of the technology might impact your plan. In Chapter 9 we will provide a simple roadmap and tips to help you choose the tools that will drive your sales. We will begin with Facebook.

Part Two

SOCIAL MEDIA OUTLETS—
WHAT WORKS BEST WHEN AND HOW
TO BEGIN

Chapter 9

Sales Meets Facebook

In the previous two chapters we discussed what your company needs to do to prepare for a Social Media Sales Strategy. We examined Purpose, Plan, and People. You saw how important it is to target your audience, but at the same time how you must expand your network (quality plus quantity equals access). You looked at some questions to help you determine the purpose of a social media strategy and how ready your company is to launch it. Are you interested in broadcasting or netcasting? Are you interested in being in the Test Mode or the Join Mode? Finally, you saw some specific ways various social media can help you qualify leads, grow new prospects, and target your market.

In the next several chapters we want to give you a roadmap. After having considered all the questions in Chapters 7 and 8, you are ready to move into the realm of technology. What tool works best and how do you set up that tool? While examining the tools, you must keep in mind that the technology will change. That is a given. Once you have established the three P's part of your strategy, however, you can always adjust to the technology changes. That is another reason the questions raised in the last two chapters are so important. So many clients reject implementing a Social Media Sales Strategy because they ask, "Why launch it now when things will be different next week?" If that is your attitude, you will never begin. Recognize that the majority of the work is in the three P's part of strategy development, not the T part. Furthermore, by the time you read this book, the technology will have changed. What we hope to do is prepare and guide you given the changing world of technology.

Remember what Kathy Tito said, "The big question around social media is *why not.*"[1]

As we examine each of these tools, we will share examples from companies and people who have used the tool. You can evaluate what others have experienced and learn from them.

WHAT WORKS BEST WHEN

We will look at the current major players and examine how to best use them. Each tool has certain strengths and weaknesses. You may wish to begin with just one tool and add others once you get comfortable. Since we are devoting Chapter 13 to blogging, we will postpone talking about that tool. We separated out blogging because it is such an important piece of the Sales 2.0 and social media strategy, and it has survived the test of time.

WHO ARE THE MAJOR PLAYERS?

At this writing three major players exist at the forefront of the social media landscape: Facebook, LinkedIn, and Twitter. In Chapter 12 we will talk about applications and tools within and beyond these major players, and it is there where we will give you specific suggestions about how to get the most out of your networks. We will discuss Delicious, Digg, and StumbleUpon, which will supplement what you do on Facebook, LinkedIn, and Twitter. Although there are other players (Plaxo, Ning), we contend that over time these lesser-known players will likely become absorbed or a part of the major players in some fashion.

Furthermore, the three major players could be eaten up by bigger entities such as Google or Microsoft. Some people believe that the business strategy of both Twitter and Facebook is to be acquired. At this writing, however, if you understand and become active with Facebook, Twitter, or LinkedIn, you will position yourself for whatever changes that will occur to the playing field. Remember, you must stay alert to change. If you get too comfortable and relaxed using any one tool, you may discover it gone the next day.

We will begin by looking at the strengths of each player and explain how a Sales Social Media Strategy might evolve using each. In this chapter sales will meet Facebook.

FACEBOOK

At this writing Facebook is the largest social media tool with over 400 million users worldwide recorded in December 2009 and more joining each day. Furthermore, Facebook is expanding its applications to respond to competition from Twitter and other outlets. Let us start at the beginning. It helps to understand how Facebook evolved in order to determine how to best utilize the platform. Just because everyone is on Facebook is not sufficient reason to put up a profile. Going back to your purpose and plan, think about what a profile on Facebook might mean to your overall objective, particularly related to sales.

Bear in mind that Facebook began in 2004 to help college students connect with one another. Because of the network's birth among college students, its power to reach the 30-something market is no surprise. MySpace targeted high school-age children while Facebook went after the more mature population. Initially, the purpose of Facebook was to build a strong network of people across a college campus, namely Harvard. In time, however, the power of Facebook grew beyond the college-age student. In fact, Shih said, " … although [Facebook] maintains an 85 percent or greater penetration among four-year U.S. universities, more than half of the users are out of college, and those 25 years and older represent the fastest-growing demographic."[2] One reason for the network's growth has to do with the maturity of the college student.

Take Mark, for example, who used Facebook during his college life and now finds himself searching for a job in another city. He contacted his Facebook friends for help. Lynn, who grew accustomed to sharing what movies she enjoyed with her college friends, began sharing information about the best place to open a checking account. Sandra, who used Facebook every day during her college career, turned once again to Facebook when she wanted to know which graduate school offered the best program of study. In other words, the college students grew up and their needs changed, but their method of communication did not. With these changing and expanding needs, these young people turned to Facebook, which had become part of their lives. As we discussed in Chapter 2, the communication revolution that the social media sparked happened because people changed the way they interacted with one another. Once that change occurred, the growth of the social media became inevitable.

Today Facebook still occupies the front-row seat in the field of social networking. It has the most user-friendly applications. As far as sales applications go, Facebook offers many options. Some of the people we interviewed for this book use Facebook extensively; others have not explored the Facebook waters and prefer LinkedIn or Twitter instead. As you examine some of Facebook's features, think about your own unique goals and that all-important question: Where are your customers?

WHAT MAKES FACEBOOK UNIQUE

- **Friendly, social site.** On Facebook you can post both professional and personal information. Facebook allows you to upload pictures as well as YouTube and personal videos. You can create in-depth information about yourself on the bio page. In fact, the bio page on Facebook targets your personal interests. You answer questions that identify your favorite movies, television shows, and favorite music as well as your hobbies and interests. Your Facebook profile presents less about you as a professional person in the workplace and more about you as a person. It is not uncommon to see photos of family members and close friends posted on Facebook. As a sales professional, you can create a professional profile that might look like a résumé. On Facebook you have an opportunity to either create a professional or personal profile. Most people choose the latter. Even on a personal profile, however, your responses to who you are and what you love doing could relate indirectly to the things you sell, but you must be careful not to overdo the "selling" part. Following is an example of what we found on a realtor's profile: "*In my experience, a home isn't a dream home because of its room dimensions. It's about how you feel when you walk through the front door. And the way you can instantly envision your life unfolding there. It's about more than real estate. It's about your life and your dreams. Let me help you realize those dreams.*" This person created a professional profile that includes job history. Even with that, you learn that the individual enjoys coaching soccer and is the dad of four sons. If you remember that Facebook is a social medium first and foremost, you can use it to best describe who you are in a way that invites others to share about themselves. We would not suggest making your Facebook profile too much of a sales pitch or too professional. Your "friends" want to know you as a person.

- **Status updates.** Facebook allows you to tell your friends what you are doing each day or what you are thinking about that day. You can see what your friends are doing and you can comment on their status. Status updates are visible to your friends only. These updates enable you to touch base with people daily. Imagine for a moment what this tool might mean to sales professionals. Are we not always wondering when and how to reconnect with someone or to reestablish a relationship with someone? With Facebook status updates you can touch your contacts each and every day, and you can read about what is happening in their worlds. It is like saying "hello" to someone every morning. Because you see only your friend's status updates, you do not get inundated with "hello's" from everyone. Again, you want to make your updates interesting and inviting. You don't want the status updates to constantly "sell" something or to constantly "advertise" what you are doing. Use some variety. One day you might say that you are enjoying a beautiful walk through your neighborhood with your dogs and another day you might say you are preparing for a presentation with a top client. The nice thing about Facebook is that people can keep a daily pulse on each other's lives. When they see one another face-to-face or talk on the telephone, they might ask, "How's your mom?" or "Did you get your kids off to camp?" You become a real person to them, not simply a salesman trying to push your product. By keeping up with your client's status updates you can send birthday greetings. You can contact someone if you notice they just received an important award or if they are having a particularly difficult time. Imagine how much it would mean when you pick up the phone and say, "Jack, I noticed you just completed your certification. Sounds as if that was a tough challenge. Congratulations!" Even leaving that message on voicemail could win you huge brownie points over your competitor. If you are a B2B sales professional, you will learn when your client just closed that important deal they were working on. It will alert you that timing might be right to invite this client for lunch to talk about your product. The possibilities for sales professionals are endless.

- **Communication versatility.** On Facebook, you have three choices for sending or posting messages. The status updates look more like a broadcast post because they go to all your friends at once. Wall-to-wall posts enable you to say something to just one friend, but all your friends can see it and all the people who happen to be friends of the person whose wall you posted on can see it. A wall-to-wall post then is not private. The third option enables you to send something privately to one person. As a sales professional, you will want to carefully consider which method gives you the best visibility. Recently Kyle van Hoften told us that he posted a message on someone's wall even though a direct private message would have been more logical. "I wall posted the message because I wanted others to learn more about my photography business," he said. "Even though that person asked for more information by private message, I answered on a wall post. I then sent her a private message explaining why I posted it."[3] What van Hoften did was use the wall post to answer a specific question from someone, but he explained to that person why he posted the response on her wall.

- **Fan pages.** Facebook gives you an opportunity to create a fan page that highlights a product, service, or activity that you love. Your friends can become fans of that product or service and they can invite their friends to do the same. The purpose of a fan page is to create a group of people who identify themselves as "fans" of your product or service. It also enables them to post on the page by making suggestions and/or responding to suggestions. This application gives you a chance to broaden the visibility of the products and services you like or you might wish to sell. Check out the fan page we created for this book by logging in to your Facebook account and putting "The New Handshake" in the search.

- **Facebook ads.** Facebook ads are very similar to Google ads. Anyone can create her own ad, target the population exactly as she wishes, and then pay only for clicks. This gives businesses an opportunity to netcast their products directly to their target populations and to pay only when someone clicks through.

- **Confirm friends.** Facebook allows people to invite you to become friends no matter who they are. You do not need to prove that you know the person before inviting him to be your friend. The person can choose to accept your invitation or not. If you accept someone's invitation and later decide that it was a poor choice, you can remove that person as a friend. The process is simple. You cannot see someone's profile until you are a friend. Once you become a friend, however, you can read the other person's wall posts, status updates, view their photos, read their bios, and browse their friends.

- **Create private sites on Facebook.** You can also lock your site and only allow certain people to view it. This is rarely done, but if you are working for a company, you may not wish your boss or coworkers to view everything on your site. This application might also make sense if you are a B2B sales professional who wishes to narrowly target your Facebook friends to those B2B businesses in your niche. If that were the case, you could set up a private site and only invite certain targeted people. That would limit not only your friend invitations but also your requests for invitations from others who may not fit your criteria. If you want a public site but wish to limit who can see what, the privacy settings on Facebook allow you to do that.

- **Highlight your blog post.** Facebook allows you to put your blog posts or your Tweets from Twitter on your status updates. Whenever you post on your blog, with the push of a button all your Facebook friends can read that post from their Facebook homepage. In Chapter 12 we will share options you can use that link Facebook status updates and Tweets.

SOME DISADVANTAGES OF FACEBOOK

Remembering that Facebook is primarily a social site, some companies worry that the platform is too relaxed. Trish Bertuzzi said, "I don't want to see photos of you dancing on the table."[4] She prefers to use LinkedIn or Twitter because she feels that Facebook gives people license to let their hair down.

Others worry that Facebook might violate privacy. Some salespeople do not wish for their customers to know too much about them. They do not want them to know what they like to do during the weekend or what music they enjoy listening to. These are issues of openness. As we discussed in Chapter 4 when we looked at the Johari Window, openness creates trust. But how much openness is too much?

Kathy Tito explained that one thing her company Call Center Services does is help people create a Facebook presence. She said that one of the concerns of the B2B companies she deals with is the time involved with not only creating the Facebook profile, fan pages, business pages, and ads, but also with how much time people will spend on Facebook. Her company helps B2B companies generate leads through social media and Facebook in particular. "Many companies find it more efficient to outsource social media lead generation through sites like Facebook. What we do is guide a company along by helping them develop their social media presence based on their company objectives."[5]

As you consider the advantages and disadvantages of Facebook, keep in mind that the most important thing is to get out there. You can set up guidelines within your organization to deal with most of the disadvantages. As Tito said, "If salespeople are not involved with writing press releases now or with putting information up on the corporate Web site, should they be writing status updates on the corporate fan page? These are questions each company must answer for themselves."[6]

CREATING A FACEBOOK PROFILE

As a salesperson you may want to create a Facebook profile for yourself. If you wish to self-brand, this is an important part of that brand. When you meet people face-to-face at networking events or conventions, that person will look you up on the various social media sites. It is important that you have a complete profile. Following are some tips to help make your profile interesting and professional:

- Include a photo. Make sure your photo is one of you and not one of your dog or your child. Your customers want to see you.
- You can put your birthday, but you need not include the year.
- Put where you are from, the city, state, and country.
- Include all your links on your Facebook profile. Be sure to put your Web site in a prominent place, but also the links to other sites your customers might find interesting.
- When you list movies, books, songs, remember who will be reading the profile. Whenever possible include items that might be of interest to your customer. For example, Joan lists books related to management,

MARKETING AND STRATEGIC GROWTH CONSULTANT AND FITNESS INSTRUCTOR, KYLE VAN HOFTEN, TALKS ABOUT USING FACEBOOK

"One of the ways to determine success for my fitness classes," he explained, "is the number of people who sign up for a class. As an example, on Tuesday I posted on Facebook under the status update what Tuesday's class would include and thanked friends for their input on the playlist. I had asked someone beforehand to comment on the status so it wouldn't be out there alone. This comment created a groundswell. We ended up with 30 different comments and a full class before the class even began. Part of the response was people posting things like, 'Kyle, I totally forgot you were teaching classes. When can I come?' One person contacted me from outside the state and said they'd like to come the next time I teach it. I responded to the naysayers who said spin classes were too tough by suggesting some less intense exercise. This, too, created dialogue. People see me in the community in the conversation. From a brand awareness and an expansion of interest people begin talking about my classes from all over and I'm able to generate a buzz around what I'm doing. Don't need to make the sale but to stimulate the energy for the others involved."[7]

leadership, coaching, and communication. She also tosses in the biography of Marie Antoinette and Lee Smith's *Fair and Tender Ladies* to give her viewers a well-rounded view of her tastes. Barb list includes *Naked Conversations* and the *Science of Success* as well as *Getting to Heaven on a Harley.*

One of the biggest challenges for today's solo entrepreneurs is to generate interest in their classes. Many clients struggle with ways to get the word out there to fill up the classroom. Kyle van Hoften explains that Facebook not only enables you to get the word out but to do it in a way that creates energy, interest, and dialogue. Simply announcing your program will not cut it. When you announce and encourage comment, you extend *the new handshake.*

Chapter 10

Sales Meets LinkedIn

LINKEDIN

Before examining the unique features of LinkedIn, we need to understand its origin and evolution. LinkedIn began not as a social network but as a business network. In contrast to Facebook, LinkedIn disallowed opportunities to post photo albums or to converse freely with the contacts. In the early days, the founders of LinkedIn saw an opportunity to create a social media site that was a little less "social" and a little more "professional." Valerie Buckingham, director of technology and marketing at Nokia, said of Reid Hoffman, founder of LinkedIn, "Hoffman redefined online professional networking, making a seminal contribution to the rise of social media. Now Hoffman is once again setting his sights on the future, exploring how companies will use the growing base of online social networking information as a foundation for business innovation."[1]

Even though LinkedIn has expanded with applications to allow for many of the things we can do on Facebook and Twitter, it maintains its identity as a professional networking community. Some of Joan's connections on LinkedIn, for example, opted not to become her friends on Facebook. Why? One said, "I like to keep my Facebook friends purely personal and my LinkedIn friends professional." In today's social media world these distinctions are blurring. Nonetheless, LinkedIn provides us with a social media option that eliminates some people's fears about having their privacy invaded. In quick answer to that fear, however, remember, we can post anything we wish on our profiles and make anything we wish public. If we want to post a photo of ourselves in a compromising way but do not want our boss to see it, perhaps a social media site is not the best choice.

In the early days LinkedIn began as a job search resource and an important recruiting tool. Headhunters as well as human resource professionals used LinkedIn to identify potential candidates. LinkedIn still serves this purpose, but it has grown to be a lot more than a hotbed for people looking for jobs. A strong professional network of trusted connections gives you a career advantage. Furthermore, the ability to quickly gain access to information and resources in this global economy will give you a significant competitive edge. If you see LinkedIn as merely a place for job hunting, you have missed a lot! Following are some of the other important benefits of LinkedIn:

- Gain credibility as an expert in your field.
- Create business partnerships.
- Keep up to date on trends in your industry.
- Set yourself apart from your competitors.
- Connect with people all over the world.

LinkedIn reigns as the largest professional social networking site with over 80 million users. Surveys tell us that nearly 60 percent of those users have high personal incomes and hold positions at the executive level or higher. According to Hitwise.com, LinkedIn traffic in the United States increased 323 percent from 2006 to 2007.[2] A more recent study by Anderson Analytics shows the users of LinkedIn fall into four unique categories,[3] as follows:

- **Savvy networkers.** These represent people who began using the social networks early. They understand the power of the media, and they are active users on LinkedIn with more connections than most. These people have high personal incomes and often have the word "consultant" in their profiles. The Anderson survey showed 30 percent of LinkedIn users fit this category
- **Senior executives.** These include people in power jobs that they want to keep. They are not as tech savvy as the savvy networkers, but they use the network to make connections and build partnerships. These people have the highest personal incomes and have the name owner, partner, executive, or associate in their titles. The Anderson survey showed 20 percent of LinkedIn users fit this category. (Often, these people only participate on LinkedIn. They do not participate on Facebook or Twitter.)
- **Late adopters.** These people joined LinkedIn because they received requests to do so from family and friends. They are not active users

and are not tech savvy. They are still learning what LinkedIn can do for them. These people have less personal income and have teacher, medical professional, and lawyer in their titles. The Anderson survey showed 22 percent of LinkedIn users fit this category.

- **Exploring options.** These people are looking for possible career changes. They are tech savvy and use the social media for personal and professional reasons. They make up 20 percent of the LinkedIn users.

It is clear that LinkedIn is top heavy with users who are key decision makers, have high personal incomes, and who understand the power and value of social networking. To salespeople, a presence on LinkedIn opens the door to connections that might otherwise prove impossible. Through LinkedIn, you can identify top-level executives without having to work your way up through the bottom of the organization. You can learn more about those people and what matters to them before you ever make a contact. "We started using LinkedIn several years ago," said Mike Damphousse, CEO of Green Leads. "After working hard, I became the expert in Lead Generation on LinkedIn. What I realized is that expert status created a lot of activity because hundreds of thousands of people look at this."[4]

Let us examine some of the unique features of LinkedIn:

- **A professional network.** The LinkedIn profile feels very much like a résumé. You can add information to highlight yourself, but you will not see hobbies, favorite songs, or favorite movies on a LinkedIn profile. You will not see photos of the person skydiving or sitting by the swimming pool. You will not know if the person is married or single or if he has children.
- **LinkedIn Groups.** Although Facebook has groups, the LinkedIn groups give you an opportunity to interact with business professionals on a deeper level. You may have 500 people in your LinkedIn contact network, but you could have thousands more among the people with whom you share common group interests. Joan, for example, belongs to 17 groups comprising 30,360 people. Through LinkedIn groups you can post blogs, respond to discussions, start discussions, directly contact members, invite members to connect with you, post news events, and much more. Active participation in groups specific to your business focus increases your visibility within the LinkedIn network and lets you establish yourself as an expert in your field. With thousands of groups to choose from, LinkedIn makes it easy for you to search for groups that fit your target audience. For example, Marc Perramond, who works for InsideView,

a Sales 2.0 company, joined the Sales 2.0 group on LinkedIn. Furthermore, he told us that all the salespeople in his company are members of this group and other groups related to their sales niche. If you do not find a group that fits your niche, you can start and manage your own.

- **LinkedIn search.** Unlike Facebook, which only allows you to search friends, LinkedIn lets you search for companies, jobs, and answers to questions as well as search for people. For salespeople, the ability to search companies and locate additional network connections within those companies gives them a competitive advantage over others not using LinkedIn to the fullest. Here is how it works. You can place the name of any company or any job category in your search, such as vice president of sales, and gain access to all the people matching that company or job specification in your network. By your network we mean not just your direct contacts but secondary and lesser contacts as well. For example, if you put vice president of sales in the search, and Joan, as one of your contacts, has 15 vice presidents of sales in her network, those 15 people will be listed as a secondary contact through Joan who you can then contact to make an introduction for you. Remember, all your group contacts constitute primary connections. In Chapter 8 we showed you the power of the Advanced Search on LinkedIn, which is one of the most valuable lead-generation features of the network. Mike Damphousse told us his company uses LinkedIn to help him identify leads for his clients.

- **Question and Answer.** When LinkedIn began, the Question/Answer section of the site was a powerful place for you to showcase your knowledge. You could either post a question to the entire LinkedIn population or to segments of the network. You could answer questions other people posted. Many members answered questions and became experts in that area. For example, Joan became an expert in the area of staffing and recruiting because that area fit the topic of her first book. Updated and expanded functions on LinkedIn enabled members to ask and answer questions within specific groups in which they are members. By becoming an active giver of information, you create credibility and trust with a wide range of people. Remember the Johari Window we discussed in Chapter 5. Once you create trust and respect, you move people into the Open Area, and that is where sales are made. You also create brand and name recognition. Before long people recognize you as someone they can go to for information. LinkedIn groups tend to be much more active than Facebook groups. Most people on Facebook join groups when asked, but the groups do not interact the way they do on LinkedIn.

- **Recommendations.** On LinkedIn you have an opportunity to publish recommendations and testimonials. Peer recommendations and testimonials hold weight and power in the eyes of your potential buyer. Through the eyes of others you showcase your products and services, further building on the idea that you are a credible player in your field. To secure a 100-percent-profile-completion status, LinkedIn requires you to have a minimum of three recommendations. Most people have many more than three, but remember this is not a numbers game. Your recommendations should be credible and authentic; otherwise people will suspect that something is not quite right. For example, Barb ran across one LinkedIn user with several hundred recommendations for his work. Upon closer inspection it was discovered that many of those recommendations came out of a training class the individual conducted. Recommendations that look contrived can work against your credibility. Our suggestion: Be careful! Furthermore, when someone recommends you, you want to return the favor only when you feel confident in your ability to recommend that person's work. Who you recommend will say as much about you as it does the other person. Just as the LinkedIn network has expanded beyond its early history as a job board, the recommendations feature has also grown. It now serves as a place for customer feedback about your products and services.
- **Blog posts.** Using one of the blog posting applications included with LinkedIn, you can publish your blog posts directly to your LinkedIn profile and to any and all of your groups. This feature enables you to give your blog much broader visibility across the LinkedIn network. Instead of merely posting your blog to your profile or on the status update as is the case with Facebook, you can post it to an unlimited number of groups within your profile. Again, as is the case with Joan, instead of posting to just 350 friends on Facebook, her blog post goes to 30,000+ people in her LinkedIn group network. LinkedIn sends her a digest where she can quickly scan comments to these posts. If you wish to post your blog to your entire list of connections on LinkedIn, it is a bit more difficult, depending on the size of your network. LinkedIn limits the number of people you can communicate with and the frequency of communication. The blog, however, is posted on your profile where your connections can read it whenever they wish. Your connections do not get a notice when a post is made, however, and few people check each other's profiles daily on LinkedIn. Figure 10.1 shows one of Joan's blog posts in the News Section of the Public Speaking Network on LinkedIn. Note the tabs for Overview, Discussions, Job, and Subgroups. These tabs show how much you can do with LinkedIn groups.

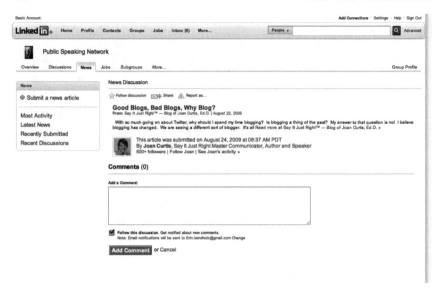

FIGURE 10.1 Joan's blog posted in the Public Speaking Network on LinkedIn (Reprinted with permission from LinkedIn.)

- **LinkedIn Polls.** On LinkedIn you can create a poll. You can target the poll to a segment of the LinkedIn population, or if you wish to pay a fee you can send the poll to all LinkedIn users. Imagine being a sales professional in the Test Mode. Perhaps you wish to find out how people are using your product or service. Perhaps you want to know what day of the week would be best to run a teleclass. The ability to access LinkedIn users in this way is worth the fee. If you want to create a free poll, however, you can do so. Depending on the size of your network, the free polls can also have widespread visibility. You can send the poll to all of your connections, say 350 people. You might then want to write a blog post that includes the link to the poll, and as we pointed out above you can post that blog to all your groups, say 20,000 people.

- **LinkedIn Reading List.** Amazon hooked up with LinkedIn to provide a book list application that lets users tell others about the books they recommend and love. The savvy sales professional will use the reading list as a way to showcase and recommend books that she believes her network will find valuable. You can also use the reading list as a way to drive traffic to your profile. For example, Barb often references information and ideas from books she has read during her keynote speeches. Instead of providing a "hard copy" book list, she encourages

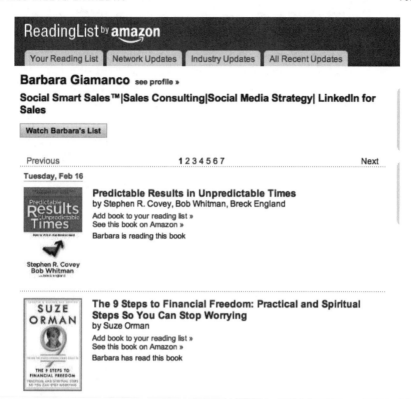

FIGURE 10.2   Barb's reading list on her profile page on LinkedIn
(Reprinted with permission from LinkedIn.)

people to view her book list on her LinkedIn profile. Recommending books that fit with your expertise may pique someone's interest enough that they decide they would like to connect with you. People can "watch" your book list (and you can watch theirs) and receive network notices when you have added new books to your list. Figure 10.2 shows you Barb's LinkedIn reading list.

From the interviews we have conducted with people in sales and marketing, LinkedIn is the most widely used social media tool for business networking and lead generation. Blogging follows closely on its heels. While many people are beginning to experiment with other social networking tools, they have been part of the LinkedIn network longer and have thus established themselves within the LinkedIn business community. Mike Damphousse said that in his company all the salespeople have LinkedIn profiles, and he asks each person to submit a status update at least two times a week.

InsideView is a business-to-business company specializing in helping sales professionals increase productivity. Since 2007 the company launched a Sales 2.0 social media strategy that heavily involved both sales and marketing. Product manager, Marc Perramond, explained it this way. "We recognized the tremendous growth of the social media and realized we wanted to leverage that growth in sales and marketing." Perramond told us that all the company's sales professionals use LinkedIn and Twitter to participate in the conversation. He explained that marketing adopted the new media earlier because of their one-on-many mentality. The sales department came on board later because it deals more with relationships.

Today, InsideView hires salespeople who understand the social media. Once hired they go through a vigorous on-boarding process to bring them up to speed with how to leverage traditional sales data as well as tap into the social media outlets. "We want a complete view of the customer," he said. "The new buyer has lots of information about you, not just from your company Web site. They learn about you from all the information on the Web. Matching sales with social media is about arming our salespeople with information about prospects. It helps eliminate the imbalance of information."

InsideView boasts a 410 percent increase in sales growth from 2007 to 2008 during the onset of the national downturn. The mission of the company is to maximize sales growth by taking advantage of the convergence of traditional media with the social media.

Perramond told us that the salespeople use Twitter to help establish their own brand within the company. On Twitter they can mini-blog what is happening within the company as well as join the conversation with customers. He gave one specific example that resulted in an important sale for InsideView. Perramond met someone on Twitter because they both were talking about similar topics. They connected. That person introduced him up the chain into management of another company. "From that contact, we made an important deal," he said.

LinkedIn is an important tool for InsideView. Perramond explained that everyone at the company has a LinkedIn account, and when hired each connects with everyone else. This process broadens the company's overall base of contacts. The salespeople are very active in the LinkedIn groups. They join groups that are relevant to their products and then they participate in the conversation.

Because this technology is new and ever changing, the people at InsideView work to stay ahead of the game. They are constantly monitoring what is going on so they can help their clients make adjustments. Perramond said, "We want to make sure we're not drinking from a fire hose, but from a stream of focused information." That will be the challenge of the future, he added, to use the growing sea of information to make salespeople more productive.

For more information on InsideView go to www.InsideView.com.

CREATING YOUR LINKEDIN PROFILE

If you are a first-time LinkedIn user and finally getting started, congratulations! Now that you have put together your purpose and plan, you have the information you need to create a public profile designed to target your ideal buyer.

In today's online world your profile has become your virtual calling card. As such, it must clearly communicate the value you deliver in the products and services that you sell. You want to create a profile that feels approachable and authentic. Leave the corporate buzzwords at home. If the task overwhelms you, hire a professional writer who can capture the essence of your message.

Always keep in mind who may be reading your profile. What message are you creating? Is that message consistent with your brand? Have you clearly articulated your competitive difference? In other words, what benefits do you offer that others do not? This is especially true on LinkedIn where you want your profile to look like more than a résumé. Here are some general tips:

- Post a current *business* photo. On Facebook your photo can be casual—you in casual clothes or you outside with the sun at your back, but on LinkedIn you need a professional photo. It could be you giving a presentation or your headshot in business attire. Remember that every major corporation has a presence on LinkedIn. Further, LinkedIn is also home to small and medium-sized businesses and independent consultants all over the world. Your business photo, like everything else, reflects your professional brand.
- Be specific, but compelling, about what you do. One of the first things people will see in your profile is what you do. After your name comes the keywords that identify your work. If you are the vice president for sales at Coca-Cola, that is pretty well understood. If, on the other hand, you are a sales rep, you want to draw people in with a message that engages them and propels them to find out more about you and your company versus the other guys. Think like your potential buyer. What pain are they feeling in their business? What problems are they trying to solve that would cause them to search out specific keywords that then lead them directly to you? As a master communicator with two prior books under her belt, Joan leverages her book title with a heading that says, "Say It Just Right Master Communicator, Author and Speaker." Barb wants to capitalize on her sales and technology experience while emphasizing the services she offers, so her header reads, "Sales Results, Social Media Strategy, Speaking, Coaching,

Programs, Business Blogger." Think of your header as your three-second tagline. Whenever you post in group discussions or answer questions, your "profile badge" appears with your critical keywords listed right alongside your name. That is why the right descriptive words are so important. If people notice your comments and like them, perhaps they will want to connect with you. You want to make it easy for them to understand what you do. Most folks will not invest a lot of time perusing your profile. Capture interest quickly and give them a reason to want more.

- **Make yourself shine in the Summary section of LinkedIn.** Here you can specify the value your product or service might bring to someone reading about you. Read other people's summary statements to get an idea. Joan's is divided into these parts: (1) Header or hook (2) What she or her product will bring to any organization (3) Why she is on LinkedIn (4) Highlights in her career, including her writing and speaking awards (5) her specialties. Be sure to make this section interesting, crisp, and inviting. Unfortunately, once you get below the Summary section on your profile, LinkedIn moves into questions that sound résumé like. Even though LinkedIn asks for your current and past experience as part of your profile, you do not have to default to boring. As you think about who you are and what your company offers, remember to highlight experiences that really support your current brand offering. You need not include every detail of your personal work history on your LinkedIn profile. Always remember that online attention span is short.
- **Use SlideShare.** Using the SlideShare application enables you to post up to four PowerPoint presentations on your LinkedIn profile. Not only can you use SlideShare presentations to showcase your work, but you can also increase your search visibility inside the LinkedIn community as well as on the World Wide Web. Mike Damphousse told us, "I encourage all our staff to include a SlideShare program on their LinkedIn profiles, and I ask them to keep that program up to date."[5]
- **Check your ratings and recommendations.** Your LinkedIn profile also displays when you have received an "expert" rating on your responses to questions. It shows the people you have recommended and highlights recommendations that you have received from others.
- **Update your profile twice a week.** At a minimum, update your status several times a week. Be strategic in your status updates. Let people know what you are doing, but also use updates to highlight and promote the work of others. For example, if you have just attended a conference and enjoyed what the speaker had to say, compliment that

person in your status update. If you are a sales rep and you just landed a big deal, post your good news without naming the company. As you roll out new products and services or take on volunteer projects, add that information to your LinkedIn profile. Keep in mind that each time you update your profile, LinkedIn alerts your network. It is a subtle way to maintain visibility within the LinkedIn community.

- **Limit highly personal information.** LinkedIn gives you an opportunity to add your marital status and birthday. This is new to LinkedIn and clearly an attempt to look more like Facebook. For a professional profile, this information is unnecessary. It is not likely that LinkedIn professionals will send you birthday greetings like people do on Facebook. Adding your telephone number and e-mail address is an option and depends on whether you want someone to contact you directly through traditional means or reach you through your Web site.

- **Be selective in the groups you join.** Your profile also includes a list of the groups you belong to. Your group membership says a lot about you. Do not join any group that invites you. Join groups that fit your sales niche and actively participate in those groups. If you do decide to join a group that fits your personal interests, such as photography or fine wines, keep your readers in mind. Because your profile reflects your business brand, think carefully about the messages you share.

Chapter 11

Sales Meets Twitter

TWITTER

One of the most important things you can get from this book is to determine which tool will work best for you to generate revenue and which may become time wasters. Twitter seems to be the least understood tool out there at this writing. No one knows where it will go and what will become of Twitter. Our contention is the future of Twitter is not a relevant question for you. The relevant question is *whether a Twitter presence can produce better productivity with your sales force.* As we pointed out previously, to answer that question you must consider what your product is and how your customers purchase your product.

In addressing these questions, you must refer back to all the questions we posed in Chapters 7 and 8. When asked why people love Twitter, the following are the most common responses: "I can ask a question and get instantaneous responses," and "I can bounce ideas off people I could otherwise never have contact with." These two answers help us understand the value of Twitter. In addition, when we interviewed sales and marketing people using Twitter, most agreed that Twitter offers a great way to research. Trish Bertuzzi said she can find out more on Twitter about what is going on in her industry than she can on her own. Mike Damphousse said he and his team use Twitter to help them extend their blog reading. Instead of having to read and subscribe to thousands of blogs, he simply uses Twitter to keep up with what is happening. In a *Wall Street Journal* article titled "Follow the Tweets," the authors wrote, "We believe executives can make accurate predictions about sales trends by analyzing Tweets that mention their products and services."[1]

In essence we recommend that you consider Twitter if you are a B2B company interested in promoting your brand and credibility within your industry. Here are the values that Joel Comm listed from his experience with Twitter:[2]

- **It builds deeper relationships with partners, clients and entrepreneurs.** As Marc Perramond discussed regarding InsideView, he met people on Twitter that he would have never met, and through those people he developed deeper relationships both as partners and as customers. His Twitter contacts opened the door for him. As sales professionals, we know that getting our foot in the door is half the battle. Twitter is about more than relationship, according to Mike Damphousse, it is about information.
- **It extends and broadens the brand.** Sales 2.0 combined with social media extend branding beyond the grasp of marketing. Perramond called it "smarketing"—a blend of the sales and marketing mentality. He said he sees this as the trend in sales. "Instead of branding who you are as a company, I see branding expanding to who you are as a sales rep." Mike Damphousse told us that Green-Leads.com has a company account on Twitter, but they also have six separate employee accounts in which employees can niche themselves according to their expertise.
- **It enables information flow from experts you might not find elsewhere.** Karen Russell, a public relations professor at the University of Georgia and named as one of the 100 smartest social media people by Smarter Social Media, said she uses Twitter to keep up to date in her field. Experts post the newest developments, which she can explore at her leisure and later share with her students. Trish Bertuzzi said, "People I follow share fantastic information. I follow vendors and analysts, not clients. I run a business. I can't be doing research 24/7. If I look at Twitter a couple of times a day, I get great information on what people are reading, and I've developed some unbelievably great relationships with some of the vendors."[3]
- **It adds people to your network.** Through Twitter you can increase the number of people who visit your Web site and who stay informed about new developments in your company. Damphousse said, "Once we started using Twitter, we saw immediate results. Within a month or two we saw a noticeable increase in inbound leads. People were saying things like, 'I've been reading your blog' or 'I heard about you on Twitter.' It all came back to our stepped up activity on Twitter. We've closed business with this."[4]

Like Facebook and LinkedIn, Twitter launched in one way but morphed in directions not predicted by its founders. In the beginning Twitter started as a way for people to send short messages to one another in order to keep up to date in real time. The founders soon realized that they enjoyed this process. The micro-blogging (140 characters) function of Twitter saved time. Instead of having to develop paragraphs of content, they whipped out short, daily messages. By doing so, they touched one another quickly. Creating short messages evolved because Twitter began as a platform for handheld devices. No one could text long messages. As the handhelds became easier to use with the introduction of keyboards, people could type more, faster.

Nonetheless, Twitter maintains the 140 character limit. Why? Because people like it. No matter how busy you are, you can send a 140 character Tweet, and you can send that Tweet from anywhere in the world. You do not have to be at your computer. The ease and efficiency of Twitter helped it grow to more than 12.1 million users at this writing. Today, Twitter users have become the on-the-scene reporters throughout the world. When news happens, instead of reading about it in the newspapers or waiting for a report on CNN, people go to Twitter. Through the eyes of Twitter ordinary people Tweet the firsthand accounts. When Michael Jackson died, for example, so many Tweets overwhelmed the system that it crashed. Twitter enables us to stay far ahead of the information game.

There are big differences between Twitter and Facebook and LinkedIn. Twitter is more than a social network. It has followers, but Twitter was not designed to build long-lasting deep friendships, like Facebook. You cannot post photos on your Twitter profile. You cannot join groups on Twitter. However, Twitter enables you to send brief messages multiple times a day to many people. The one-on-many concept explodes with Twitter. "Twitter is a communications tool," said Joel Comm. "It's a channel that lets you speak to lots of people and enlighten them about your life and your work."[5] The Facebook and LinkedIn status options grew in response to Twitter. On Facebook, however, only your friends read your status updates. On Twitter, all of Twitterville can read your Tweets. Unlike LinkedIn you cannot showcase your career on a professional profile. Twitter profiles are brief, just like the Tweets. Given these differences, let us examine what this means to a Social Media Sales Strategy and the special features Twitter offers users.

- **Search function.** Twitter enables you to search for people and topics that fit your unique niche. What this means is you can find out what people are talking about. Marc Perramond searches "Sales 2.0." From that search he learns everything that is being said about Sales 2.0. He can also search his company, InsideView. He quickly gauges what people are posting, good and bad about his company. From the search function you can click on all the people you would like to follow. Although Twitter allows users to lock their following, most people do not enable this function. Most Twitters want new followers. They desire to build the quantity with the quality. As we learned from Perramond and Damphousse, it was through Twitter that they closed sales that they would not have closed otherwise.

- **Monitoring function.** Twitter enables you to monitor what is being said about your product and services. You can also monitor what the competition is doing or not doing. The ease of the searches gives you access to specialized information you might not have otherwise. Imagine as a sales rep you might wonder what your customers are saying about a generic product, such as airline service for example. You learn that people are frustrated with long waits or with lost luggage. You learn that people like the new movies shown on one airline but not another. You can use all this information to tailor your pitch to new customers.

- **Build a large base of followers.** On Twitter, unlike Facebook and LinkedIn, you can opt to follow anyone you want (unless they have locked their following—which is not common). When you search a topic or a brand or a profession, you will uncover many people you might wish to follow. You do not have to "prove" you know someone (as on LinkedIn) nor do you have to get confirmation (as on Facebook). You simply hit the "follow" button and you are now following that person. If, at some later point, you do not wish to follow that person, you can simply block them. It is as easy as that. This function gives you access to many more people quickly. Quick is the name of the game with Twitter. We offer one caution, however. Do not automatically follow everyone who follows you. There are many pornographic sites on Twitter. Using a simple tool called Twitter Karma (http://dossy.org/twitter/karma/), you can view people who are following you, but whom you are not following. From the photos and name descriptions, you can weed out unwanted followers. For example, you may not want to follow someone called "Asian Funny Girl2 or Myhotcomments2." If you are not sure of someone, you can go to their profile and take a look at their Tweets and their bio.

- **Exposure to your products.** Even though Facebook and LinkedIn expose people to your products and services, nothing does it faster than Twitter. As we pointed out in Chapter 1, when you Tweet about your product to your following, say 2,000 people, and someone sees it and re-Tweets it to their following of 7,500 people, you create instant visibility to 9,500 people in a matter of seconds. Remember, this exposure goes both ways. If people are unhappy with your product or service, they can just as quickly expose their displeasure. That is why the monitoring function of Twitter is so important. You need to know what people are saying, and you need to enter the conversation.

- **Brand yourself.** Some companies use their brand on Twitter and create a brand profile. Most do it the way InsideView and Green Leads do it in that they allow the sales reps to brand themselves within the company. In this manner, people follow people, not companies. Your customers might know you as someone who works for Dell, but when your customers know you as a person, it is much easier to develop the know, like, and trust factors. That is why Stephanie reached such high popularity at DellOutlet on Twitter.

- **Micro-blogging.** For many people creating frequent blog posts is not possible. Either they are not writers or they do not have the time to blog. The opportunity to micro-blog on Twitter gives you a chance to share information quickly without having to write long, well-thought-out content. Micro-blogging offers a great opportunity for sales. The marketing people can write the blog posts and the sales rep can post the link to that blog on Twitter. The sales rep need not write the blog herself. Here are some of the things you can micro-blog about: inspirational or motivational quotes; someone else's interesting blog or online article; a fun or funny YouTube video; a short survey (e.g., How many of you enjoy movies over two hours long?); links to quality blogs (yours if you have one), resources, or products; announce new applications to your product or upcoming events; and a personal tidbit, particularly if you are Tweeting over the weekend.

- **Tweet with a purpose.** Alan Sicinski wrote a great blog post titled, "How to Twitter: A Beginner's Guide."[6] In it he suggested some important sales fundamentals for every Tweet. (1) Include a call to action. It can be as simple as "check this out." (2) Use key words that are commonly searched for in your niche. Remember the Twitter search function includes searching key words in Tweets as well as people and professions. (3) Tweet something that will catch the attention of your followers, such as a Tweet titled, "I love using the new Twitter application that organizes my Tweets."

- **Time sensitive.** Because Twitter was designed to happen in the moment, it is the most time-sensitive social media tool. You need to Tweet during "prime" times. If you Tweet during the wee hours of the morning or during holidays and weekends, you may miss your audience (be aware of time zones). No one can read all the Tweets flooding onto their Twitter Deck. Unread Tweets are gone within seconds. Twitter gives you an opportunity to Tweet often and to take advantage of the moment. "Twitter is real time and micro and takes place in a micro time span," said Tom Canning. "The old sales cycle was three to six months. Blogging sped things up. Now with Twitter we've gone from zero miles per hour to 100 miles per hour."[7]

- **You can respond to people in three ways on Twitter.** (1) The @ symbol is used to respond directly to someone's Tweet. This response is public, available for everyone to read. Although similar to writing on someone's wall on Facebook, there is a visibility difference. On Facebook, only your friends and the friends of the person you wall posted can see it. On Twitter, when you @ Tweet, everyone in Twitterville can see it. Make sure you respond with the bigger audience in mind. Otherwise, what is the point of a public response? (2) RT means "re-tweet." This is the highest compliment in Twitterland. When you RT someone, you are saying that you like what they have Tweeted so much, you want to send that Tweet out to your followers under your name. Whenever someone RT's you, it is customary to respond to them with a thank you. And, even more important if you "steal" someone else's Tweet without the RT symbol, it will not bode well for you. (3) DM means a direct and private message. You can only DM your followers, and the DMs are private. It is through DM that you can create a stronger relationship with someone. There you can arrange for telephone meetings, direct e-mail correspondence, or other information that you wish to divulge privately.

CREATING YOUR TWITTER PROFILE

As we discussed above, each tool poses different questions within a different framework. You will note, however, similarities and differences as well in the profile development. One thing is consistent: Post a photo!

- Post a photo. If you develop a product profile for your company, you will post the company logo, but you will also want your sales reps to have their own profiles. They will post photos of themselves with the company logo in the background. The worst thing you can do is not post a photo. If you do, you will have an ugly default image in place of your photo.
- Describe who you are and the benefits of knowing you. On Twitter you have very few words for describing yourself. Imagine creating your three-second elevator speech. That is what you are doing on Twitter. You must uncover what it is about you that makes you interesting enough to follow. Take a look at what Barb's bio on Twitter says: "Sales & Social Media Consultant, Author, Speaker, Technology Lover, Internet Radio Host."
- Keep your profile up to date. If things change, make sure you update your profile. When Joan published her second book, for example, she changed her three-second bio to read: "Say It Just Right Master communications coach, author and speaker."

- Make sure you put your company Web sites on your profile. Twitter allows you to put your Web site on your headline page. If people like what you say, it is the first place they will go.
- Brand yourself with your background. Twitter gives you an opportunity to create your own background colors and logo. If you take a look at people's Twitter pages, you'll see all kinds of interesting, colorful background. It is better to put your own logo up in the background, using the company colors than to use one of the default selections Twitter offers. Even photos of you placed in an interesting way can attract people to your site. Remember, Twitter is about branding. Take a look at Joan's Twitter profile and the way she incorporated the *New Handshake* logo.
- The most prominent thing you will see on the Twitter profile are your Tweets. If you are constantly "in your face" with Tweets that sell, sell, sell, that will turn people off. Most people look for a variety of Tweets. They look for @ symbols that suggest that you are interacting with people. They look for RT's that suggest that you read other people's Tweets. They look for links that suggest that you share information, and they look for questions suggesting that you do not know all the answers.

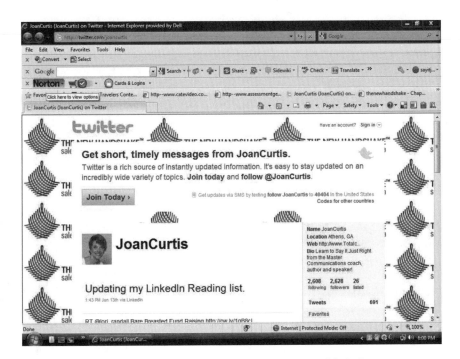

FIGURE 11.1   Joan's Twitter profile page using The New Handshake logo.
Source: Twitter.com

People often ask if you can make money using social media. The answer is yes, but you must work your plan consistently. We have been very successful in securing paid speaking and consulting engagements, but that has happened as a result of knowing exactly who our target market is and our ability to use social networking regularly. Barb invests time daily, as part of her sales plan, to make business connections for others, to participate in group discussions, and to share tips with others to help them increase their business. Joan uses the applications feature to include presentations and her blog posts on her profile. All of these moves create visibility and awareness for who we are and what we have to offer. Do not forget DellOutlet on Twitter where the company boasts $6.5 million in sales. Take a look at how Mike Damphousse is incorporating social media into his company. He said that he is seeing a real return on the investment of his time and money.

GREEN LEADS SUCCESSFULLY IMPLEMENTS SOCIAL MEDIA

Green Leads is a five-year-old, business-to-business company that helps marketers find leads. On a pay-for-performance model, Green Leads represents its clients with prospects to set up appointments for sales reps. For example, Company X hires Green Leads to work with five sales reps to book appointments for those reps. A Green Leads sales rep pitches as if he works for Company X. When the prospect starts showing an interest, Green Leads secures a meeting. Company X does not pay anything until the meeting takes place.

Green Leads Chief Executive Officer Mike Damphousse explained that the company began looking at social media in two ways and for two reasons. First, for the internal lead generation for its own business and second as a service it would provide to clients. Being a small company with 30 people in the United States and eight in Europe, Green Leads operates with sparse marketing resources. Hence, it was searching for ways to do more for less. Enter social media. "We began dabbling one year ago with the blog," Damphousse explained. "The blog was generating a lot of activity. So we wanted to find a way to radiate out from the blog. Twitter works to propagate information from the blog." He said Twitter is all about sharing information with people of similar interests.

From the blog the company moved slowly into LinkedIn. Damphousse became active with the Lead Generation group and soon became an expert by answering a lot of questions related to lead generation. Currently he intends to expand LinkedIn usage within the company. The company plans to create a phased-in social media strategy as follows:

- **Blogging.** In the beginning Damphousse contributed to the blog—Smashmouth Marketing. He is now grooming three other people in the organization to post on the blog.
- **LinkedIn.** Damphousse and several staff have LinkedIn profiles, but only Damphousse has been active. The new goal is to get everyone in the company on LinkedIn with updated profiles. He will train and encourage people to make regular status updates and to add a Slide-Share program to their profiles. They will all connect with one another. Green Leads also uses the LinkedIn poll service to find out how things are changing in the world of lead generation.
- **Tweeting.** In addition to the three new bloggers, Damphousse will add three more people. All will have Twitter profiles related to their niche. He explained, "We have a company account on Twitter. In addition to this account we will have more presence with six additional staff with individual accounts. We've got a guy on the staff that is an outbound dial-up guru. He will brand himself this way; another guy is a data researcher, who is talented using the social media. He will brand himself that way. Everyone will have a certain area of expertise—it will be focused but personal."
- **Facebook.** Green Leads will phase in Facebook. The company currently has a Facebook fan page but they want to expand more. "That is on the drawing board," Damphousse said.

In addition to phasing in the social media tools as noted above, Green Leads has figured out how to deal with the time issue. "If we aren't careful, the place could come to a grinding halt," Damphousse said. "We don't want people to ignore these tools but to use them at their own pace." The junior marketing person on staff dedicates a third of her time to coordinate the social media activity. She reads 75 to 100 RSS feeds and when she finds something of interest to someone's online persona, she forwards it to them to Tweet. She spends a few hours a day doing this to make it easier for everyone else. Her job is to keep everyone active and if that means nudging them, then that's an accomplishment."

Green Leads also believes in training the staff on how to use the social media. They will spend time with the initial training and then, as Damphousse termed it, "baby-sit" people until they feel comfortable using the new methods of communication. "We see it as a win-win. Once we understand how to incorporate these tools into our own lead gen(eration) efforts, we can provide a similar service to our clients."

For more information about Green Leads, visit the Web site http://www.green-leads.com.

As we will talk about in a later chapter, there is an art to how you create a sense of community and build relationships with people that ultimately lead to sales. It requires patience and consistent participation, as the Green Leads example shows. The tool you pick matters less than picking a tool and using it to the fullest capacity. In Chapter 12 we will give you some tips on how to deepen your use of the technology by adding applications to each of the three major players and bookmarking what you uncover as you explore the Web.

Chapter 12

You Digg It, I'm Delicious, We All StumbleUpon

LET US TAKE THE MYSTERY OUT OF SOCIAL BOOKMARKING

Social bookmarking is emerging as a popular part of the social media movement. Though a bit misunderstood, social bookmarking provides the opportunity to align with your customers as a trusted advisor and research resource. Consider that executives face the challenge of staying current on massive amounts of business information. They must often slog through inaccurate or irrelevant information. On top of that, the biggest complaint we hear about social media is that they consume massive amounts of time.

Imagine creating a social bookmarking strategy that not only gives your clients relevant information but helps them save time. All you need to do is gather and consolidate the mountains of information that inundates all of us every day. How might you do that? Creative use of social bookmarking is your answer. This chapter explores a few of the popular social bookmarking tools and shows you how to integrate those tools into your sales and service processes.

Before we show you how to integrate bookmarking into your sales process, let us address the concern about time management.

SOCIAL MEDIA TIME MASTERY

Whenever we mention social media in a business context, the response we hear is this: "I don't have time for social networking." This attitude springs from a belief that you are adding on to an already overloaded business day.

Instead of thinking about *adding on*, consider *integrating* sound principles into your sales day. How do you do this? Let something else go in order to free up time for targeted social selling. Let us face it. Every one of us have time wasters disguised as results-driven activities hidden somewhere on our calendar. Many hide in plain sight, and it is time to weed them out.

Try this exercise. Write down how many face-to-face networking events you attended in the past month. Even if you wrote down one per week, you probably spent at least three hours when you include driving there, parking, and the event itself. That adds up to 12 hours, more than a full business day, each month. Next, consider your hourly billable rate and ask yourself if you secured enough clients from those networking activities to justify the time spent. From our experience and the responses we have received from every group we polled, the answer remains a resounding no! That is why the effective use of social networking tools like LinkedIn, Facebook, and Twitter offer such an attractive alternative. Done right, you spend less time and you get better results.

To take managing your time one step further, let us examine how social bookmarking and social media aggregators can help you organize and manage the information exploding before you each day.

TOP PLAYERS IN THE BOOKMARKING WORLD

When it comes to social media, people scratch their heads in confusion about how social bookmarking fits in. They even understand Twitter better than they do social bookmarking. To respond to this mass confusion, we turn to Chip and Dan Heath and the suggestions they provide in their delightful book, *Made to Stick*.[1] The authors advise creating a simple analogy about something most of us can relate to in order to dispel the confusion. The Heath brothers tell us that with the right analogy something as confusing as social bookmarking can stick to you. Think of the file cabinet you have sitting in your office. When you look inside, you discover file folders arranged in some orderly way, for example by alphabet. Now, reach in, search for what you want, and retrieve the file. Voila! The arrangement enables you to find what you need easily.

The social bookmarking process differs little from that file cabinet in your office. With social bookmarking you save file locations that are housed in your own personal file cabinet on the Internet. Instead of labeling file folders, you use an informal tagging system that lets you create keywords and categories for easy reference and retrieval. You "tag" the Web address of articles, videos, blogs, audio files, and Web sites that you know you will want to access in the future. What makes social bookmarking even more attractive to a sales rep is that you can "share" your tags with other people. For some of us, sharing our filing system in our own file cabinet might not prove so easy.

From a sales perspective, social bookmarking offers a way for you to create categories that represent a particular client's interest. Imagine, for example, Joan is your customer. You know that Joan is a communications expert. You watch for interesting articles, blog posts, and videos about communication, and you tag them for Joan. In sales we know that it commonly takes 7 to 10 touches, depending on the complexity of the sales cycle, before we can move the buying relationship forward. Those touches may include a follow-up phone call after an initial meeting, making a business introduction, or sending a personal, handwritten note to your prospective buyer that includes a relevant business article you clipped from *Fortune* magazine. Add to that mix tagging a great blog post on communication you just ran across and sending it to Joan. Though the handwritten note never goes out of style, using social bookmarking hastens the process and makes it easier for salespeople to keep up with the various interests of their clients.

Another benefit of the bookmarking tags that we do not have with our traditional file cabinet is we can make them public or private. In other words, if you choose to make the bookmarking account public, then anyone who has an account with a particular site—like Delicious—can access the information that you have tagged. Conversely, you can opt to keep your tags private, sharing them only with the people in your private network. With the vast amounts of information available on the Internet, your ability to become an information aggregator and resource for your customers and prospects gives you a substantial competitive advantage.

For the modern-day sales manager, use of social bookmarking and aggregation tools speeds up the on-boarding process for new people on the team. Faster ramp-up time means a faster contribution of revenue to the bottom line. If you are the manager responsible for multiple geographies, you can use these social tools to listen and gain broader perspective on the conversations taking place in your geographical community. We already know that customer loyalty increases as clients feel engaged and appreciated.

The New Handshake is all about building community, collaboration, and creating a forum for conversation. Social bookmarking adds another dimension to your sales toolkit to help you extend the new handshake. You can make it your goal to get your contacts signed up and participating in your bookmarking community. When one person finds information she believes of value to others in the community, she shares her bookmarking tags with everyone else in the group. Before long, everyone is sharing with everyone else. Learning how to integrate the use of social bookmarking into your CRM approach will *differentiate* you, your products, and your services from the competition and will create a sense of open sharing within your network. Remember the Johari Window? The name of the game is openness in the online world—giving to receive. Information tagging makes it easier than ever to share valuable information that benefits others.

Let us examine the three most recognized content tagging services: Digg, Delicious, and StumbleUpon. Each service has a slightly different twist to its approach. Just like your study of Facebook, LinkedIn, and Twitter, you will want to evaluate these services to determine which might fit your Social Media Sales Strategy.

Digg

The Digg community encompasses a place for people to find and share content from anywhere on the Web. Digg differs from the other services because the community votes on what it considers the most popular items. In other words, people locate information anywhere from the largest and most popular online sites to the most remote places, and then they vote on that information's content—do they "digg" it? Digg employs no editors. Instead, members collectively determine the value of content, using what we would call the Join Mode. The "Digg" approach definitely changes the way individuals consume information online.

Here is how Digg works. Users in the community submit everything from videos to images to news items. Once a user submits something online, others see the information and "digg" (the popular term for voting) what they like best. When a submission gets the most "diggs," that item appears on the front page of Digg's site in plain view of millions of visitors. You know you have hit the big time when your content gets enough votes to place you on Digg's home page.

The real power of the Digg community lies in the conversation that can ensue around content. In other words, when your article appears on the front page of Digg, people talk about what you wrote. Digg encourages dialogue and provides tools for the community to discuss topics that interest them. From a sales point of view, Digg is a place for you to learn what people are talking about. Keeping a close watch on the content that receives the most "diggs" enables you to let your customers know what others are saying and helps you stay ahead of the trends. If there was ever a great model for diversity, Digg would certainly be it. Digg believes that every piece of content on the Web enjoys an equal opportunity to be seen and heard and given the chance to be the next big thing. Figure 12.1 shows Digg's front page and what was hot at the time of this writing.

Delicious

Delicious gives users the ability to tag, save, manage, and share Web pages from a centralized source. Going back to our file cabinet analogy, imagine that Delicious enables you to create one gigantic file cabinet in cyberspace. With

FIGURE 12.1   Digg's front page screen shot. Reprinted with permission from Digg.com

the wealth of information that bombards us every day, it is easy to lose track of that great article you just read. Delicious allows you to not only remember the article but also to retrieve it for later use. As an example, in the course of writing this book, we used Delicious to tag, save, and share information with each other. These articles served as reference material or as additional insights from experts in the world of social media. Considering how much information on the Web comes out every second about the social media, without Delicious we would have spent untold hours trying to catalogue data.

Using Delicious, you can bookmark any site on the Internet and retrieve your bookmarks from any location. Instead of storing different bookmarks on every computer, Delicious keeps everything in sync in a single set of bookmarks in one spot. Even when your own computer is not handy, you can retrieve your bookmarks on the Delicious Web site. Users in your community also benefit from the interesting information available to them each time they log in. Finally, you can create RSS feeds of Delicious groups and consolidate them into dashboards.

Again, from a sales point of view, Delicious provides a way for you to send and retrieve information to your customers often and regularly. It also gives the sales team access to each other's content in an organized way no matter where each person resides. With widely dispersed sales teams, this function helps link everyone together. Figure 12.2 shows you Barb's Delicious files.

StumbleUpon

StumbleUpon helps you sift through search information from your typical search engine sites like Google. When you Google something, you get many pages of results. To find what you want eats up a lot of time and sometimes produces nothing.

FIGURE 12.2 The files Barb tagged in Delicious. Reproduced with permission of Yahoo! Inc. © 2010 Yahoo! Inc. DELICIOUS and the DELICIOUS logo are registered trademarks of Yahoo! Inc.

StumbleUpon changes this model and removes some of the guesswork from the process. Rather than sifting through search lists, StumbleUpon community members go directly to Web sites that match their personal interests and preferences. Imagine that! StumbleUpon collects opinions and interests that match your own and from that data source helps you filter the search process. To understand the value of this service, let us look at how the dynamics of business have shifted in this digital economy.

Your buyers surf the Internet looking for what you have to offer. They view Web sites, videos, special reports, and blog posts to research the options available to them. Next, they peruse recommendations from peers and colleagues about which products to buy. Indeed, as we discussed earlier in this book, buyers opt to learn from a variety of sources about their buying choices. Anderson Analytics reported that some 9.2 million Americans use the Internet each day, with 78 percent of those people doing research on products they want to buy. On a daily basis some 20 percent of those online users are sourcing information about a product or service that they specifically plan to purchase now.[2] Will they find you?

To respond to this change in buying behavior, companies invested large sums of money for search engine optimization techniques, for paid sponsor links, or for paid advertising to move their Web site to the head of the search list line. What we know is that people will stop looking at Web site suggestions by the time they have gone through the first page. In the traditional search model, your Web site, which might offer the buyer the best product for the best deal, might appear on page two, never to be found. Enter StumbleUpon.

StumbleUpon offers technology that filters through the information pool and directs you to Web sites that are relevant to your specific needs. Knowing that the staggering speed at which information on the Internet changes and how difficult it is to keep on top of the changing options in the virtual market-place, StumbleUpon responded by aggregating, filtering, and directing in order to keep you up to date. Similar to Digg, StumbleUpon uses a ratings system driven by community members to help the service maintain the highest-quality database of information.

SOCIAL MEDIA DASHBOARDS

In addition to the three social bookmarking tools, other aggregation tools exist that you may want to use to help you streamline your social media time. Clearly, becoming a trusted advisor and research resource requires that you stay on top of vast amounts of information. The social bookmarking tools Digg, Delicious, and StumbleUpon can help you do that. In addition, other tools will help you organize the information and better manage your social media time. These include various social media dashboards. You will want to build a system for yourself that keeps you abreast of the current buzz in the online world relative to your customer's preferences. Here are some well-known dashboard tools that you may wish to incorporate into your online arsenal:

- **Digsby.** This dashboard tool allows you to combine your e-mail, instant messaging, and social networks into one easy place.
- **TweetDeck or Seesmic Desktops.** These tools are your personal browsers for staying in touch with what is happening in the world of Twitter and Facebook. Their power comes from the ability to customize your Twitter interaction columns, groups, saved searches, and automatic updates, making it easy for you to zero in on the people and conversations that have the highest priority to you. For example, Barb has set up a group comprised of top technology bloggers. Each time she logs in, she quickly scans the Tweets in that group, responds as needed, and moves on. Many new users to Twitter complain about the overwhelming amount of information flowing in the Twitter stream. TweetDeck and Seesmic help you organize the conversations you want to hear most in order to keep you from getting lost in the noise.
- **XeeSM.** This new Social Relationship Manager (pronounced "see sam") helps highly connected individuals and teams keep track of all their relationships. Friends, colleagues, and customers can find you more easily in the social Web and connect with you whether they know exactly what social sites you use or not. You organize your social presence by putting your XeeSM on each social site you participate on and then you use your XeeSM account to manage your data from one location and not from multiple social sites.

- **Ping.fm.** This terrific social media service lets you update your status with Twitter, Facebook, LinkedIn, and more on one convenient site. The motto of Ping.fm is "post from anywhere to anywhere." Rather than worry about posting status updates to multiple social sites that you frequent, you use Ping.fm to streamline your approach—one step versus two or three.
- **Alltop.** The brainchild of Guy Kawasaki, Alltop mimics the magazine rack you might find in your local bookstore. When you use the Alltop service, however, you are creating an online space that you customized to meet your unique sales and marketing needs. For example, you have clients in the financial, technical, and pharmaceutical vertical markets. To deliver increased value to your customers, you can create a MyAlltop page that aggregates the topical information important for them to stay current in their respective fields. The Alltop motto says "we give you aggregation without aggravation." Using the Alltop technology, you take this service one step further with your customers and buying prospects by handling the information aggregation for them.

In summary, social bookmarking can shift your role from simply being viewed as a vendor selling a particular product or service to a trusted advisor and resource for information. The sharp salesperson recognizes the competitive advantage of mastering social bookmarking and information aggregation tools. It is not only a way to help you manage your social media time (which is important enough!), but it is also a way for your to become indispensible to harried executives who face information overload. Many of today's sales approaches are largely outdated and in desperate need of a refresh. Buyer behavior has changed. The integration of social media into your sales strategies will enable you to meet the buyers where they are. You can, as Tom Canning says, "even the playing field."

Chapter 13

The Blogosphere

In December 1997 a man named Jorn Barger coined the term weblog. It did not take long for the idea to catch on. Most of us remember asking our friends, "So . . . what's a blog?" We may not admit to that question today either to ourselves or to others. In Julie Powell's bestselling book, *Julie & Julia*,[1] the author talks about blogging as if none of us ever heard of it. In 2002, when the book was written, most of us had not heard of blogging. Blogging has sneaked into our lives in much the same way as television. It was never there; it suddenly appeared; and now we cannot live without it. Or can we? What is the future of blogging, and how will blogging play a role in the way we do business?

Andrew McAfee coined the term, Enterprise 2.0, to describe how Web 2.0 technology sneaked its way into our daily business activities. Here's what Barb told *Success Magazine* about blogging and creating an online presence: "You need to remain in front of people, providing them with relevant, meaningful information that delivers real value to them before they've made a purchase."[2] In the world of sales, blogging remains the best way to do exactly that.

In this chapter we explore the history and evolution of blogging and look at ways you can incorporate blogging into your life as a sales rep. Finally, we will give you some tips on how to blog successfully.

HISTORY OF BLOGGING

Just like the other forms of social media, blogging began as one thing and evolved into something quite different. When Barger coined the term, he created a way to talk about his Internet wanderings on his Robot Wisdom Web site.

The word "wanderings" clearly describes the early blogs. They were simply ways for people to share their thoughts as one might in a journal. Early blogs not only contained important industry information but also information about the person. You learned who that person was. Julie Powell's blog about her cooking project talked not just about cooking but also about her relationship with her husband, with her friends, and with her coworkers. She shared very intimate details about her life on her blog. In the beginning bloggers put themselves out there in an open way because they had no idea who might be reading their posts.

There was some anonymity in the vastness of the World Wide Web. As late as 2006, Debbie Weil wrote, "The very best way to get to know us, how we think and what we're passionate about is to read our blog."[3] As blogging grew, things began to change. One big change was the introduction of blogging into the corporate world. Even so, Jonathan Swartz of Sun Microsystems said, "Good bloggers are chatty and into relationships."[4] Today, blogs have come to dominate the Web. Many people prefer blogs to Web sites. Some companies and people with Web sites combine the Web site with a blog.

The growth rate of blogs continues to astound us. Jenna Wortham reported in her blog post titled "After Ten Years of Blogging, The Future Is Brighter than Ever," that Technorati, a search engine that monitors blogs, tracked more than 8 million online blogs in March 2007, up from 100,000 two years earlier. Technorati reported that a new blog is created every 7.4 seconds. That adds up to 12,000 new blogs a day, 275,000 posts a day, and 10,800 updates an hour.[5] Today, the number of online blogs has jumped to 112.8 million.

With the blogosphere exploding, what changes have we noticed? First, the blogosphere has evolved into a profound source of information. Unlike in the early days, we care less about building a relationship with the blogger than we do with what the blogger has to say. One reason for this change is the growth of other social networking sites like Facebook. Because we can build a relationship on Facebook, we seek information from your blog. There is a new platform for you to tell us about your weekend with your dog or to blog about the great movie you just saw.

This does not mean that online readers are not interested in who you are. They will check out your Facebook and LinkedIn profiles. Many will check out your Tweets. Most bloggers include direct links to the social media sites and invitations to connect. Even so, people still like to interact with the blogger. Chris Brogan's blog contains tons of information about how to use Twitter.

He shares his experiences when he goes to conferences related to social networking. People respond to his posts as if they were "talking" to Chris, as if they personally know him. Once when Brogan broke his arm and could not type, he videotaped his blog. The tape showed him sitting on a couch wearing a T-shirt. He looked like an average guy talking to us from his own den. The informality of the blog, particularly in the comment section, remains.

Scoble and Israel wrote in *Naked Conversations*, "Come as you are. We're just folks here. We're not concerned with typos or grammar errors, which remind readers, that it's just a human speaking."[6] Weil said that the blog writing style needs to be informal. By informal she advises bloggers to think about the way they would write to their mom. "Dear Mom, Great news about the big case I've been working on. . . . "[7]

A second major change in blogs is that blogging has become a corporate activity. Instead of a few Internet geeks blogging here and there, blogging has become part of the corporate public relations machine. The corporate nature of blogging takes away some of the informality that Scoble and Israel spoke about. Spelling and grammar take on a new importance as blogging becomes part of the corporate brand. Nonetheless, because blogs are blogs and not press releases, they retain their informality and their transparency—two things press releases never had.

Third, blogging has become an important source of industry information. People expect to see well thought out paragraphs of data and information in article format. They do not expect to see sales pitches or wandering paragraphs that reflect a "stream of consciousness." Blogs provide you with a real opportunity to differentiate yourself as an expert in something. The strategy Mike Damphousse told us about where he identified sales reps with certain unique skills that he intends to leverage through blogging is a strategy that will pay off for his company. Identify the talents of the people working for you and allow them to share their expertise either through blogging or providing guest blogs or commenting on other people's blogs.

A fourth change in blogging is that people blog less frequently. Twitter enables people to micro-blog several times a day. Through Twitter, people can send out little tidbits of information often. Daily blogging overwhelmed many people in the early days. What could they possible say to their readers every day? Now, you need not worry about blogging once a day. You can blog twice a week and still maintain a Web presence. Kathy Tito explains that staying active in the social media is now embedded in her job. She does it as naturally as she does picking up the telephone. Blogging need not be a burden but a part of your daily and weekly activities.

In 2006 Scoble and Israel described six reasons blogs are different than other kinds of communication. Although these six reasons still describe why online 2.0 communication differs from other forms of communication, they no longer describe why blogging reigns supreme. We now explore Scoble and Israel's six reasons and look at what has changed and what has not changed given how blogging fits on the new landscape next to other social media platforms that include Facebook, LinkedIn, and Twitter.

Publishable

Scoble and Israel point out that *anyone* can publish on a blog. This factor continues to be true; blog writing is very democratic. In the corporate world, however, certain designated people may publish on the corporate blog. Most corporate blogs carry restrictions not only with regard to who can post but also to who can comment on other industry-related blogs. Blogs help develop and maintain the corporate brand. You can always start your own blog, but you must be sure that you do so in a manner consistent with your company's corporate blogging policies. Yes, today there are company corporate blogging policies, and that is a good thing. Furthermore, a new type of blogger has emerged, the professional blogger. Companies hire people to blog for them. These people are the best of the best in the blogging world. That does not mean those of us who are "unprofessional" cannot publish, it just means that the blogging world is changing. In an October 22, 2009 blog post by Kit Eaton titled, "Blogging Is Dead—Long Live Journalism," she talks about the evolution of blogging, pointing out the high salaries of professional bloggers. She ends the article with this quote: "Blogging's about to shed its ugly caterpillar stage and emerge as journalism's future."[8]

Findable

Andy Wibbels tells us in *Blog Wild* why Google loves blogs: frequent updates. Blogs, unlike Web sites, are not static. In addition, they are linked and networked. Good blogs contain many ingoing and outgoing links, which increase your page rankings. Wibbels tells us that the underlying HTML behind blogs is simple and clean and that makes them easy to index. Blog posts are archived and organized—characteristics the search engines love because it's easy for Google to read.[9] Therefore, if you want to be found, you must blog frequently, but now you can also Tweet. Technoati added a search called "Twittorati" that monitors Tweets for search purposes. Micro-blogging as well as blogging are ultimately findable, but Tweets are not yet linked to search engines.

Social

Even though Scoble and Israel say the blogosphere is social, it's not as social as it used to be. Blogs that are not posted on the highly social platforms like Facebook and MySpace are becoming less a social tool and more an information-sharing tool. The blog has become the new press release, albeit more informal and interactive than the old-fashioned press release.

Viral

Blogs are still one of the fastest ways to share information. It is, however, no longer *the* fastest way. Twitter outshines blogs in terms of speed of information. People no longer use blogs to share timely, immediate happenings. They turn to Twitter instead. Nonetheless, when looking to share something about your product or new information important to the industry, you should both blog and Tweet. As Mike Damphousse said, he uses Twitter to propagate his blog posts. According to Marketing Profs research, those companies that have found success with Twitter now use Tweets to get the word out fast for new products, promotions, and special events.[10] If you examine most Tweets, however, you'll see links to people's blogs.

In fact, Tweeting creates more activity on your blog. What comes with more activity? More participation and more visibility, which equals more opportunities to hit that purchase button. Your blog then becomes part of your Social Media Sales Strategy. Posting good content with well-written, well-researched information that others in the industry find meaningful further contributes to your status as an expert. That kind of content development will help create your following on Twitter, Facebook, and LinkedIn. People want to follow people who deliver the goods. Blogs, therefore, are one part of the social media strategy, not the be-all-end-all.

Syndicatable

Blogs are still very accessible through the RSS feeds. This feature enables people to get your blog posts immediately. Furthermore, sites like LinkedIn and Facebook enable you to post your blogs to certain niche groups. These features make your blog post more syndicatable than ever. In addition to being syndicatable, the blog posts are more accessible. If you miss a Tweet, you'll never find it again. When you subscribe to RSS feeds, you can keep up with your favorite bloggers and what they are saying about the industry. As we explained in the last chapter, you can bookmark and rank blog posts as well.

Linkable

You can link your blog to other blogs. Although this feature still exists, the process is slower than on a platform like Twitter. The links in a person's blog refer readers to more information about something or reference material rather than simply share an interesting blog post.

To summarize, three major changes have affected blogging, namely:

1. They have become more corporate and less informal.
2. Social networks like Facebook have usurped the "social" part of blogging.
3. Twitter has usurped the speed and efficiency of blog information.

Do these changes suggest you should not blog or that you should simply Tweet or post status updates on Facebook? Absolutely not. What these changes suggest is that blogging has evolved. Here is what Darren Rowse wrote about the future of blogging: "I don't think blogs are past—but I would say we are in a period of consolidation and extension."[11] He predicted that bloggers would add authors, cluster themselves around similar blogs, network with one another, and add services and features.[12] Many of his predictions have happened or are happening. We might add that blogs are also becoming money generators by adding ads and special give-aways. All these changes do not suggest that blogging has disappeared. In fact, we would argue that blogging has matured into a very effective communication tool that businesses in the twenty-first century cannot ignore.

HOW TO BLOG AS A SALES PROFESSIONAL

Now that you have an idea of what the new face of blogging looks like, how might you add blogging to your Social Media Sales Strategy?

Trish Bertuzzi has a great blog called Inside Sales Experts Blog, http://blog.bridgegroupinc.com/blog. The following are some of the tips she shared with us on blogging:

- **Invite guest bloggers.** You do not have to write every post. When you invite others to participate on your blog with their posts, you bring other points of view to the table. In some larger organizations several people blog for the organization. Seagate, for example, reports that it has six regular bloggers. What Bertuzzi suggests goes beyond allowing more people within the organization to blog; she advises bloggers to invite people within the industry to post on their blogs. For example, you might invite a notable university professor, who recently published a book on a topic of interest, to guest blog. The Bridge Group also includes six regular bloggers, including Bertuzzi. Photos and bios of each of these bloggers reside on her site with links to their LinkedIn profiles.
- **Do not promote yourself on your blog.** Remember the Procter & Gamble example when the company created a community for girls. It did so by answering personal teenage-related questions that the

girls would never have asked their parents. In answering these questions and sharing information, they placed the name of the company discreetly at the end of each entry. That is what you do on your blog. Although Trish Bertuzzi cringes whenever she thinks of people who promote themselves on their blogs, if you look at her blog, you will see her company banner and logo. You will also note that all the regular bloggers are from The Bridge Group and there is a tab titled "What We Do." The promotion is subtle; it is discreet, tasteful, and not in your face. That is the challenge of blogging. If you are always ending by selling, people doubt your credibility. "Sales 2.0 is an approach not a sales process," Bertuzzi said. "It requires you to transform your business from one that is focused on *selling* to one that is focused on letting the market *buy* from you."[13] In other words, once you are established as an expert by posting quality information and adding to the conversation, people choose to purchase from you.

- **Maintain transparency.** Count the number of instances this word appears in *Naked Conversations*. We bet you will find it hundreds of times. The entire point of blogging is to be genuine and transparent. "The essence of blogging is being real,"[14] Weil said. You must be willing to hear some blind spots, and you must be willing to share some hidden area information. Only then will your customers share blind spots with you. Even though blogging has largely become a part of corporate public relations, you must be willing to respond openly when you are criticized and never engage in "cover-ups." Rich Harris of Seagate said companies must be flexible and use out-of-the box thinking in order to be successful using the social media. He said, "To be successful in this model, companies will have to be a bit more transparent and nimble."[15] In our view this is the real challenge of the next decade. Those companies that can let down the traditional barriers, participate openly in the social networks, and maintain corporate integrity will lead us into what Daniel Pink calls the Conceptual Age.
- **Do not shy away from controversy.** All industry faces some kind of controversy. On the Inside Sales Experts blog, Bertuzzi brought up cold calling because sales professionals are in heated debate about this issue. Some feel it is dead; others think it remains an important sales tool. On her blog Bertuzzi asked the question and challenged cold calling. This blog post created more comment than any other they posted. In fact, she said months later she still gets comments on that particular post. Your blog is not designed to simply spill the corporate line; it is designed to explore and share information in an open format. When you create controversy, you encourage people to

share views. One caveat, however. Do not feed controversy just for controversy's sake. Corporate blogs exist for more reasons than drawing traffic (You are not Jerry Springer!). Weil quotes from Kevin Holland's blog in which he takes offense at controversy for controversy's sake on blogs. He points out that corporate blogs exist to support the organization, sell products, and interact with customers, not to simply pick fights.[16] Part of what the social media enables is for companies to listen. Blogs give you a platform for listening. You want to hear both sides.

BLOGGING OPTIONS FOR SALESPEOPLE

Now that you know how blogging has evolved and some of the important considerations you might need to make about blogging, let us examine some of the options. All of the companies we spoke with had blogs. Each dipped their toe in the social media waters first with blogging. From there they branched out. If you were going to dip your toe into the blogging waters, what would you do?

As a sales rep you must first find out whether or not your company has a blog. If your company does have a blog, is it possible for sales reps to offer guest posts? When customers read a post that you have written, you can form a stronger connection with that person. If your company does not allow you to guest post, you could connect with the corporate blogger and channel information that might affect your customers. Sales reps have first-hand information from customers that could prove quite useful for blogging purposes. For example, you might learn that customers like or dislike certain features of your product. You might learn that customers prefer certain ways to communicate. You might discover an interesting link to another blog or to a book that your customers might find useful.

How effective is your writing? Some people write well; some people talk well; some people do both well. What do you do well? If you are not a good writer, but you wish to post content to the blog, consider creating a video post. More and more blogs are dominated with video streams and podcasts. Sales reps often have strong communication skills. Furthermore, if you are primarily an inside sales rep, your customers might like to "see" you via a video blog post. Anneke Seley in *Sales 2.0* told us that the best use of inside sales includes some opportunity for face-to-face interaction. Perhaps you cannot make a trip, but you could create a video to visually touch your customers. Take a look at YouTube. Not only is it an easy format for creating video blogs, but it is also a great resource for locating quality information that other people have posted.

How much time do you have for blogging? How much time is your organization willing to allow you to blog? Salespeople face quotas and deadlines related to selling products and services. How much time is your organization willing to allow you to spend blogging versus direct selling? Mike Damphousse tells us that he considers one hour per day not too much time devoted to social media. Trish Bertuzzi felt one hour per day was exorbitant for salespeople to be away from the business of selling. What is your company's line in the sand?

If you are a small organization and you are the CEO and want to begin with blogging, we suggest that you explore Wordpress.com. Some people still use other blogging sites, but Wordpress has become the most user-friendly and cost-efficient platform at this writing. You can create a Wordpress blog for very little money (or no money) and in a matter of hours versus months for a Web site. Typepad and Blogger.com also provide good services for blogging. You need not invest in expensive software to create your first blog.

GENERAL TIPS ABOUT BLOGGING

Once you decide to create a blog, you are not finished. For your blog to succeed it needs to have two very important pieces: readers and useful content. If you work hard on your content, do not expect the readers to simply "show up." That no longer happens (if, in fact, it ever did on the Web). With so many blogs out there, you are competing with hundreds of thousands of other people for the reader's attention. Take a look at our tips on how to attract readers to your blog as well as how to make your content interesting and inviting.

Attracting Readers

The other social media tools we have already discussed, Facebook, LinkedIn, and Twitter, will help attract readers. We have shared with you the importance of posting your blog on these sites and posting inviting links to these sites on your blog. Your Social Media Sales Strategy needs to be integrated and interconnected. In other words, you do not create a blog and then a LinkedIn profile and not link the two. Everything must connect to everything else, and it all comes back to you. We have also shown you the importance of sites like Digg, Delicious, and StumbleUpon to help people bookmark your information. Take a look at Joan and Barb's blog in Figure 13.1. If you explore that blog page, you will see how we invite visitors to join us on Twitter and Facebook.

Here are some additional ways you can attract readers:

1. **Comment on other relevant blogs.** Subscribe to the RSS feeds for blogs in your field. When you comment on someone else's blog be sure to include your blog address. When people read your comments, if they find them insightful, they will visit your blog. Because so many people are publishing their blog posts on LinkedIn groups, you can easily find relevant blogs to follow by examining the groups.

For example, take a look at the Sales 2.0 group on LinkedIn. Examine the blogs posted under the tab in the News section. There you may find relevant blogs related to Sales 2.0. Explore those blogs and begin commenting.

2. **Put your blog post titles up as a stream on the corporate Web site.** Again, this is another way to integrate your online presence. People visiting your Web site will look at those items that interest them and visit your blog. Many people also put their Tweets as a stream on their Web site.

   1. **Include your recent blog posts in your e-mail signature.** When you create your profiles for Twitter, Facebook, and LinkedIn, include your blog site as well as your Web site.

   2. **When you write your blog post, add links to other people's blogs and ping back to them.** That way your blog and their blog are linked. People who read the other blog can find you and you them. As we said earlier, one of the values of blogs is their linkability. Search engines look for links. The more you link, the greater the chance Google will find you. Deborah Weil's book on corporate blogging preaches about links. She tells readers over and over to include links in their posts.

   3. **Put your blog site on all your product packaging and all online sales confirmation e-mails.**

   4. **Tag your blogs with appropriate keywords to optimize searches.**

   5. **Include your blog address on your business cards and other brochures and newsletters.**

   6. **Publish a blog post regularly.** Set up a schedule that encourages you to post at least two times a week. Remember, every time you write a post, Google notices.

   7. **Just do it!** What do you have to lose? The time is now. You do not need all the answers, you simply need to take the risk, place that toe in the water, and begin swimming. You can always tweak and refine as you go along.

Developing Interesting Content

Besides writing about what is important to your readers in a clear, concise manner, the following are some other tips that make blogs more attractive to readers:

- **Write in the first person.** Weil encourages you to find your voice. By that she means write as if you were talking to someone. Make your blog interesting with stories and anecdotes. Your blog should not be written in a dry, stiff fashion. Weil suggests you write your blog as if you were writing an e-mail. "Write from the heart," Weil said. "Take a few risks. Be passionate. Be honest. Know what you're talking about but don't be afraid to ask readers for help or feedback."[17] Here is an excerpt from Chris Brogan's blog to give you an idea of how he found his voice: *"I'm plotting how to use my Jet-Blue-All-You-Can-Fly pass. Are you near any of these cities? Do you think you could get a bunch of people together and buy up 100 books for a book signing. . . . "*[18] This post created a groundswell around Chris's new book, *Trust Agents.*

- **Post photos and videos.** As we have already mentioned, YouTube provides an excellent service for creating simple videos. Flickr enables you to post photos you have created. If you develop a video blog post or if you have seen a good video that someone else created, post the video on your blog. Photos also bring readers into the blog. If you do not want to take your own photos, you can find and upload photos from any number of Web sites. Some bloggers simply write a one-sentence introduction before posting a video or a powerful photo.

- **Begin your blog with a question.** "What is the future of cold calling?" for example. A question tends to hook your reader. It also suggests different answers. It opens the floor for discussion.

- Use many links within the blog to share more information or reference information. Online readers love links. Early on in blogging some people believed that if you provided links, people would navigate away from your blog and read something else. What we have learned, however, is that most online readers are skimmers. They read some from the link and come back to your blog, particularly if it is well-written. When you share valuable information and resources, you create a following.

- **Be short and sweet.** Blogs are longer than Tweets, but they are not several pages. Most blogs should not run more than one page. Seth Godin's blog rarely runs more than seven to eight sentences. If the blog goes over one page, you are no longer blogging; you are writing an article. Keep your readers in mind. Online readers cannot spend hours at their computer reading. Weil advises using lots of white space, snappy subheads, bullets, short paragraphs, and, most importantly, illustrations—graphs, photos, videos. Your readers want quick spurts of information. That is what has made Twitter so popular.

- **Vary your blog posts just like you would your Tweets.** One day you might blog about the effects of social media on the economy and the next day you might blog about your great customer service experience at Best Buy. The following are some of our suggestions as well as those from David Pollard's blog, How to Save the World, taken from *The Corporate Blogging Book.*[19]

- Blog about original research, surveys, and so forth. You can also take a survey in your blog. Ask your readers to participate to get information. The Bridge Group did this in its blog post dated, August 21, 2009, "New Survey: The Impact of Sales 2.0." You can also publish the results of a poll you took on LinkedIn. We discussed the polling feature in Chapter 10.
- Great resources, blogs, essays, reports, statistics. Do not limit yourself to your own data. Find good information from other key experts. Tom Canning posted a video from Andrew McAfee talking about Enterprise 2.0 on his blog.
- Testimonials from customers.
- Benchmarks.
- Personal stories, experiences and lessons. Chris Brogan nearly always begins his blog with a story of something that happened to him. Sales reps have tons of these!
- First-hand accounts. What actually happened to you when and how that relates to some area of interest. For example, Joan experienced a very rude clerk at a large car-rental agency. She blogged about the incident and then talked about the importance of good customer relations.
- Live reports from events, conferences. We discussed Seagate's creative use of a live event using Twitter. Reporting after a conference is another great way to keep your content interesting and up to date. You could blog about what you specifically learned.
- Book reviews, particularly related to sales or the selling industry. Your blog could set up an affiliate link to Amazon or Barnes & Noble. You could periodically suggest reading, and when readers purchase the item from your blog you receive a small income stream.
- Relevant "aha" graphics.
- Useful checklists and tools.
- Quizzes, self-evaluations. There are excellent online sources to create quizzes and assessments for little money. You could use these or create your own. People love to learn more about themselves.
- End your blog post with a question. "What has your experience been with cold calling? Do you think it is dead?" These kinds of questions suggest you do not know all the answers and they encourage your readers to comment. When readers comment, answer those comments. Participate in the conversation.

Take a look at the blog we created for *The New Handshake* and join us there. Blogging has evolved, but it remains a powerful social networking tool. Hugh MacLeod, early in his book titled *Ignore Everybody,* he tells his readers

FIGURE 13.1   Blog post from the New Handshake blog.
Source: www.TheNewHandshake.com

that the book was born on his blog, gapingvoid.com. He credits blogging for the book's success. He advises his readers to " . . . put some of your ideas on a blog and get them 'out there.' Eventually the fish will start biting. Just remember that it doesn't happen overnight."[20] It took MacLeod several years to build a trusting following on his blog. It took Chris Brogan 10 years. How long will it take you?

In Chapters 9, 10, and 11 we examined the three major social media players, Facebook, LinkedIn, and Twitter. Chapter 12 provided you with tools to expand, augment, and organize your online presence with Digg, Delicious, and StumbleUpon. Finally in this chapter we gave you an overview of blogging and how it has evolved into a key communication tool for business in the digital economy. Chapter 14 will explore the area of netiquette. What is appropriate and what is not? We will warn you against doing things that could destroy the online presence you spent so much time creating.

Chapter 14

Netiquette

Loose lips sink ships as the old saying goes. Whether you are sitting in a coffee shop or having a meeting with a potential buyer or Tweeting on Twitter, you must not lose sight of where you are and what you say. In the online world in particular, one misstep could sink your ship. Rather than use fear of making a netiquette mistake as justification for not participating in the online space, become savvy about what is appropriate and what is not and set clear, concrete guidelines and expectations. We are not talking about the kind of policies that will completely hamstring your salespeople from using social media effectively. The way we see it, it is like setting performance expectations in advance of a review cycle. Everyone needs certain clear understandings, namely:

- What is expected in their job role?
- What is appropriate when communicating with customers and what is not?
- How will their results be measured?

As we have reinforced throughout the course of this book, tools like LinkedIn and Facebook are amazing for creating a sea of new sales opportunities *if...*

- You develop well-written, up-to-date profiles that contain a professional headshot.
- You coach salespeople on how to contribute effectively to group discussions.

- You create guidelines for how to "get in and get out" without blowing a day with online chatter.
- Everyone, including your salespeople, exercise patience.

In this chapter we explore all the issues related to netiquette. We will define the term, and we will relate netiquette to traditional business etiquette for networking. We will examine some concrete examples of missteps we have seen online, and finally we will give you some tips on how to toe the netiquette line without destroying your or your company's reputation.

WHAT DOES NETIQUETTE MEAN?

A blended word for "network etiquette," Wikipedia defines netiquette as "a set of social conventions that facilitate interaction over networks, ranging from the Internet and mailing lists to blogs and forums."[1] While there are no formal rules, so to speak, there are generally three principles for your salespeople to keep in mind when navigating the online waters.

Principle #1: Do Not Sell

This philosophy may seem counterintuitive if you intend to use free online tools to sell more quickly to a large number of people. We will warn you, however, that nothing turns people off faster in the online world than having some "slick Willy" enter the scene and within minutes hawk his latest product or service. The number-one goal for your salespeople is to create trusted relationships with others in the community based on honesty, transparency, and integrity. How do you do that? Make contributions to group discussions in ways that benefit everyone in the community without clogging up the group discussions with sales pitches.

As we have said throughout this book, using social media will absolutely speed up the sales cycle when used effectively to support your sales objectives. We stress, however, that throwing up a LinkedIn profile today will not result in sales tomorrow. The principles of do not sell and exercise some patience to develop trust are no different than you believing that you can attend one networking event and expect to close sales the very next day. Trish Bertuzzi tells us when she explored the LinkedIn groups, she was appalled at the self-promoting going on. Turned off by what she saw, she started her own group which she monitors carefully. "I spend time on the group every day deleting self-promotion from the discussions. I tell people this is not the place for self-promotion or open networking. I wanted a place where people could share."[2]

The push sales approach has given sales a bad rap for years. It is not the profession that is tainted with over-selling, it is the people. Some salespeople cannot comprehend that the sharing of relevant information, making connections for others, tooting the horns of their colleagues, and adding value to the community conversation will ultimately produce benefits and result in sales. The bottom line for the new handshake is no different than the old handshake. We must develop a reputation for giving to others first without expecting anything in return.

Principle #2: Give to Receive

Robert Cialdini's best seller, *Influence*, reminds us of the power of reciprocity. According to Cialdini, "The impressive aspect of reciprocation with its accompanying sense of obligation is its pervasiveness in human culture."[3] Basically, this unwritten cultural rule means that when someone does for you, they naturally want to find a way to return the favor. The art of great selling embodies this concept through a series of people relationships that your sales reps cultivate with potential buyers. Tom Peters tells us in *The Pursuit of WOW!* that 70 percent of customers hit the road not because of price or product quality issues, but because they did not like the human side of doing business with the provider of the product or service.[4]

Research conducted by The Forum Corporation supports this fact and indicates that 45 percent of these customers said they switched to another company because the attention they received was poor in quality (see http:// www.forum.com/library/the_forum_blog-307.aspx). Keep in mind that the other company's product or service does not necessarily have to be of similar or better quality. Consumers will purchase a product with fewer bells and whistles if they enjoy working with the people at the company. In the end, customers want to work with those businesses that demonstrate a sincere desire to help them with anything they need, and they will to pay for it. Yes, they want products to work and services that meet their needs. More importantly, however, they want someone to care when something goes wrong.

Heather Lalley, in a blog post, "Twitter for Hire. More Businesses Hire Tweeters," tells us that when Coke learned of a disgruntled Tweeter, the company responded quickly. The individual Tweeted his disappointment with Coke's claim to give away an all-expense-paid trip through his MyCokeRewards program. Within half and hour, a Coke representative telephoned this person and resolved the problem. The Tweeter was so pleased with the response, he changed his Twitter avatar to a photo of Coke Zero.[5]

The nature of the social media demands that salespeople recognize that to succeed with their sales efforts utilizing the new handshake they must build strong relationships within the community by giving first and receiving second. Social media sites are not the place to deliver a feature dump or to promote the benefits of your product or service. Instead, answer questions, help others, and let people get to know you.

It occurs to us as we continue to see abuses on the social media that the netiquette principles are more easily violated in the online world than they might be elsewhere. In fact, most salespeople understand the importance of relationship to sales. In earlier chapters where we examined the history of sales, we saw that sales professionals learned this principle the hard way. Why, then, violate it in the social media arena? The answer may lie in two areas: lack of understanding of the social media which we hope reading this book will dispel and the anonymity of the World Wide Web. For some reason salespeople believe they can get out there, push, and self-promote because they cannot see you and you cannot see them. The new handshake lends itself to abuses and thereby demands greater caution.

Principle #3: Be Human

While technology is an amazing enabler, people still pull the strings on the other side. Think carefully about what you say and do. It is certainly okay to be yourself and share your opinions, but always treat others with courtesy and respect. If you would not say it to someone's face, then do not say it online. If you are angry or annoyed, then take a breath before you type those words and click the send icon. As many have learned the hard way, (Remember the Domino's Disaster) what is said on the Internet definitely stays on the Internet. Here is an example that appeared on a blog post in the comment section. *"Hmm a Twitter feed that is Miss Manners polite, never blogs about sex, politics or re(li)gion, and won't acknowledge me if I do follow them. Sounds pretty f-ing boring to me."* This comment shows an unprofessionalism that could seriously tarnish the sender's reputation. Whenever you write anything that you post online, think about what your boss might say if she reads it.

How might you be human in the virtual world? Indeed, we know how much harder is it to turn down an offer with a person standing in front of you than it is on the telephone or in an online interaction. Take a look at this real example of the humanness created by the social media. If one of your friends asks you to become a fan of a Facebook page, you might think twice before you hit the ignore button. You might even hit the accept button just because your friend asked.

Recently a colleague of Joan's worried because a friend asked her to join his group of Facebook fans in his bid to run for mayor of their town. She liked the man but did not agree with his politics. She fretted over this invitation and came close to agreeing to become a fan simply because he is a friend. With great reluctance, she decided to hit the ignore button. Imagine your salespeople creating those kinds of strong relationships as human beings with others online. The power of the human touch reigns supreme particularly when you extend the new handshake.

SELF-MONITORING

Who makes the rules online? Who sets the netiquette standards that put these three guiding principles in place? The interesting thing about the Web is the way it monitors itself. The community is a powerful watchdog with little or no mercy.

When Wikipedia came on the scene, we witnessed online self-monitoring at its best. Though many people may think of Wikipedia as an online encyclopedia, Wikipedia never made that claim. Wikipedia's goal from the beginning was to provide a space where users post articles that cover existing knowledge, rather than expect them to create and contribute original works of knowledge and research. Requiring no special skill or credentials, Wikipedia accepted articles from visitors of all ages and socioeconomic backgrounds. Users need not worry about accidentally damaging Wikipedia when adding or improving information because other editors correct obvious errors. Wikipedia enforces no formal policing or watchdog groups to monitor content. The platform works because individuals who violate the online code of conduct receive quick and certain repercussions from others in the group.

The self-monitoring activity via an online group or community compels others to conform to group norms. Wikipedia illustrates the power of group monitoring. All the social media, however, have their own form of self monitoring. For that reason, your salespeople must realize that whether they are posting in LinkedIn groups, talking to friends on Facebook, participating in blogs, or Tweeting on Twitter, they must clearly understand that netiquette covers both common courtesy and the informal rules of the road of cyberspace. If they are not conscious of how and what they are saying, they risk tarnishing your corporate brand, tearing down their own professional credibility, or offending people who will vigorously pass on their displeasure to everyone they know. Ask any police officer about the power of the neighborhood watch. Self-monitoring online is like the neighborhood watch on steroids.

THE BUSINESS OF NETWORKING ONLINE

If you think about the social networks as one giant networking event, you will grasp the informal rules of cyberspace that comprise networking. Problems surface because most of us do not know how to network. When we think about going to networking events, we cringe. Some of us prefer to sit at our computers and interact simply because we feel safer there. Unfortunately if you network at your computer, you must recognize you are still networking and you must apply similar rules that govern that behavior.

When you first meet someone at a networking event, do you shove your card in their hands and launch into your elevator pitch? Do you talk about politics or religion? Do you immediately challenge their world views with your own?

Do monopolize the conversation by talking about yourself and your accomplishments? In Lalley's blog post, Ford employee Scott Monty asked, "You wouldn't burst into a cocktail party and just start handing your business cards to people and leave, would you? The online space is no different."[6]

Let us examine some of the rules of in-person networking and relate them to the online world of social media.

- **Break the ice.** For person-to-person networking we suggest you introduce yourself in an informal way. Do not take yourself too seriously and do not try to sell yourself or your product in the first five seconds. Be open and honest about who you are and what connects you to the person. Give the person you are meeting something that will engage her. These etiquette rules stand up in the online world as well. You want to introduce yourself in a simple manner without selling who you are or what you do. Joel Comm in *Twitter Power* talks about using humor and some playfulness when introducing yourself on Twitter.
- **Listen.** Pay attention to what the other person says. How does she introduce herself? How is she connected to that particular online community? Ask open questions and use humor when you can. Continue to share bits about yourself.
- **Look for a connection between you and the person.** Do you like the same sports? Do you live in the same town, state, or country? Do you both like to travel? What similar books have you read? This advice works for both face-to-face and online networking. In fact, online you can learn a lot from a person's profile before you extend the new handshake. You can read their Tweets to learn their interests. You can study their Facebook or LinkedIn profiles to determine the books they recommend or the groups they belong to or the causes they support.
- **Talk about up-to-date current events that are non-political.** Steer away from controversial subjects. This rule applies to in-person networking as well as online but intensifies when networking in cyberspace. If you assume the person agrees with you and spout your political thoughts, you will lose the opportunity to create a relationship. Furthermore, by bringing up controversial topics just for the sake of controversy, you threaten to turn people off who might otherwise connect with you. We tend to speak more freely online where we feel anonymous. Even though dealing with tough subjects on your blog creates dialogue, be careful to approach those subjects with a listening ear and not a closed mind.
- **Do not always be the one to tell the story.** Instead, be the one who encourages the other person to tell her story. Listen to what the

person says and allow her the opportunity to share. Salespeople want to jump in with their stories and their solutions. It takes great discipline to wait until just the right moment. That moment happens when you hear, "So, tell me more about what you do?" Until you hear that question, wait and listen.

- **Set a networking goal.** For in-person networking, we encourage people to set small goals, such as aiming to meet five new people at an event. For online networking, you might set a goal of adding 10 new quality contacts to your LinkedIn connections per day. When you have a goal that includes quality and quantity, you will get enough followers within each platform to give you access. People shy away from what is called open networkers. On LinkedIn there are groups of people who will connect with anyone. They do not care about quality; they want numbers. Beware of the connecter who wants to add you as a notch on his belt. Instead, find people who fit your niche, people with whom you relate. Considering how many people are out there, you will still get the quantity you want. Quantity is easy; it takes time and a strategy to get quality.

- **Do not monopolize a person's time.** For face-to-face etiquette, the rule says to let the person go after 10 minutes. For online networking, we suggest you limit the number of times you make a contact with someone. Do not fill up a person's inbox even if you think you are sending quality information. Make a single contact and wait for a response. If you do not hear a response after one day, you might send a follow-up e-mail to make sure the person received your first message. If you still hear no response, move on.

- **Introduce others to the people around you.** When you are at a networking event, if a new person walks up, we encourage you to bring that person into the conversation by introducing her to those around you. When you connect with someone online, you build a stronger relationship with that person when you connect her with others in your network. Think of whom this person might like to meet. Make virtual introductions. Suggest friends on Facebook. Be one of Malcolm Gladwell's Connectors (see Chapter 2).

- **Remember it is better to give than to receive.** This principle applies to all networking, both online and offline. We talked earlier about not thrusting your card at someone. Instead, ask for their card, and they will respond by asking for yours. If someone does not ask for your card, move on. Clearly that person is not interested in what you have to offer. Online, you want to share information. You can send an interesting article you ran across in the *New York Times* or a relevant blog post tagged in Delicious. Share information that the person seems to be seeking. How do you know what they are seeking? Check out their profiles, read their Tweets, *do your homework.*

- **Use humor to ease an awkward situation.** For a face-to-face situation, you might run into a person who knows your ex-spouse or who is in a legal battle with someone you know. Humor helps ease tension. Online the same principle holds. Recently Joan and Barb met two researchers whom they thought might provide information for this book. In the course of the conversation it was clear that the researchers had different goals. How to gracefully exit? We diplomatically noted the value of the research, but also suggested in a pleasant manner that our book would not add to their database. The awkward moment ended and everyone agreed to keep in touch in the event anything changed, knowing it would not.

HOW TO TOE THE NETIQUETTE LINE

One of the most important things you can do if you participate in conversations whether on blogs, Twitter, Facebook, or LinkedIn, is cut out the noise. By noise we mean do not clog up the systems with unnecessary information, Tweets, or other kinds of clutter. Particularly if you are representing a company, you need to constantly ask yourself, "Would I want to read this?" Most of us are getting hundreds of e-mails daily. The amount of content on the Web is not shrinking, but exploding. How do you manage all that content? The biggest complaint Joan and Barb hear from businesses is the amount of time it takes to participate in the social media. Recently a colleague asked, "How do you stop? Isn't it a bit addicting?" The answer to that question is yes. Social media are addicting. As a company you must help your employees draw the line. As far as netiquette is concerned, ask yourself if you are adding to the clutter. The following tips might help you find a way to toe the netiquette line and participate more meaningfully.

- Do not talk constantly about yourself or your business. We have discussed how important it is to listen. Online you listen by responding to other people's Tweets and by joining a conversation in the LinkedIn discussions, not by promoting yourself but by sharing useful information or by noting a response from someone else. Augie Ray told us in his blog post, "Eight Twitter Habits That Might Get You Unfollowed or Semi-Followed," about a printing company in North Carolina that constantly Tweeted about its products, new services, and what great offers it had. TweetLater (www.tweetlater.com), a service that monitors followers, reported a 50 percent drop in followers for that company. Why? People do not want to hear you constantly talking about yourself.[7] Please note this applies to both the real world and the virtual world!

- Do not use the public messaging option when a private message works just as well. Both Twitter and Facebook allow for either a public or private response. On Facebook the public response or "wall" response goes to all your friends. On Twitter the public response or @name response goes to all of Twitterville. For example, when you write @*name Great fun last night* or @*name here ya go*, what does that mean to me? All it does is clutter my Tweets. We shared a Facebook example earlier in the book when Kyle van Hoften used a public response option when he would have ordinarily used a private response. He did this specifically to give airtime to his photography business to his friends, but he toed the netiquette line in two ways: he wrote a longer response that enabled him to explain what he was doing rather than a cryptic message that only the wall receiver would understand, and in a private message he explained to the wall receiver why he chose to write on her wall rather than send a private message. Twitter is clogged with public responses to Tweets that most people do not understand.

- Send links on Twitter and Facebook, but include why you are sending them. Twitter shortens the link name. A link comes to your attention without a clue as to what it is. On Twitter, in particular, share a title or a comment that helps others decide if they want to click on that link. Whenever you add a link on Facebook, a description and a few words follow automatically. Remember to check the link. Sometimes links get broken when shortened.

- Avoid automated direct messaging or responses. As we all juggle the various social media and weigh our time constraints, we search for ways to organize. Automatic messaging on Twitter is one way to manage our time. In the beginning when Twitter was young and just out of the gate, it was polite to thank people for following you. That practice has quickly become an obsolete nicety. What is even more annoying is when the "thank you" becomes a marketing strategy. We have discussed how some Twitters send automatic messaging that includes links to their site or special freebies. Again, this kind of self-promotion does not engage and assumes your followers need something before you know them. There is a site that began late in 2009 that is called StopAutoDM. com. The goal of this site is to get rid of these messages once and for all. Instead of an automatic thank you that means little to most of your followers, turn off that function. It is best not to say thank you than to add to the clutter.

- Automate your Tweets and Blog posts. One way you can save time and use an automation function is to create several Tweets or blog posts and then schedule them for release. That way you do not have to worry about being on Twitter all the time. You can create a backlog of blog posts and Tweets that you can schedule throughout the day or week. Mike Damphousse uses this function for Twitter, and it enables him to stay active without eating up too much of his day. Check out SocialOompth.com and other similar services that enable you to schedule your Tweets.

- Link Twitter to Facebook status updates. Another time saver is to opt into the application that combines your Tweets and Facebook status updates. In other words, when you Tweet something, it automatically appears as a Facebook status. Or the reverse, when you write a Facebook status, it Tweets automatically. Beware of this function! Facebook status updates give you more than 140 characters. You can explain more. When that option becomes a Tweet, it makes sense. The reverse is not true. When an RT@name Loved the quote, becomes a Facebook status update, it clogs your follower's inbox. If you use this function, make sure you are Tweeting from Facebook and not from Twitter to Facebook.

- Publicly recognize people on Twitter through #followfriday. On Friday, people recognize their fellow Twitters by encouraging others to follow these Twitters. It is a great way to show respect for other people's Tweets.

- Do not publicly thank people. There are two schools of thought on this. Some people like to publicly thank others for re-Tweeting them or for a comment they made or for recognizing them on #followfriday. Other people feel that the public thank you clogs the system. We tend to agree with the latter. You are less likely to clutter up your follower's e-mail if you send a direct message rather than thank people publicly. Yes, thank them, but in private, please!

- Do not make useless comments on a Facebook status update. All comments on a status update are sent to the person who posted the status and to all people who comment. When you make a two-word comment, like, "I agree," or "This is great," how does that add value to your friends? Facebook allows you to click a "like" or "dislike" button. Use that option unless you have something meaningful to add to the status update.

- Limit your open announcements on LinkedIn. If you manage a group on LinkedIn, you have an option to send announcements to the entire group. One way to lose group members quickly is to use this function too frequently. You might use the announcement function to announce new applications on LinkedIn that pertain to your group or to announce an event that you feel group members

might wish to attend. It goes without saying to never use this function to self-promote.

- Do not spam your friends with quizzes or Tweets that say things like,
  "Gain 1,000 followers a day." This tip nearly goes without saying, but
  because we still see it so frequently, we mention it again. If you have
  a poll or assessment you created for a target group, by all means
  Tweet that. However, quizzes that say things like, "Find out how
  smart you are" or other such generic spamming devices leave your
  followers frustrated and annoyed.
- Do not pitch your blog right after following someone. This often happens in an automated response to a follow-on Twitter. We have
  already talked about automated responses. When you pitch your blog
  at me before you know me, it feels intrusive.
- To find a complete and good list of Twitter netiquette tips, check out
  Chris Brogan's blog post at http://www.chrisbrogan.com/a-brief
  -and-informal-twitter-etiquette-guide/.

CASE EXAMPLE OF HOW QUICKLY YOU CAN
TARNISH YOUR BRAND

Brand is all about perception. What message are you sending to prospective buyers with every post, group comment, or newsletter you send out?
Self-promotion is the biggest no-no that we see abused every day on the social
media. One place where people often abuse each other is when they extend a
LinkedIn invitation. When it comes to sending LinkedIn invitations, you
should reach out by saying to someone why you would like to connect with
them. What is it about that person's profile that draws you to him and where
do you see similar interests? Please stop trying to sell something to your
connections before you know anything about them. Below is an example of
an invitation Barb received that illustrates how you can tarnish your brand
simply by ignoring the rules of netiquette:

On June 19, 2009, 2:27 PM, Mary Ann, salesperson for XYZ company wrote:
*I'd like to add you to my professional network on LinkedIn. I have worked with Jimmy
L. in the past & he recommended you to me as far as someone who would probably benefit from XYZ company's industry intelligence. Please call me as soon as possible at . . . ,
so I can help you grow & be the most consultative person you know!!*

Netiquette Buster Analysis

Mary Ann does not know Barb, but she knows that she can help her be *the*
most consultative person in the world. This assumption feels both rude and
presumptuous. What does this person know about Barb's consultative

sales skills? This is exactly why people are annoyed by vendors and their arrogant, untrained salespeople who assume that what they have to offer is just what everyone on the planet needs. We might also note that Mary Ann did not do her homework. In doing her homework she could have crafted a message that told the recipient what was in it for her. Such an invite might have caused Barb to sit up and take notice. Mary Ann lost the opportunity to sell what she had to offer. From a netiquette point of view, Mary Ann scored zero.

Another example of a netiquette faux pas occurred during a LinkedIn Discussion thread. The discussion began with someone stating an opinion. From that point on things got nasty. Below are some excerpts taken directly from the discussion:

> "Guys, I don't want to rain on your parade but . . . this happens to be my area of expertise for the last 10 years. Dolly, it has nothing to do with the intended audience or whether it is formal or informal learning. Roger, when I refer to hard baked I am referring to static content which is a blog and not easily maintained or all that intelligent. Roger, I will need some time to educate you. I am not sure there is enough space in this forum to do so."
>
> Brenda

Netiquette Buster Analysis

Rule #1: Do not insult other people by making your comments personal. Everyone has his or her opinion. Be careful not to confuse your sales agenda with contributing ideas to the discussion. This is not about winning or insisting that people believe in your point of view. The Discussion area of LinkedIn provides a forum for exploration, learning, and sharing, not for boasting about your credentials or putting down the responses of others.

> "Sorry, Brenda, It looks like you haven't been paying attention for the last 10 years. Maybe you should find a new career. Your ideas are strictly 1997, and you clearly haven't been looking closely at the online collaboration and learning repository technologies that have evolved in online tools such as ours, or in Rapid intake's new online version, or in Atlantic Link etc."
>
> Roger

> "As I stated, Roger, there is not enough room in this forum for me to educate you. I know your system; I know Atlantic Link and the many other online authoring tools. I don't think you are as smart as you give yourself credit for. Do your homework. LCMS's have matured over the

last 10 years. You don't have a clue what you are talking about. Duh, what do you think tools like Lectora and yours for that matter use to animate objects in a browser? Scripting Languages or proprietary authoring tools like Flash. I know more about web services than you could even imagine."

Brenda

Netiquette Buster Analysis

Rule #2: Do not spout out everything you know at the expense of other's knowledge. The LinkedIn Discussions encourage people to ask questions to get information, not to be browbeaten. When you have to self-promote saying you know more about something than anyone else, one wonders why we have not heard of you. What do you think of Brenda's company? Would you buy from her? Her haughty responses that belittle others only turn people away and tarnish the brand her company may have spent years building.

"Wow, Brenda, I really hadn't intended to turn this forum into a personal vendetta, your arrogance is as deep as your ignorance. You are the classic case of the salesperson becoming indoctrinated by her own BS."

Roger

Netiquette Buster Analysis

Rule #3: The verbal abuse on this thread clearly indicates that neither party is paying attention to what the other is saying. Do not fall into the trap of getting defensive and angry. When Roger took up the mud and slung it back at Brenda, he stooped to her level. On the other hand, had Roger responded professionally to Brenda's abuses, he may have maintained the upper hand. People like Brenda will self-destruct. Do not allow them to pull you into the fight.

What we have here is a classic case of a salesperson who ventured far, far off the reservation. Brenda was so caught up in winning that she evidently lost her mind. She wanted to push herself on everyone else as the smartest person alive and as such she forgot about common courtesy. Giving no thought to the fact that she risked damaging the reputation of the company that she represented, she kept mouthing off. For those people reading, clearly her image was forever tarnished in their minds. Whenever we see her name we will say to others, do not buy from her! Unfortunately, there are more examples like this online. The anonymity of the social media somehow gives people license to let it all hang out. The danger is that the conversation is public. Imagine what will happen when Brenda's boss reads this thread, and believe me, he will.

This example illustrates the importance of netiquette. As we have discussed earlier, cyberspace challenges companies to create clear, specific guidelines for online behavior that includes accountability. You do not wish to hamstring people with oversight, rigid control, and micro-management, but you must draw the line against certain types of behavior. Examples like the dialogue between Brenda and Roger will help salespeople see what inappropriate behavior looks like.

Respect and appreciation for the diverse viewpoints of others are as critical in the online world as in the offline world. Would Brenda have really said those insulting things to Roger if she were talking to him face to face? Would he have said those things to her if they were standing toe to toe at a networking function? And that is the moral of the story. Loose lips definitely sink ships. Be careful what you say online!

Part Three

DEVELOPING A SOCIAL MEDIA
SALES STRATEGY

Chapter 15

The First 15 Days of the 30-Day Social Media Sales Challenge: What You Need to Do to Get Started Now

Throughout this book we have talked about the necessity of getting started. We have made a compelling case for companies to take the plunge into the world of social networking. You have read examples from CEOs who took up blogging to build community with employees, with customers, and with business stakeholders. You have read about marketing executives who started online communities to build customer and brand loyalty, and you have heard about how salespeople are using public profiles like LinkedIn, Facebook, or Twitter to expand their sales reach. We have talked about the why and what of social media, and now it is time to talk about how to get started.

If you focus on the dizzying array of social tools that exist today, you will likely feel overwhelmed. *Do not let that stop you.* Rather than shy away from embracing the opportunity, focus on what you want to achieve. Core questions you may be ask include: What are the key business questions you need to address before you jump in headfirst? What policies and guidelines do you need? What resources—people, technical, training—are required? How can you implement and monitor a Social Media Sales Strategy in terms of the return on investment?

Even though we realize that every company, business, and individual operation is different, beginning with this chapter we offer you a roadmap that might set in motion your approach to integrating social media into your sales framework. Let this 30-day roadmap serve as the impetus to jumpstart your efforts. The time for you to take a risk is now. The changing world of business will not wait. In the pages that follow we challenge you to reach out to your customers and prospective buyers in a new way with *the new handshake*.

To guide you through the 30-day Social Media Sales challenge, let us take a look at a typical sales rep in a medium-sized company. As you follow her progress, be sure to think about your own business situation and make adjustments to fit your organizational and/or professional requirements.

A CASE FOR PDQ SHELVING TO GO SOCIAL

Sandra works as a sales rep for a medium-sized company, PDQ Shelving. Her company specializes in manufacturing computer accessories, equipment, and furniture that suit the unique requirements of small to medium-sized businesses. Her territory consists of the Southeastern states. A typical sales week for Sandra involves travel throughout her territory to make customer service calls or to conduct sales meetings with prospective buyers. She's usually on the road three to four times each week. Sandra also attends trade shows where she showcases the PDQ unique line of products. Today, PDQ's net revenue is $1.5 million. Sandra is one of four sales reps charged with achieving the company's sales goals. Launched as a family-owned business in 1984, PDQ has enjoyed consistent growth since its inception. In the last year the founders sold the company to Sandra's boss, Mr. Morris.

Like many business owners who feel the pinch of the downturn in the economy, Mr. Morris plans to initiate some financial cutbacks. He asked his salespeople to reduce their travel time and to scale back their attendance to only one trade show during the year. At their most recent sales meeting, Mr. Morris announced his decision, telling them, "Look for more efficient ways to get our product out there. We've witnessed a significant reduction in sales over the last six months which has resulted in scaling back our resources. For our business to weather these challenging times, we must explore more creative sales approaches which include everything from generating leads, qualifying sales opportunities to maintaining solid customer relationships." The only problem was that he did not suggest how to achieve a more creative sales approach. Ironically, in all this talk about cut-back the company neglected to trim from its budget an expensive print advertising program with several targeted trade journals.

As Sandra ponders her CEOs words, she realizes it is time to get educated on these social networking tools she has been hearing about. She knows her team must find a way to create new sales leads and maintain existing customer relationships without always meeting them face to face. Sandra has heard the term "the new handshake," and she realizes that the world of sales is changing. She decides to take the 30-Day Social Media Sales Challenge.

Day 1: Getting Started

As we discussed in Chapters 7 and 8, a good starting point for Sandra was to examine her company's culture. On Day 1, Sandra asked herself some important questions related to PDQ's readiness to launch into the social media. Some cultures were more apt to adopt the new handshake philosophy than others. For example, Web-based companies or organizations heavily involved with information technology seemed more likely to experiment with the new media. Nonetheless, other companies were beginning to come along. Working for a previously family-owned company, which tended to be more conservative, Sandra began by rating her company's social media readiness with the questionnaire found in Chapter 7. Second, Sandra knew that she had to address one question upfront, namely, how social media might benefit sales. Day 1, then, required Sandra to determine the company's readiness as well as do some investigative work to determine how social media might improve the company's overall sales process.

Day 2: Engaging the Sales Team and Setting Objectives

Sandra suggested to her boss, Mr. Tweeds, the vice president of sales, that the sales team meet to discuss their current sales process, which was largely spent making cold calls and working to convert those calls into qualified leads. During the meeting, a few of the sales reps grumbled that they have been doing this work for far too long and they were not willing to learn new methods. They argued that they had no time to learn new approaches. One rep expressed concern that using these online tools would burn precious time that few of them could afford to lose. Everyone felt the pressure of declining sales. Sandra reminded her peers of the CEOs directive to find more efficient ways to market their products and services. "Before our meeting today, I rated our company's social media readiness," she said. "I learned some things that might help us figure out how to move ahead." She said they scored high in some places, namely strong company leadership, a flexible IT organization on the cutting edge of new technology, and a strong relationship with marketing despite the fact that there are ways to improve.

According to the readiness indicator, Sandra listed the company's opportunities for improvement: monitoring what is being said about PDQ, its competitors, and its industry; embracing less formal communication channels, and gathering real-time customer feedback and service data. Following Sandra's presentation, the team agreed that improvements in the current sales process could lead to shortened sales cycles, higher quality and quantity of leads in the sales pipeline, faster repeat orders from current customers, and the ability to tap new markets with the social media.

With these primary objectives in mind, Sandra volunteered to lead an internal pilot using social media to drive sales. Acknowledging that a few of her peers remained skeptical, she asked them to keep an open mind. "It would really help us if you could share your candid input and feedback from customers as we venture into all this," she told them. "None of us really knows what to expect." The team agreed to move forward and Sandra's boss gave her the nod.

Day 3: Getting Upper Management Support

Sandra and Mr. Tweed worked on a pilot project plan to present to Mr. Morris. For any new business initiative to succeed, especially when it represents a significant departure from the way people currently conduct their business, executive support and participation are essential.

In the meeting with Mr. Morris, Sandra outlined a new strategy of using social media to increase the sales revenue and improve efficiencies in the sales process. The plan included piloting creative uses of the social media to shorten the sales cycle and to attract new buyers in currently untapped markets. Mr. Morris endorsed the plan and gave the team a firm commitment by saying he wanted to actively participate in the process. He called the vice president of marketing into the meeting and immediately engaged her in the process.

Day 4: Research and Benchmarking

The overall purposes of this new virtual approach were to increase sales and to improve efficiencies. The ability to measure the ROI throughout the course of the pilot relied on creating clearly defined success metrics and a foundational benchmark at the onset of the pilot. The integrity of the data would play an important role as a key performance indicator of success. To kick off the creation of a Social Media Sales Strategy for PDQ, Sandra documented the steps taken throughout the current sales process. She set out to answer the following questions and to set goals around those questions:

How does the sales team currently prospect for clients?

Most of PDQ's prospects came from a leads list generated by marketing. Using this list, Sandra and the other reps spent a minimum of four hours a day making cold calls. Not only was this activity time consuming, but it also led to poorly qualified leads, which often did not convert to a sale. In talking with her peers, she heard similar feedback.

Goals.

- Improve the quality of the leads list and reduce the amount of physical time it takes to make cold calls.
- Examine cold calling to determine its effectiveness as a strategy given the various ways potential buyers elude a vendor's phone calls.

*How does PDQ create visibility and product demand through
its marketing activities?*

Currently, PDQ marketed the business through traditional means such as
trade shows and face-to-face sales meetings. Sandra calculated that she spent
40 percent of her time traveling to visit current customers onsite or to attend
trade shows. The amount of time her peers spent traveling was similar to
hers with the exception of one team member who often traveled as much as
70 percent of the time. The company also relied heavily on referrals. The
referral process meant sales reps invested a significant amount of time chasing down leads passed along from sources other than marketing. The trade
magazine ads generated some leads for the sales team, but those leads were
few considering the cost invested in advertising.

Goal.

- Team up with marketing to examine the current lead-generation
  model and determine what tools helped sales reps remain visible in
  the minds of their customers and potential buyers now that the company was reducing face time.

*What qualification processes do Sandra and her peers use to determine
if a buyer is indeed ready to purchase?*

Sandra typically called prospects for the purpose of scheduling an introduc-
tory meeting. Once she scheduled the meeting, she visited her buyer's Web site
to learn about their philosophy, service offering, and delivery approach. Next,
she organized a face-to-face visit. In most cases, her prospects wanted more
information or time before they decided to purchase. Sandra often visited a
new customer six times before a sale happened. This analysis showed Sandra
that the sales leads were not properly qualified to ensure that the potential buyer
had a need, had the budget, and was ready to purchase in the next 30 to 60 days.

Goals.

- Put a social media prospecting plan in place to target ideal buyers.
- Use results of the lead-generation list to create opportunities to
  engage her prospective buyers in conversation.
- Tighten the phone qualification process, including the creation of a
  top-10 list of qualifying questions.

What percentage of the company's sales processes was internal and external?

The majority of PDQ sales efforts consisted of the traditional field selling
model of meeting buyers face to face. To date, PDQ had not incorporated
any Sales 2.0 tools into the operations. Sandra saw a great opportunity for

PDQ to experiment with a few Sales 2.0 strategies to meet the goals of increasing efficiency and increasing sales.

Goals.

- Create a LinkedIn profile to build an external network of potential buyers and referral partners as well as integrate the use of the Slide-Share application to create a visual presentation of what her company offers.
- Review the LinkedIn profiles and company pages of PDQ's top competitors to determine how they are using social networking to reach customers.

Once Sandra determined these benchmarks and goals, she visited with Tim, her liaison in marketing, to share her analysis and to get his input before moving forward.

Day 5: Online Presence

Sandra recognized that PDQ's online presence would be a critical component to succeeding in this new digital economy. The company had a Web site, but she was not sure how well the site actually preformed. With the help of colleagues in IT, Sandra learned more about PDQ's online presence.

A team of IT professionals maintained the PDQ site and did a good job keeping it up to date. Sandra, along with the other sales reps, encouraged clients and prospects to visit the site to see the new innovations in shelving, new accessories, and custom furniture options. The marketing staff posted new product innovations and specials on the site. The Web site, however, looked more like a static company brochure than a dynamic tool that might compel prospects to want to learn more. Sandra learned from Tim that PDQ's Web site visits had leveled off in recent years. Sandra looked for efforts to drive people to the site and found few with the exception of word-of-mouth. When Sandra Googled computer shelving and furniture, PDQ came up 20 pages down. Clearly, not much had been done to optimize the Web site with terms and key words that buyers would likely search. Sandra also noted that PDQ's chief competitor, Fowler's Furniture, popped up in the number-one position on page one with a blog post. As Sandra had learned in Chapter 13, search engines love blogs because they contain fresh information. She also noted that effective blogging might produce even better results than the best SEO maintained Web site.

Day 6: Create a Company Blog

Sandra and Tim agreed to create a corporate blog with the purpose of engaging current customers and new buyers. With the help of IT, they launched the company blog on Wordpress called, "The P's and Q's of Computer Furniture." Tim and Sandra agreed to publish posts three times a week. By the end of Day 6 Sandra published her first blog post. She sent the post to Mr. Morris and encouraged him to weigh in with comments. She also asked him to contribute a post once a week called, "The CEO Corner."

Day 7: Establish a Listening Post

One of the core values in using social media for business is the ability to "listen" to conversations. Sandra wanted to select tools that would enable her and her team members to hear what people were saying about her company, about the industry of work furnishings/ergonomics, as well as keep tabs on the company's top competitors. Before developing her own strategy, she decided to listen to the buzz to learn how the conversations flowed and to pick up on the informal "rules of the road." Sandra began listening on Day 7 in the following ways:

- Sandra set up a Twitter account under her name within PDQ. She posted her photo on the profile with the PDQ logo in the background and referenced PDQ's Web site. She conducted a Twitter search of the industry, and she began reading Tweets. She learned two things immediately. First, Fowler had three staff on Twitter, and they were already in conversation with many customers. Most of the Fowler Tweets were sales offers. Second, she picked up on a general frustration with shelving designs that did not fit the smaller, more streamlined offices. Because PDQ specialized in a line of custom design for small offices and home-based businesses, Sandra alerted the sales team to try and capitalize on this frustration. She also made a note to talk with Tim about how to call this out in the marketing materials the company prepared.
- She set up Google Alerts to notify her when PDQ and Fowler were mentioned online. Being alerted to references to the company gave her a chance to connect with people talking about PDQ or to help someone resolve a problem. Knowing what its key competitor was up to potentially gave Sandra and her sales team a decided edge during their sales meetings. Ironically, the first alert she received was Tim's blog posted earlier that day.

Day 8: Buyer Assessment

Now that Sandra had examined her company culture, analyzed the sales process, set up listening posts, and partnered with marketing, it was time for her to investigate buyer behavior. Whether you are a B2B company or a

B2C company, your buyers will be more or less active online. Sandra dealt with B2B buyers who must make significant financial commitments when deciding to purchase a product. PDQ's clients took an average of six field visits before committing to the sale. Sandra suspected that some of these people were online, but she had no data to indicate that they would make a decision to purchase online.

Nonetheless, she realized that she and her peers had to keep an open mind, think outside the box, and communicate with buyers in their preferred manner. She knew that they needed to find new leads and learn to cultivate trust through an engaging online presence. She revisited the goals she and the team set for the Social Medial Sales Strategy in Day 2, namely to shorten the sales cycle, to create higher quality and quantity of leads in the sales pipeline, to speed up repeat orders from current customers, and to tap new markets.

Demographically, PDQ buyers represented executive decision-makers working with multiple budgets. They typically tended to be well educated, roughly 35 to 55 years old, with a solid background in design and manufacturing. For the most part buyers did not find PDQ. Instead, the company found the buyers most often at trade shows. On a rare occasion a buyer surfaced from an ad and contacted PDQ directly.

At this stage Sandra had no idea about her current buyer's online behavior. She did not know if they were creating blogs, responding to content, joining social media groups, or simply watching. Sandra could engage Forrester to run a Social Technographics analysis of her buyers. PDQ, however, being a smaller, conservative company, had not invested resources for this kind of analysis. Nonetheless, Sandra made a note to recommend doing so, depending on the results of this pilot. In the meantime, she Googled her main clients to get a rough estimate of their online behavior.

Day 9: Join the Social Media Sites

Sandra's analysis of the PDQ's buyer helped her see how important it was to create a strategy that would enable potential buyers to find the company even if they were not ready to purchase immediately. As she began thinking about joining the social media sites, she set out the following objectives: to find out where her target buyers tended to participate online and join those sites and to discover what type of dialogue her buyers engaged in and look for ways she could join the conversation.

She began by joining LinkedIn and Facebook. She completed the profiles, inserting her own business photo and ensuring that each profile included keywords specific to PDQ's business. In Day 9 Sandra also worked with Tim to create a Facebook fan page for PDQ. However, they decided not to publish the Facebook fan page until they each had at least 50 friends whom they could invite as fans.

On Day 9 Sandra also explored the LinkedIn groups by going to the Group Directory. She typed in ergonomics and found seven pages of groups. She sifted through the groups and selected three that fit her company objectives. She explored the profiles of group members to find people who fit her niche: decision makers in medium-sized companies. Using a personalized message in which she communicated the value she believed they would both receive by connecting with one another, she invited members to connect. By using this personalized approach she increased her connections to 75 by the end of the day. Sandra also posted the following question to the Applied Ergonomics group: "What are your biggest physical stressors with current computer furniture?"

Responses to this question opened up three opportunities for Sandra: (1) Thank responders and share additional comments with them. (2) Invite those who responded to her question to connect with her on LinkedIn. (3) Publish the new blog link and PDQ Web site at the end of each interaction. Furthermore, she began a dialogue with two people. For both, she made small suggestions that she thought would help make their workspaces less stressful. By Day 9, Sandra had begun engaging in the online conversation with potential buyers.

At this point, Sandra was recognizing the value of the blog. She asked IT to add the blog application on LinkedIn to feed PDQ's blog posts to her LinkedIn and Facebook profiles and appropriate LinkedIn groups.

Day 10: Increase Your Following

Sandra was now set up on Twitter, Facebook, and LinkedIn. By Day 10 she also had a blog where she had published several short articles. From her monitoring and from the cautions presented in this book, she had learned that a cardinal sin in the online world was overt selling on the social networks. She carefully avoided this kind of selling. In this early stage, Sandra focused more on listening and watching.

Day 10 found Sandra focused on increasing her following with Twitter. Rather than focus on all the social sites at once, Sandra decided to take one at a time. Today's goal was to build a network on Twitter that represented both quality followers who fit her niche and a sufficient quantity that would give her greater visibility. She recognized that numbers for numbers sake would not help her achieve her sales objective. Furthermore, she knew from reading Chapter 11 that she did not wish to follow everyone who chose to follow her. As a result, she used the search function on Twitter to find the customers and buyers she was targeting as well as industry thought leaders. She then returned to the Fowler employees on Twitter and spent some time mining the people following Fowler, carefully selecting those people who met her sales criteria. At the end of Day 10 Sandra had increased the number of people she was following to 210.

To more effectively manage her online time when using Twitter, Sandra downloaded Tweetdeck to enable her to search and keep up with Tweets. She established groups on her Tweetdeck dashboard so she could access information quickly. From Tweetdeck she quickly re-Tweeted an excellent blog on office organization. She posted a Tweet called Ergo Tip of the Day and sent that directly to one of her clients.

Sandra asked IT to integrate the new Twitter, Facebook, and LinkedIn profiles with the company blog. By that, she wanted them to add the Twitter, Facebook, and LinkedIn icons to the blog home page. This feature invited the visitors to the blog to join her and Tim on the social media sites. She also linked the Facebook status updates with her Tweets using Ping.fm (see Chapter 12). Now when she posted on Facebook, she automatically Tweeted to her following. She noted that this feature immediately increased the number of people reading the company's new blog posts even though they had not yet created a conversation on the blog.

By the end of Day 10 Sandra had 143 Twitter followers (even though she was still following more people), 75 LinkedIn connections, and 54 friends on Facebook.

Day 11: Post Your Fan Page on Facebook

Sandra and Tim updated Mr. Morris on the progress thus far. They presented their analysis of PDQ's target buyer, noting particularly that some used Facebook exclusively, others used LinkedIn exclusively, and many used both. Furthermore, she explained that Twitter was a great place to listen and to monitor activity. She took this opportunity to show Mr. Morris her Twitter page, noting several more people following her than yesterday. She mentioned that she searched Fowler and started following key people who fit the PDQ's buyer profile in Fowler's Twitter population. Recognizing that Facebook appealed to a younger business audience but was also a favorite of smaller businesses, Sandra and Tim showed Mr. Morris the fan page they created for PDQ. He made a few suggestions and approved publishing it.

Sandra and Tim invited their friends on Facebook to become fans. They also took out an ad that showcased one of PDQ's newest products. They agreed to run the ad for a month at minimal cost and evaluate the number of leads generated. They also planned to compare the results with the current advertising campaign running in key trade publications. Tim agreed to monitor the statistics from both advertising activities and share those results with Sandra.

Sandra met with the other sales reps and encouraged them to post a profile on Facebook and become fans of the new PDQ page. Two of the reps already had a presence on Facebook, and they immediately linked with Sandra and Tim, expanding everyone's network.

Day 12: Work LinkedIn

By Day 12 Sandra had over 100 connections on LinkedIn, and she was ready to use the advanced search function to uncover new leads in her niche. She proceeded as follows:

- Sandra searched for purchasing managers in computer-driven companies. She acknowledged that purchasing managers in other companies could benefit from PDQ, but she decided to focus on this sector first. She uncovered 25 primary and secondary contacts from her list.
- She examined the profiles of each of the people she uncovered. Some were not in her territory; some were in other countries. Five direct contacts remained. Sandra decided to focus on those direct contacts before moving on to the secondary contacts in her network.
- Sandra looked at the groups these five people participated in and studied the Web sites for each of these prospects. At the end of each LinkedIn profile, members listed their particular interests. Sandra paid close attention to these interests because her goal was to find something they shared in common. She wanted to make a personal contact that would resonate with their needs.
- She created a plan to contact the five people. She would begin with a LinkedIn e-mail to share information that might be useful to them without making a sales pitch. Her second touch would be a direct contact with a request for a telephone conversation.

To continue building a network on LinkedIn, Sandra read the group discussions and added comments and helpful responses. She continued going through the group members to invite people to connect with her. Her connections now exceeded 200.

Day 13: Expand and Access

After 13 days, Sandra and Tim had discovered the power of the social media. They had created strong networks on all three social media sites. Sandra was cultivating five strong leads through her LinkedIn connections. Tim was posting to the blog on a regular basis and was monitoring the responses to the Facebook ad and the growth in the numbers on the company fan page. He was also tracking the number of visits to the company Web site. Tim had alerted Sandra to a number of blogs that he thought she might wish to follow. From this list Sandra identified six blogs that she bookmarked through Delicious. She signed up for the RSS feeds to these blogs and now received daily posts. She commented on these posts, Tweeted them to her following and sent them directly to the other sales reps.

Day 14 through 15: Listening and Responding

Day 14 began with Tim alerting Sandra to a negative Tweet about PDQ: "PDQ is a company not to be trusted. Doesn't keep its promises." Mr. Tweed saw this Tweet and told Tim that Mr. Morris wanted the company to shut down all the social media sites. Tim, Sandra, and Mr. Tweed met with Mr. Morris to explain how to handle negative comments without overreacting. Sandra said she would like to respond to the post to try and resolve the problem. Mr. Morris worried that other customers might see the negative comment and decide not to purchase the company's products. "Whether we have a presence on the Web or not, there will be negative comments. Because we are set up now, we can respond to our customers' input, both positive and negative," Tim explained. Even though Mr. Morris was skeptical, he agreed to give it more time.

Sandra sent an @ response to the person, who had Tweeted that PDQ did not keep its promises and requested a telephone conversation. She added this person to her following so he could direct mail her back. She received a fast response. She immediately called the customer. During that phone conversation Sandra learned that the furniture this customer had ordered had been delayed, and the CEO was breathing down his neck. One of the problems PDQ has had over the years was manufacturing delays. This customer said he had been waiting two months even though the sales rep had assured him that the furniture would be delivered in a matter of weeks. Sandra agreed that PDQ was responsible, and she apologized. She contacted Mr. Morris and asked if the company could do anything to appease this customer. He agreed to a percentage reduction in the costs, and he called manufacturing to expedite the order. Sandra contacted the customer and told him what had been done. The customer was grateful for both the action and the attention.

Later that day, Sandra noted that the same customer Tweeted a thank you note to her for her fast response to his troubles. This note went to his following of 741 people as well as Sandra's following. It also appeared on all searches of PDQ. That same day Tim blogged about the incident and apologized for any inconvenience customers may have had in awaiting delivery of their orders. For the first time, comments came into the new blog. The comments gave PDQ high marks for admitting to a problem and taking care of it.

During the sales rep meeting that occurred on Day 15, Sandra encouraged the sales reps to recognize that manufacturing cannot deliver products as quickly as they were telling customers. Rather than set up false expectations, Sandra encouraged the reps to give more realistic delivery dates and to stay in close contact with customers until PDQ completes the delivery. This problem, however, would have never surfaced had Sandra and Tim not been monitoring the social networks.

At the end of Day 15, Sandra and Tim sat down to evaluate their progress. They looked at their original goals and noted that even though they had done a lot, particularly with increasing sales efficiencies, they still needed to work on the goal of generating more quality leads. As they geared up for second phase of the 30-Day Social Media Sales Challenge, they agreed to redouble their efforts and focus on quality lead generation.

Chapter 16

Seeing the Finish Line: Meeting the 30-Day Social Media Sales Challenge

Let us take a look at Sandra's progress and the key steps she has taken in the first 15 days of the 30-Day Social Media Sales Challenge:

- She examined her company culture and readiness.
- She enlisted support from her boss, the sales team, upper management, IT, and marketing. (You might need to add legal, human resources, or other components of your organization.)
- She benchmarked the company's current sales process and set specific sales-oriented goals.
- She informally measured buyer behavior online.
- She joined key social media sites to drive visitors to the new blog and to watch and listen to the conversation.

Her steps from this point onward will focus on working the new media to create specific sales opportunities, namely: re-establish contact with previous customers, generate new leads in new markets, unearth prospects that come to PDQ via the social media, and add functions to increase the efficiency of Sandra's social media time.

DAY 16: ORGANIZE TWEETS AND BLOG POSTS

Sandra logged onto Tweetlater.com. There she wrote several Tweets. She sequenced them to release over the next five days. These automatic Tweets will go out two per day, and she will add one per day, giving her a minimum of three Tweets daily. Chapter 11 gave her ideas for the kinds of Tweets to include. She varied her Tweets from Ergo Tips of the Day to interesting blog posts that she had bookmarked to questions she had about the market. She planned to use one daily Tweet to re-Tweet others whenever possible or to enter conversations using the "@" function.

She also wrote four new blog posts that she scheduled for future publication on her Wordpress blog. Tim was monitoring and maintaining the blog. He planned to intersperse her posts with his. She will plan to write four more blog posts each Monday afternoon and get those to Tim.

DAY 17: BUILDING A FOLLOWING ON FACEBOOK

In addition to the friends Sandra accumulated on Facebook, she decided to go through some of her friend's networks to locate more followers. She had confirmed quite a few over the last week, but she wanted to expand her Facebook friends number past 100.

Sandra spent time responding to her friend's status updates. She then placed a comment on someone's wall about the upcoming reception that PDQ was hosting for new clients in Chicago. She placed that notice on the events calendar and invited friends from the Chicago area. One Facebook friend responded that he would be in the area when the event was scheduled even though he lived in Atlanta. She encouraged him to attend. This friend was a former client who had not purchased from PDQ in several years.

DAY 18: TWITTER AND THE TRADE SHOW

As Sandra entered the third week of her 30-day Social Media Sales Challenge, she decided to put Twitter to work during an upcoming trade show. She departed that morning for a show in Charlotte, North Carolina. Before she left, she Tweeted about the show. She got two Direct Messages from people saying they would be at the show and would come by her booth. She made the following offer via Twitter: "If anyone hears about our booth on Twitter and comes by, we'll give them a five percent discount on any purchase made."

During the show, she Tweeted about the people she met. She Tweeted about the other booths at the show and what they had to offer. She began a conversation with someone on Twitter who wanted to know more about the purpose of the trade show. In addition to the contacts she made at her booth (which doubled from this time last year because she brought in 100 people who said they saw her Tweet.), she increased her following on Twitter by 20 percent.

DAY 19: TRADE SHOW BLOG POST

Sandra wrote a blog post about her experience at the trade show. She posted photos of the booth and testimonials from people who attended the show. She Tweeted this post and got six comments. She responded to those contacts. Three of them turned into qualified leads that she immediately followed up on. When Sandra Googled office furniture, she saw her blog post from the trade show as the first entry on the first page.

DAY 20: YOUTUBE ON THE BLOG

Tim and Sandra created a 2-minute YouTube video that demonstrated PDQ shelving. They demonstrated an office before PDQ and after PDQ. The stunning change using the ergonomically sound innovations unique to PDQ produced 14 comments on the blog. Four people that day asked for quotes. Sandra asked IT to post the video on the PDQ Web site.

Tim agreed to create a new 2-minute video twice a month, post it to the blog and the Web site, and follow the YouTube sightings.

DAY 21: VIRTUAL DEMO

One of the CEOs stated goals was to cut down on travel. In the last four weeks since Sandra had been working with the social media, she had identified eight new prospects. She had been in touch with them by telephone and arranged demos for each. Working to reduce cold calls and better qualification of leads up front, her work using social media had now led to these eight highly qualified buyers to agree to a demo onsite. Furthermore, one of Sandra's goals was to tighten the phone qualification process by creating a list of qualifying questions. She used that list to make sure these prospects had all the information they needed if they decided to make a purchase. Even though Sandra planned to carry out these demos onsite, she still wanted to incorporate virtual demos into the initial stages of the sales process.

To that end, Sandra and Tim met with IT to begin the process of creating the virtual demo that would illustrate the unique qualities of PDQ furnishing and enable viewers to request price quotes. This virtual presentation would make use of video technology and the telephone. Sandra also wanted to entice people to ask for a demo. She created a short PowerPoint SlideShare show that she posted to her LinkedIn profile and a short YouTube teaser video.

DAY 22: KEEPING UP WITH THE TECHNOLOGY

Sandra realized as she worked with the social media and learned new applications every day that she would have to keep up with changes in technology.

Not long after Sandra posted her profile on LinkedIn, the company added new applications. She realized that she needed to dedicate time to keeping up with the quickly changing world inherent with the new media. She and Tim signed up for a free webinar hosted by Hubspot, titled "Getting the Most Out of Social Media." They agreed to attend online conferences and webinars once a month.

DAY 23: CONTINUING TO GROW THE NETWORK

Sandra spent Day 23 inviting more people to connect with her on LinkedIn. She joined three more groups from the seven-page list she had uncovered. She read through the group discussions. From the questions and answers she read, she contacted people directly to invite them to connect with her using her personalized approach. Her goal was to uncover five new prospects.

Other strategies Sandra used to expand her LinkedIn connections included the following:

- Sandra added her most recent blog post to the News sections on each of the groups she belonged to. She singled out the people whose blogs she liked, commented on their blogs, and invited them to connect with her.
- She invited 10 of her connections to join her on Twitter and Facebook.
- She scanned the profiles of 30 of the secondary contacts she had uncovered previously. She learned that these people all belonged to a group she had not yet joined. She joined that group and then invited each of those people to connect with her. Those who agreed to the invite would become a primary connection.
- She sent these new primary connections her personalized letter. This action resulted in a direct contact to eight new highly qualified leads.

DAY 24: UPDATE YOUR PROFILE

Sandra returned to her Facebook, LinkedIn, and Twitter profiles to make updates. Even though she had only been involved in the social networks for just over four weeks, her profiles needed regular updates. She took the following steps on Day 24:

- She added books to her reading list on LinkedIn.
- She added a new SlideShare program on LinkedIn.
- She posted a new Ergo Tip on her Facebook status update.
- She added sales information to the PDQ fan page.

- She updated her Facebook profile with a new photo.
- She changed the color of her Twitter background.

DAY 25: REEVALUATE AND REASSESS YOUR GOALS

Sandra spent Day 25 reevaluating her goals to determine what else she could do to make the most out of the networks now that she had just five days left in the 30-day challenge.

- She analyzed her Twitter account. Sandra used Twitter for two purposes: to find out what others were saying about PDQ and similar products and to find new and interesting blog posts that she could share with potential leads. She noticed that her most productive Tweets were articles she had found online. She decided to spend more time mining the people in her network to determine where she could add more followers.
- In looking over Facebook, Sandra noticed that some of her status updates did not receive any comments. The update that received the most comments had been a video program she had found on YouTube. It was a spoof on inefficient office furniture. She also had several comments to her blog posts on ergonomics. Status updates that merely said something she was doing that day got few responses. She decided to only post status updates when she had something substantial to say. Furthermore, she noted that she had not done any wall posting. She set a goal to wall post more frequently to her friend's Facebook pages. She also decided to post more events since the Chicago event generated several new and returning customers.
- On LinkedIn Sandra realized she had the most activity, particularly with finding new leads. She had answered several questions in the ergonomics area of interest and had received "Best Answer" for two of them. In response to someone's question, she had also posted an article on how to avoid physical stress when working at a desk, including photos of exercises people could do. That article won her expert status in the area of ergonomics.
- The new blog that Sandra and Tim created was already getting comments. Sandra realized that most of the views came from Tweets. She made a note to ask IT to enable the TweetThis tool to encourage blog readers to Tweet the PDQ blog posts. Sandra was already seeing the benefit that regular blogging was having in helping sales and marketing achieve their goals. Commenting on other key industry blogs was also creating new visibility for PDQ. She decided she

would encourage her peers to become more active with their own blog posts.

Sandra's personal sales goal was to cut down or eliminate cold calling altogether. Using social media sites, Sandra had reduced her cold calls by 35 percent as of the Day 25. Most of her current calls were to people she had already connected with on one of the three social networks. She had eight client demos set up, and one client had agreed to view the virtual demo as a pilot.

DAY 26: TAGGING INFORMATION THROUGH THE SOCIAL MEDIA

Chapter 12 gave Sandra ideas that might expand her status as an expert in ergonomics. She had found a number of articles that she had tagged on Delicious and on StumbleUpon. What she had not done was decide whom to send what information to. She put together the following plan:

- Spend some time each week on LinkedIn to discover what people wanted to learn about ergonomics.
- Put together a spreadsheet with names of contacts and interests.
- Go through the articles she tagged and earmark them for certain contacts. Note when these were sent on the spreadsheet.
- When sending an article to someone on LinkedIn, Tweet the article to her network.
- Save particular blog posts on Delicious and send the link to Twitter-mates with similar interests.

DAY 27: LEAD GENERATION FROM SOCIAL MEDIA

Sandra had started generating prospects, particularly from LinkedIn and from the blog posts. She wanted to build on these and create new prospects using all the tools. She began by creating a lead-generation list using the LinkedIn search function. From that function she put together a list of leads. She saved her search. Now any time a buyer who met her criteria surfaced, she would receive a weekly e-mail alert. Using these dynamic updates, she not only kept up with new people joining the network, but she added them to her prospect pipeline and began to build a relationship with these potential buyers.

Additionally, on Day 27 Sandra turned her attention to companies. Using the LinkedIn company function and the Facebook search function, she compiled a list of small to medium-sized companies that had done business in the past with PDQ. Next, she searched for those companies on LinkedIn and on Facebook. From there she made a list of potential leads with whom she could connect or friend.

DAY 28: TRAIN OTHER PDQ STAFF ON THE POWER OF THE SOCIAL MEDIA

As Sandra and Tim became believers in the potential of the social media, they agreed it was time to include more people within PDQ. With the 30-day challenge nearing its end, they wanted to share their success results with the other sales and marketing reps.

Sandra and Tim co-hosted a companywide webinar in which they talked about the leads and prospects generated through LinkedIn, Facebook, and the blog. They discussed the power of Twitter to drive traffic to the company blog. They demonstrated how Twitter Search allowed them to quickly research both the industry and their competition. They showed others how to develop a Twitter and LinkedIn account. Sandra walked them through the process she used to set up accounts, invite people to the network (including a sample of her personalized invitation), join groups, add quality content to the blog, participate in groups, ask questions using Questions & Answers on LinkedIn, post events, add presentations to their profiles, and create dynamic lead-generation prospecting lists.

DAY 29: INDIVIDUAL BRAND ASSESSMENT AND SALES STRENGTHS

After the webinar, two other sales reps came forward who wished to add their strengths to the PDQ brand. Sandra covered ergonomics. Mark knew all about the organizational components of the products. Lucy was their technology whiz. Each of the sales reps had different strengths that they could capitalize on to extend and deepen the PDQ brand. The following strategy resulted:

- Each sales rep created a Twitter profile within the narrow niche related to their strengths. They followed Sandra's lead by mining the contacts among both hers and Fowler's followers.
- The sales reps expanded their LinkedIn group membership to reflect their individual strengths.
- Mark and Lucy agreed to add blog posts related to their area of expertise and to publish those posts on their Twitter, LinkedIn, and the PDQ Facebook fan page.

DAY 30: EVALUATE THE SOCIAL MEDIA SALES STRATEGY DURING THE 30-DAY CHALLENGE

Sandra had spent over two hours each day educating herself on how to make the most use of the social media sites. Now that she was more informed and had a strategy as well as a solid network, she could reduce her time to one hour each day. She put together the following Time Mastery Strategic plan:

- Focus one hour a week on increasing following.
- Focus one hour a week on preparing Tweets and blog posts.
- Focus one hour a week on LinkedIn for lead generation, profile updates, and adding applications.
- Focus one hour a week on commenting on other blogs and bookmarking relevant blogs and information for later Tweets and Facebook activity and tagging to prospects.
- Focus one hour a week on YouTube programming to strengthen the power of the company blog.

OVERALL ANALYSIS OF THE 30-DAY CHALLENGE

As we traveled through the 30-Day Social Media Sales Challenge with Sandra we saw several key points that could apply to anyone wishing to pick up the challenge:

- **Work within your company culture.** Do not embark on a social media sales strategy as a lone ranger. Sandra knew she needed support from the top, marketing support, and the blessing of the sales team.
- **Keep an open mind as you go through the process.** Sandra assumed that her customers would not make purchase decisions without an onsite demo. As she created relationships with customers, she saw a shift from this assumption. We predict that she will cultivate more opportunities to use the virtual demo and that she will experience a willingness to make purchase decisions without face-to-face interactions. This phenomenon has been confirmed by Anneke Seley and OracleDirect with their experience with Sales 2.0.
- **When things get tough, keep going.** The negative feedback that the company heard on the Web nearly frightened them away. You must remember that customers will make both positive and negative comments. The goal is to position yourself so you can listen and respond. Sandra did not shy away from hearing what the disgruntled customer had to say. She listened, and she responded. Furthermore, Tim wrote an open and honest blog post about the incident.
- **Stay tuned into the changes in technology.** Things will change as you proceed through the 30-Day challenge. Attend frequent webinars or teleseminars to stay up to date.
- **Do not violate the informal rules of netiquette.** As you watch and listen, pay attention to what people are doing that works and what they

are doing that offends. Do not just follow along. Listen to what the thought leaders are saying about appropriate uses of the social media to build business.

- **Take a good look at the old methods.** Some work and some do not. The trade shows had been a very effective method for generating leads for PDQ. Rather than toss that out, Sandra found a way to make the trade show experience even more powerful. The ads in the trade magazines may prove too costly. Once the data come in regarding the Facebook ads and the leads generated through the social media, PDQ may scale back its traditional advertising. It may also wish to explore placing ads on the trade magazine sites rather than in print media.

- **Evaluate your goals throughout the process.** Make sure you are staying targeted. Sandra continued to keep an eye on the company goals. The initial assessment of readiness showed that the company was not monitoring the Web nor were they active participants in the conversation. In just 30 days she changed both those factors. She and Tim accomplished the overall goal to make it easy for people to find PDQ by the end of 15 days.

- **Do not let the social media consume you.** Sandra restricted herself to two hours daily in the initial work. At the end of 30 days, she crafted a plan that would restrict her time on the social media sites to just five hours a week.

- **Phase in new components.** Once Sandra and Tim report the results of the 30-Day challenge to Mr. Morris, they may consider phasing in other components that might further strengthen their Social Media Sales Strategy. These could include: professional lead-generation services that focus on the social media (see Appendix); professional aggregation services (see Appendix); professional social media strategy services (see Appendix); refocus a marketing rep's responsibilities (possibly Tim) to feed constant information to the sales reps; and utilize the money saved from traditional advertising for expanded social media services.

YOUR CHALLENGE

This book offers you the challenge. It provides the resources you need to reach out with the new handshake. As we pointed out in the early chapters, we are experiencing a revolution in communication in which the social media are active players. Indeed, social media have reached their tipping point and are here to stay. Business and particularly sales must wake up and embrace this opportunity, not with overt selling and spamming but with relationship building and trust. B. L. Ochman said in his November 10, 2009 post:

> "Big companies have moved cautiously for eons. While many corporations *are* making forays into social media, very, very few are taking huge risks. Instead of jumping in, they're still standing on the edge of the pool, dipping a toe in the water. As a result, getting companies to add social media into the marketing mix is still a hard sell."[1]

It is our contention that not responding to the new world around us is an even greater risk. If you doubt this contention, we'd like to share one last incentive to join the conversation. We recently heard about a musician named Dave Carroll, who on a flight from Nebraska to Chicago, watched as United Airlines crew broke his Taylor guitar. Mr. Carroll went through all the corporate channels to get compensation for his treasured instrument. When after nine months the airline told him he would receive no help, either with the replacement or the repair of his guitar, he told United he would take his message to the world via YouTube. They responded with "Good luck with that, pal."

Carroll made a YouTube video with a very catchy song titled, "United Breaks Guitars."[2] Three days after he posted the video, it received 1 million hits. At this writing, 6 million people have watched Mr. Carroll's video. United Airlines contacted the musician asking him to take down the video. His response, "Good luck with that, pal."

As we have demonstrated countless times in this book, when companies ignore the power of the social media, they pay the consequences. United Airlines, meanwhile, announced that it will use Dave Carroll's video as a unique learning opportunity. The company plans to show it internally to help build better customer relations. You may think this is too little, too late. Perhaps it is. At least for the time being, the company now recognizes the power of social media. Let United's lesson be our lesson. Will United survive this public relations disaster? Only time will answer that question.

In contrast to the United Airlines response, Taylor Guitars capitalized on the Carroll video. They not only captured many new customers, but they also made their own YouTube video showing all these new potential buyers how to protect their Taylor instruments during air travel. Wow! Taylor Guitars understands the new handshake.

The new handshake means reaching out in a different way by understanding the culture and blending it with the new tools out there. In this book we provided you with a step-by-step formula for integrating Facebook, Twitter, LinkedIn, blogging, and much more into your sales operations. We have shown you how to use these new tools to benefit your organization. We have encouraged you to embrace the social media. The rest is up to you.

Are you willing to extend the new handshake and meet social media head on?

Postscript: Accessibility and Customer Service—When Technology Fails Us

One of the things we have said repeatedly in this book is that you should embrace the new technology. However, we would like to add a few cautions. Technology without touch can produce frustration. As salespeople you know the importance of being accessible to your customers. You understand the power of a good customer interaction. We have talked about the power of the Internet to communicate bad customer service quickly and without mercy.

In writing this book, we have discovered that some of the social media platforms are more conscious of being accessible than others. Here was our experience.

We needed to secure permission to use screen shots to illustrate certain points we made throughout this book. The screen shots helped show you, the reader, what we were talking about as we described innovative ways to use the social networks. Unfortunately, we did not always experience good customer service in our efforts to secure permission to use the screen shots.

Three companies, Digg, Delicious, and Constant Contact, did an outstanding job in reaching us and helping us secure permission to use screen shots from their platforms. In fact, each of these companies contacted us personally either by telephone or e-mail. They did all they could to help us. They win the prize when it comes to combining technology with touch.

With Twitter, we received a generic response to our request, but the response had everything in it that we needed. The touch factor was lacking, but at least we got what we wanted. We have to assume, hopefully rightly, that had we not gotten what we needed, someone would have contacted us directly. Nonetheless, Twitter came through.

Unfortunately, our experience with Facebook and LinkedIn was dismal. We managed to find whom to contact by major circuitous means. In other words, there was nothing on the site of either major social network telling us whom to contact or where to go. The generic "frequently asked questions" regarding intellectual property did not help us. Once we found the proper place, however, we went for weeks trying to communicate with the company. Facebook emailed us with forms that did not make sense based on our request—they were generic in nature. LinkedIn did not even respond to our repeated e-mail pleas. We struggled and struggled looking for ways to reach a *person*—the touch part of customer service. Finally, we heard from LinkedIn and managed to secure permission to use screen shots in this book. Unfortunately, we never heard anything from Facebook. We wanted to include a shot of the New Handshake fan page. We are certain if we had been able to talk to an individual, we could have resolved this problem in moments. Instead, weeks went by and the problem remains unresolved.

We share this experience to remind you that as you begin to implement your Social Media Sales Strategy, remember what we said early in this book. Reach out and embrace the new handshake, but do not forget the value of the old handshake. Make new friends but keep the old!

Appendix

Resource Guide

Throughout this book we have highlighted certain resources. The purpose of this book is to help you create a Social Media Sales Strategy at very little cost (with the exception of time allocation) to the company. We wish to note, however, that many companies will want to capitalize on the knowledge and skills of professionals.

The following list represents innovative companies that provide a multitude of services:

1. **Call Center Services.** Focused primarily on sales and lead generation, Call Center Services provides both inbound and outbound products to help generate and convert leads. Although originally focused on telephone services, the company now offers a wide array to services to help businesses take advantage of social media. Like the other services noted in this section, Call Center Services has adapted to the new buyer. See http://www.callcenterservices.com.
2. **Connectize.** This company focuses on real-time Sales 2.0 collaboration. The applications that the company created will help you build a social network relative to your sales operation. Connectize's role is to take the mystery out Sales 2.0, Web 2.0, and Enterprise 2.0. See http://www.connectize.com.
3. **Forrester Research.** Forrester Research is a technology and market research company. Among all the services it provides to help you understand the latest trends in buying behavior, the one most

relevant to *The New Handshake* is Social Technographics, which enables companies to profile the way customers are using the social media. See http://www.forrester.com/Research/Document/Excerpt/0,7211,42057,00.html.

4. **Green Leads.** A pay-for-performance company, Green Leads generates leads whereby clients only pay for those contacts that materialize. Connecting the dots between inbound marketing, outbound marketing, and performance, Green Leads harnesses the full potential of lead generation. One difference with Green Leads is that clients pay only for quality leads that it uncovers through a combination of inbound and outbound marketing services. See http://www.green-leads.com.

5. **Hubspot.** Launched in 2006, Hubspot's purpose was to give small to medium-sized businesses the tools they need to compete in the new digital economy. Hubspot provides inbound marketing software designed to help small businesses generate and convert leads from the Internet. The company's big emphasis is on ROI. The goal is not just to put oneself out there, but to do it in a way that produces results. Among the software options available are inbound marketing tools to help customers find you online and to convert those visits into sales. In addition to software, Hubspot provides a wide array of consultative services and advice. See http://www.hubspot.com.

6. **InsideView.** This company combines the intelligence gained from social media and traditional marketing services with the business of sales productivity. Beginning in 2005, InsideView has taken advantage of the social media to create unique sales applications to identify the new customer as well as generate leads. InsideView provides software applications to help companies make the most use of their CRMs and mobile devices. It helps aggregate and analyze relevant data to enable companies to uncover new sales opportunities. See http://www.insideview.com.

7. **Phone Works.** This professional company designs and implements innovative sales strategies by building inside sales teams and making better use of existing inside sales teams. The company uses the skills and knowledge pioneered by OracleDirect when that company created an inside sales strategy. Focusing on People, Process and Technology, Phone Works helps companies develop a strategy that will accelerate sales and increase revenues. See http://www.phoneworks.com.

8. **Sales 2.0.** Nigel Edelshain coined the term Sales 2.0 and launched the company of the same name in 2007. This company helps organizations push the envelope to create a Sales 2.0 strategy using the

social media. It provides everything from consulting and lead generation to training. The focus is on sales and increasing the selling potential of companies. Companies can choose to outsource components of the selling process or to use the services of Sales 2.0 to build a new selling strategy. See http://www.sales2.com.

9. **The Bridge Group Inc.** This company will help clients develop a productive inside sales team, with the goal to create an inside sales function that will drive greater return on investment. With a hands-on approach, The Bridge Group provides many services, including sales benchmarking, sales training, and a sales playbook. See http://www.bridgegroupinc.com.

10. **Xeesm.** This company provides an array of software solutions to help companies create a better business experience using the social media. Xeesm has software to help customers find you, to help you grow your network, and to help you build stronger relationships with the new buyers. Other software solutions connect vendors to buyers through a network to disseminate content in real time to buyers. See http://www.Xeesm.com.

Finally, you can check out both Barb and Joan's Web sites:

http://www.thenewhandshake.com
http://www.talentbuildersinc.com
http://www.totalcommunicationscoach.com

Notes

INTRODUCTION

1. David Henderson, *Media Savvy in the Internet Era* (David Henderson, 2009), 4, www.mediasavvyleader.com.

2. Robert Scoble and Shel Isreal, *Naked Conversations* (Hoboken, NJ: John Wiley & Sons, Inc., 2006).

3. Registered by Nigel Edelshain, www.sales2.com, 2007.

4. Interview with Axel Schultze, http://xeesm.com, conducted on November 24, 2009.

5. *See* http://www.customerthink.com/blog/what_is_social_selling.

6. Clay Shirky, *Here Comes Everybody* (New York: The Penguin Press, 2008), 20–21.

7. Monte Lutz, *The Social Pulpit: Barack Obama's Social Media Toolkit* (Edelman, 2009), http://www.edelman.com/image/insights/content/Social%20Pulpit%20-%20Barack%20Obamas%20Social%20Media%20Toolkit%201.09.pdf.

CHAPTER 1

1. Interview with Axel Schultze, www.Xeesm.com, November 24, 2009.

2. Walter Friedman, *Birth of a Salesman* (Cambridge, MA: Harvard University Press, 2005).

3. Ibid., 1.

4. Ibid.

5. Dale Carnegie, *How to Win Friends and Influence People* (New York: Simon & Schuster, 1937).

6. In an interview with Nigel Edelshain, July 16, 2009.

7. Tom Funk, *Web 2.0 and Beyond* (Westport, CT: Praeger Publishers, 2009).

8. Ibid., xv.

9. Interview with Nigel Edelshain, July 16, 2009.

10. Anneke Seley and Brent Holloway, *Sales 2.0: Improve Business Results Using Innovative Sales Practices and Technology* (Hoboken, NJ: John Wiley & Sons, 2008), xiii.

11. Interview with Anneke Seley, July 10, 2009.

12. Michael Port and Elizabeth Marshall, *Contrarian* (New York: John Wiley & Sons Inc., 2008).

13. Ibid., 11.

14. Interview with Tom Canning, www.contectize.com, July 8, 2009.

15. Inside Sales Experts Blog, June 16, 2009, www.blog.bridgegroupinc.com.

16. Port and Marshall, 13.

17. Interview with Axel Schultze, www.Xeesm.com, November 24, 2009.

18. Daniel Pink, *A Whole New Mind* (New York: Riverhead Books, 2005).

19. Razorfish ebook, *Fluent: The Razorfish Social Influence Marketing Report* (Razorfish, LLC, 2009), 20, http://fluent.razorfish.com/publication/?m=6540&l=1.

CHAPTER 2

1. Interview, Tom Canning, www.conectize.com, July 8, 2009.

2. Interview, Tom Canning, July 8, 2009.

3. Interview with Kathy Tito, www.callcenterservices.com, July 23, 2009.

4. Clara Shih, *The Facebook Era: Tapping Online Social Networks to Build Better Products, Reach New Audiences and Sell More Stuff* (Boston: Prentice Hall, 2009).

5. Ibid., 64.

6. Charlene Li and Josh Bernoff, *Groundswell: Winning in a World Transformed by Social Technologies* (Boston: Harvard Business Press, 2009), 70.

7. Interview, Kathy Tito, www.callcenterservices.com, July 23, 2009.

8. Interview with Marc Perramond, www.insideview.com, June 30, 2009.

9. Razorfish ebook, *Fluent: The Razorfish Social Influence Marketing Report* (Razorfish, LLC, 2009), 20, http://fluent.razorfish.com/publication/?m=6540&l=1.

10. Clay Shirky, *Here Comes Everybody* (New York: The Penguin Press, 2008), 16.

11. Joan Curtis, *Managing Sticky Situations at Work: Communication Secrets for Success in the Workplace* (Santa Barbara, CA: Praeger Press, 2009).

12. Anneke Seley and Brent Holloway, *Sales 2.0: Improve Business Results Using Innovative Sales Practices and Technology* (Hoboken, NJ: John Wiley & Sons, 2008), 31.

13. Razorfish, 9.

14. Li and Bernoff, 2009.

15. Shih, 2009.

16. Razorfish, 9.

17. Interview, Trish Bertuzzie, www.bridgegroupinc.com, July 23, 2009.

18. Malcolm Gladwell, *The Tipping Point: How Little Things Can Make a Big Difference* (Boston: Little, Brown, and Company, 2000).

19. Ibid., 4.

CHAPTER 3

1. Rick Levine, Christopher Locke, Doc Searls, and David Weinberger, *The Cluetrain Manifesto: The End of Business as Usual* (Cambridge, MA: Perseus Publishing, 2000).

2. See http://en.wikipedia.org/wiki/TheGlobe.com.

3. See http://oreilly.com/web2/archive/what-is-web-20.html.

4. Anneke Seley and Brent Holloway, *Sales 2.0: Improve Business Results Using Innovative Sales Practices and Technology* (Hoboken, NJ: John Wiley & Sons, 2008), 104.

5. Matt Bertuzzi, www.bridgegroupinc.com/blog, Inside Sales Expert Blog, "What Is Inside Sales," July 21, 2009.

6. Interview with Trish Bertuzzi, www.bridgegroupinc.com, July 22, 2009.

7. Seley and Holloway, 105.

8. Ibid., 112.

9. Interview with Anneke Seley, www.phoneworks.com, July 10, 2009.

10. Seley and Holloway, 119.

11. Ibid., 128.

12. Interview with Kathy Tito, www.callcenteredservices.com, July 23, 2009.

13. Rick Levine, Christopher Locke, Doc Searls, and David Weinberger, 75.

14. See www.Xeesm.com, "10 Reasons for Sales to Think Social Media," 4.

CHAPTER 4

1. Interview with Tom Canning, www.connectize.com, July 8, 2009.

2. Interview with Axel Schultze, www.Xeesm.com, November 24, 2009.

3. Interview with Anneke Seley, www.phoneworks.com, July 10, 2009.

4. Ibid., July 10, 2009.

5. See www.thriveamerica.com.

6. Charlene Li and Josh Bernoff, *Groundswell: Winning in a World Transformed by Social Technologies* (Boston: Harvard Business Press, 2008).

7. Ibid., 121.

8. Joel Postman, *Social Corps: Social Media Goes Corporate* (Berkeley, CA: New Riders, 2009).

9. See http://tech.yahoo.com/news/ap/20090902/ap_on_hi_te/us_fea _lifestyles_professional_tweeters.

10. See http://www.dailycomet.com/article/20090919/ARTICLES/ 909099888?Title=Tweet-for-hire-More-big-businesses-hire-tweeters.

11. Keith Eades, *The New Solution Selling: The Revolutionary Sales Process That Changes the Way People Sell* (New York: McGraw Hill Co., 2003).

12. Postman, 2009.

13. See http://econsultancy.com/blog/5083-dell-reaches-6-5m-sales-via-twitter?utm_medium=email&utm_source=topic.

14. Interview with Rick Burns, www.hubspot.com, November 16, 2009.

15. Interview with Dale Underwood, www.federalappliance.com, October 29, 2009.

16. Interview with Dale Underwood, www.echoquote.com, October 29, 2009.

17. Clay Shirky, *Here Comes Everybody: The Power of Organizing without Organizations* (New York: Penguin Press, 2008), 14.

18. Interview with Tom Canning, www.connectize.com, July 8, 2009.

CHAPTER 5

1. Interview with Rick Burns, www.hubspot.com, November 16, 2009.

2. See http://www.richardson.com/.

3. See http://img.en25.com/Web/Taleo/groundswell%20taleo.pdf.

4. Harvey Mackay, *Dig Your Well before You're Thirsty* (New York: Doubleday, 1997).

5. Ibid., 14.

6. Interview with Nigel Edelshain, July 16, 2009.

7. Clara Shih, *The Facebook Era* (Boston: Prentice Hall, 2009), 61.

8. Interview with Rick Burns, www.hubspot.com, November 16, 2009.

9. Ibid.

10. Ibid.

11. Joseph Luft and Harrington Ingham, *Of Human Interaction* (Palo Alto, CA: National Press, 1969).

12. Josh Bernoff and Charlene Li, *Groundswell: Winning in a World Transformed by Social Technologies* (Boston, MA: Harvard Business Press, 2008) 163–165.

13. See www.econsultancy.com/blog, April 2009.

14. Shih, 196.

15. *USA Weekend*, May 8–10, 2009, 10.

CHAPTER 6

1. See http://blog.comscore.com/.

2. Interview with Tom Canning, http://www.connectize.com, July 8, 2009.

3. Josh Bernoff and Charlene Li, *Groundswell: Winning in a World Transformed by Social Technologies* (Boston, MA: Harvard Business Press, 2008).

4. Bernoff and Li, 2008.

5. See http://blogs.forrester.com/groundswell/2008/10/new-2008-social.html.

6. See http://www.nielsen-online.com/.

7. Gerhard Gschwandtner, "Why We Need to Stop Selling Like We Sold in the Past," *Selling Power* (June 2009: 10).

8. Berhoff and Li, 226.

9. See http://blog.digg.com/?p=74.

10. Ibid., 25.

11. Digital Marketing Profs Conference, April 1, 2009.

12. Interview with Dale Underwood, www.echoquote.com, October 29, 2009.

CHAPTER 7

1. Kermit Pattison, "Managing Your Small Business Online Reputation," *New York Times*, July 29, 2009.

2. Interview with Dale Underwood, October 29, 2009.

3. Jeff Zabin, "The ROI on Social Media Marketing: Why It Pays to Drive Word of Mouth" (San Carlos, CA: Aberdeen Group, 2009).

4. Jeff Zabin, 8.

5. Anneke Seley and Brent Holloway, *Sales 2.0* (Hoboken, NJ: John Wiley & Sons, 2009), 64.

6. Joel Comm, *Twitter Power: How to Dominate Your Market One Tweet at a Time* (Hoboken, NJ: John Wiley & Sons Inc., 2009), 163.

7. Interview with Axel Schultze, www.xeesm.com, November 24, 2009.

8. Interview with Kyle van Hoften, May 20, 2009.

9. Interview with Anneke Seley, July 10, 2009.

10. Chris Anderson, *The Long Tail: Why the Future of Business Is Selling Less of More* (New York: Hyperion, 2006), 2.

11. Interview with Kyle van Hoften, June 18, 2009.

12. Li and Bernoff, *Groundswell* (Harvard Business Press, 2008), 10.

13. Kermit Pattison, July 21, 2009.

14. Ibid., 1.

15. Jeff Zabin, 6.

CHAPTER 8

1. Interview with Trish Bertuzzi, www.bridgegroupinc.com, July 22,2009.

2. Ibid.

3. Interview with Kyle van Hoften, June 18, 2009.

4. Jim Collins, *Good to Great: Why Some Companies Make the Leap and Others Don't* (New York: Harper Business, 2001).

5. See www.marketingcharts.com.

6. Interview with Dave Mason, 2007.

7. CJ Hayden, *Get Clients Now!* (New York: American Management Association, 2007).

8. See http://training-time.blogspot.com/2009/04/dominos-employee-video-goes-viral-is.html.

CHAPTER 9

1. Interview with Katy Tito, www.callcenterservices.com, July 23, 2009.

2. Shih, 18.

3. Interview with Kyle van Hoften, June 18, 2009.

4. Interview with Trish Bertuzzi, www.thebridgegroup.com, July 22, 2009.

5. Interview with Kathy Tito, www.callcenterservices.com, July 23, 2009.

6. Ibid.

7. Interview with Kyle van Hoften, June 18, 2009.

CHAPTER 10

1. See http://www.rushprnews.com/2009/06/30/linkedin-founder-reid-hoffman-says-massive-amounts-of-online-social-data-to-result-in-cultivation-of-highly-specialized-new-products/.

2. See www.marketingcharts.com.

3. See www.marketingcharts.com LinkedIn Users Have High Personal, Financial Success, 2009.

4. Interview with Mike Damphousse, CEO, www.Green-Leads.com 8/11/2009.

5. Ibid.

CHAPTER 11

1. Huaxia Rui, Andrew Whinston, and Elizabeth Winkler, "Follow the Tweets," *The Wall Street Journal*, November 30, 2009, The Journal Report, Business Insight.

2. Joel Comm, *Twitter Power: How to Dominate Your Market One Tweet at a Time* (Hoboken, NJ: John H. Wiley & Sons, 2009).

3. Interview with Trish Bertuzzi, www.bridgegroupinc.com, July 22, 2009.

4. Interview with Mike Damphousse, www.green-leads.com, August 11, 2009.

5. Joel Comm, xix.

6. See http://blog.iqmatrix.com/mind-map/how-to-twitter-beginners-guide-mind-map, May 2009.

7. Interview with Tom Canning, www.connectize.com, July 8, 2009.

CHAPTER 12

1. Chip Heath and Dan Heath, *Made to Stick: Why Some Ideas Survive and Others Die* (New York: Random House Publishing, 2007).

2. See http:///www.andersonanalytics.com.

CHAPTER 13

1. Julie Powell, *Julie & Julia* (New York: Little, Brown and Company, 2005).

2. Joanne Eglash, "Expanding Your World with Online Networks," *Success Magazine*, February 2009, Article 566, Channel 16.

3. Debbie Weil, *The Corporate Blogging Book: Everything You Need to Know to Get It Right* (New York: Portfolio, 2006) 7.

4. Robert Scoble and Shel Israel, *Naked Conversations: How Blogs Are Changing the Way Businesses Talk with Customers* (Hoboken, NJ: John Wiley & Sons, 2006) 52.

5. Jenna Wortham, *Wired Magazine*, http://www.wired.com/entertainment/theweb/news/2007/12/blog_anniversary.

6. Scoble and lsrael, 59.

7. Weil, 105.

8. See http://www.fastcompany.com/blog/kit-eaton/technomix/blogging-dead-long-live-journalism?partner=homepage_newsletter, October 22, 2009.

9. Andy Wibbels, *Blog Wild: A Build for Small Business Blogging* (New York: Portfolio, 2006), 50.

10. Eric Bratt, "Twitter Success Stories," *Marketing Profs*, 2009.

11. Darren Rowse, "The Future of Blogging," April, 2007, http://www.problogger.net/archives/2007/04/21/the-future-of-blogging/.

12. Ibid., 2007.

13. Inside Sales Experts Blog, Trish Bertuzzi, "You Have to Walk the Walk," August, 18, 2009.

14. Weil, 98.

15. Jennifer Leggio, http://blogs.zdnet.com.

16. Weil, 104.

17. Ibid., 98.

18. Chris Brogan, "Trust Agents on a Plane," www.chrisbrogan.com, August 24, 2009.

19. Weil, 112.

20. Hugh MacLeod, *Ignore Everybody and 39 Other Keys to Creativity* (New York: Portfolio, 2009), 143.

CHAPTER 14

1. www.wikipedia.com.

2. Interview with Trish Bertuzzi, www.bridgegroupinc.com, July 22, 2009.

3. Robert B. Cialdini, *Influence: Science and Practice, 5th Edition* (Needham Heights, MA: Allyn & Bacon, 2001) 20.

4. Tom Peters, *The Pursuit of WOW! Every Person's Guide to Topsy-Turvy Times* (New York: Vintage Books, 1994).

5. Heather Lalley, http://tech.yahoo.com/news/ap/20090902/ap_on_hi_te/us_fea_lifestyles_professional_tweeters, 9/2/2009.

6. Lalley, 9/2/2009.

7. Augie Ray, http://www.experiencetheblog.com/2009/08/eight-twitter-habits-that-may-get-you.html, 8/24/09.

CHAPTER 16

1. See http://www.whatsnextblog.com/archives/2009/11/three_top_reasons_why_social_media_is_still_a_tough_sell.asp.

2. See http://www.youtube.com/watch?v=5YGc4zOqozo&NR=1.

Index

Aberdeen Group survey, 65–66, 71

Accessibility, 181–82

Accountability of employees, 32

Account reviews, 82

Addictive nature of social media tools, 148. *See also* Time spent on social sites

"After Ten Years of Blogging, The Future Is Brighter than Ever" (Wortham), 128

Age of customers, 55

Alltop, 126

Amazon.com, 14, 15, 54, 75

Anderson, Chris, 67–68

Anderson Analytics, 98–99, 124

Anonymity, 16, 18, 128

Arnold, Bob, 33

Assessment of buyers, 163–64

Authenticity, xii

Automated direct messaging, 149, 151

Barger, Jorn, 127, 128

Battelle, John, 7, 23

beinggirl.com, 33

Benchmarking, 160–62

Bernoff, Josh, 15–16, 18, 19, 33–34, 44–45, 48–49, 50, 68

Bertuzzi, Matt, 24

Bertuzzi, Trish: on blogging, 134–35; on cold calling, 8; on LinkedIn, 38, 74–75, 76; on netiquette, 144; networking with target audience, 74–75; on time spent on social media, 19, 76, 135; on transition to Sales 2.0, 24; on Twitter, 109, 110

Best-in-class companies, 65–66

Binhammer, Richard, 38

Birthdays, 45, 107

Birth of a Salesman (Friedman), 3–5

Blind spots, 48–49

"Blogging Is Dead—Long Live Journalism" (Eaton), 130

Blogs and bloggers, 127–39; attracting readers, 135–36; automating, 149–50, 151; commenting on, 135–36; creation and evolution of, 128–32; developing interesting content, 136–39; as findable, 130; Green Leads example, 117; guest bloggers, 132; highlighted on Facebook, 94; informality of, 129; as linkable, 131, 136, 137; on LinkedIn, 101–2; micro-blogging, 111, 113; organizing Tweets and blog posts, 171–72; PDQ Shelving case study, 162–63; photos and videos on, 134, 137, 173; promoting, 151; as publishable, 130; reading about on Twitter, 109; reevaluating and reassessing goals of, 175–76; as social tools, 130–31; as syndicatable, 131; time devoted to, 134; trade show blog posts, 173; Twitter vs., 129; user statistics, 128; viral nature of, 131; Wordpress.com, 135

Blog Wild (Wibbels), 130

Bookmarking sites. *See* Social bookmarking sites

Branding: advantages of using Twitter for, 110, 113, 115; credibility of, 12; managing, 37; by salespeople, 11, 16, 177

The Bridge Group, 132, 133, 138, 185

Brogan, Chris, 128–29, 137, 138, 151

Brown, Adam, 37

B2B (business-to-business), x, 15–16

B2C (business-to-consumer), 15–16

Buckingham, Valerie, 97

Burns, Rick, 40–41, 43, 45–46

Business etiquette. *See* Netiquette

Business letters, 17

Business-to-business (B2B), x, 15–16

Business-to-consumer (B2C), 15–16

Buyers. *See* Customers

Call Center Services, 95, 183

Canning, Tom: blog, 140; on cold calling, 8; on the evolution in buying, 13, 14–15, 30, 54, 114, 126; on relationship building, 10, 41; on resistance to using online tools, 32

Carnegie, Dale, 6, 7, 11

Carroll, Dave, 180

CBS television, 48–49, 58–59

Cialdini, Robert, 143

Cline, Craig, 23

Closed networks, 50

Coca-Cola, 37, 143

Cold Calling 2.0 (Bertuzzi), 8

Cold calls, 8, 36, 176

Collaboration, 10

Collins, Jim, 5, 78–79

Comm, Joel, 66, 110, 111, 146

Company culture, 178

Complaints. *See* Customer complaints

Comscore.com, 53

The Conceptual Age, 133

"Confessions of a Corporate Tweeter" (Stephens), 49

Connectize, 183. *See also* Canning, Tom

Consistency, xii, 84

Constant Contact, 83, 181

Consultative selling, 43–51; customer relationship management (CRM), 43–46; history of, x, 9, 43–44; the Johari Window, 46–51, 47f, 95, 100

Consumer education process, 3

Contrarian (Port and Marshall), 8, 9, 10–11

Controversy, 133–34
Convenience provided by Internet, 22
The Corporate Blogging Book (Weil), 137–38
Cost savings provided by the Internet, 23
Costs of sales process, 12
Craig's List, 14
Credibility, 12, 100
CRM (customer relationship management), 43–46
Crowd-sourcing, 60–61
Cuban, Mark, ix, 30
Cultural bias versus social media tools, 31–32
Curtis, Joan, 10, 17
Customer complaints: "Confessions of a Corporate Tweeter" (Stephens), 49; Domino's Pizza video example, 84–85; listening and responding to, 16–17, 37, 49, 143, 168–69, 178; monitoring online reputations, 70; spread via word-of-mouth, 11
Customer relationship management (CRM), 43–46
Customer reviews, 14, 16, 54, 64, 70, 124
Customers: buyer assessment, 163–64; buyers buying from each other, 14; as experts, 14–15; identifying target audiences, 75–76; salespeople as potential customers, 56–57
Customer service, 181–82

Damphousse, Mike, 116–17; blogging, 116, 117, 129, 131; on Facebook, 117; LinkedIn utilized by, 99, 100, 103, 106, 116, 117; time management strategies, 117,

135; on Twitter, 109, 110, 112, 116, 117, 131, 150
Dantico, Alecia, 17
Dashboard tools, 125–26
Death of a Salesman (Miller), 64
Delicious, 122–23, 124f, 168, 181
DellOutlet, 38, 60, 113, 116
Developing the corporate mindset, 63–71; death of Sales 1.0, 64; focus on buying process versus selling, 66–67; focus on revenue strategies, 65–66; sales versus marketing, 70–71; social media adoption obstacles faced by organizations, 68–70
Diamond, Jeff, 70
Digg, 60, 122–23, 123f, 181
Digsby, 125
Dig Your Well Before You're Thirsty (Mackay), 45
Direct messages (DM), 114
Disruption, 73
Diversity within media strategies, xii
DM (direct messages), 114
Domino's Pizza, 84–85
Dot-com bubble, 21–23
Dougherty, Dale, 23–24
Doyle, Patrick, 84–85

Eades, Keith M., 38
Eaton, Kit, 130
eBay, 14
Edelshain, Nigel, 6, 7, 8, 41, 45, 184
"Eight Twitter Habits That Might Get You Unfollowed or Semi-Followed" (Ray), 148
E-mail signatures, 136
Employees. *See* Salespeople
Empowering customers, xii
Engagement, 11
Enterprise 2.0, 127
Evangelist marketing, 65

Evolution of buyers and online communication, 13–20; business to business (B2B) or business to customer (B2C), 15–17; evolution of communication online, 17–19; evolution of the new buyer, 13–15; social media tipping point, 19–20

Evolution of sales, 3–12; early history, 3–7; Sales 2.0 in the twenty-first century, 7–12

Expertise, establishing on social media tools, 14–15, 110, 138, 152–53

E-zines, 83

Facebook, 89–96; accepting invitations to, 144; accessibility and customer service, 182; acts of kindness and remembrances via, 45, 107; advertisements on, 94; building a following on, 172; continuing to grow the network, 174; creation of, 18–19, 91; dashboard tools, 125–26; disadvantages of, 94–95; fan pages, 93–94, 166–67; Green Leads example, 117; links, 149, 150; Obama's utilization of, xi; PDQ Shelving case study, 164–65, 166–67; profiles, 92, 95–96, 174–75; reevaluating and reassessing goals, 175; status updates, 92–93, 150; target audience, 91; Twitter vs., 111, 112, 114; unique features, 91–94; user statistics, 18, 30, 53, 90, 91

The Facebook Era (Shih), 45

Face-to-face interactions combined with social media tools, 36, 134

Fake customer reviews, 70

Fan pages on Facebook, 93–94, 166–67

FastLane, 47

Federal Appliance, 39–40

Feedback. See Customer complaints; Customer reviews

"Follow the Tweets" (Wall Street Journal), 109–10

Ford, Henry, 5, 6

Forrester Research, 54–55, 61, 183–84

The Forum Corporation, 143

Friedman, Walter, 3–5

Funk, Tom, 7

General Motors (GM), 47

Genius.com, 41

Gennaro, Norm, 26

Gen Y'ers, 18–19

Get Clients Now (Hayden), 84

Gladwell, Malcolm, 19–20

theGlobe.com, 21, 22

GM (General Motors), 47

Goal setting, 160–62, 175–76, 179

Godin, Seth, 137

Good to Great (Collins), 5, 78–79

Google, 61, 70, 123, 130, 136

Grant, Ulysses S., 4–5

The Great Depression, 6

Green, Richard, 50

Green Leads, 110, 113, 116–17, 184. See also Damphousse, Mike

"Groundswell Approach-Avoidance Syndrome," 44–45

Groundswell (Bernoff and Li), 33–34, 48–49, 50, 68

Gschwandtner, Gerhard, 56

Guest bloggers, 132

Harris, Rich, 133

Hayden, C. J., 84

Heath, Chip and Dan, 120

Here Comes Everybody (Shirky), xi, 17, 41

The Hidden Area, 49–50

Hitwise.com, 98
Hoffman, Reid, 97
Holistic understanding of
    customers, 38
Holland, Kevin, 134
Holloway, Brent, x, 7–8, 17–18, 24,
    36, 41, 44, 66
How to Save the World (blog),
    137–38
"How to Twitter: A Beginner's
    Guide" (Sicinski), 113
How to Win Friends and Influence
    People (Carnegie), 6, 7, 11
Hubspot, 38, 40–41, 43, 46, 184
Humor, 148
Hush Puppy shoes, 19–20

Idea exchanges, 56
Ignore Everybody (MacLeod), 138–39
IM (Instant Messaging), 26
Influence marketing, described, 65
Influence marketing (Cialdini), 143
Information management, 31–32
Ingham, Harrington, 46, 50
Innovation, xii
Inside sales, described, 24
Inside Sales Experts Blog, 132–33
InsideView, 104, 110, 113, 184
Instant Messaging (IM), 26
Insults, 152–53
Israel, Shel, ix, 48, 129–31

Jackson, Michael, 111
Jericho (television), 48–49, 58–59
The Johari Window, 46–51, 47f,
    95, 100
Julie & Julia (Powell), 127, 128

Kahlow, Aaron, 61
Kawasaki, Guy, 126
Knorr, Eric, 23
Krizelman, Todd, 21

Lalley, Heather, 17, 143, 146
"Land and expand," 36
Lead generation from social media,
    18, 80–81, 116–17, 178
Li, Charlene, 15–16, 18, 19, 33–34,
    48–49, 50, 68
Linkable blogs, 131, 136, 137
LinkedIn, 97–107; accessibility and
    customer service, 182; advantages
    of using, 98; categories of users,
    98–99; discussions, 74–75, 84,
    100, 152–53; establishing
    expertise on, 14–15, 152–53;
    Green Leads example, 116–17;
    InsideView example, 104;
    insulting others on, 152–53;
    networking with target audience,
    74–75, 76, 80–81, 83, 151–52, 174;
    open announcements on, 150–51;
    origin and evolution, 97–98; PDQ
    Shelving case study, 164–65, 167;
    polls, 59, 102, 117, 138; as
    preferred social networking tool
    for business, 53–54, 80, 97;
    profiles, 76, 105–7, 174–75;
    ratings and recommendations,
    101, 106; reevaluating and
    reassessing goals, 175;
    SlideShare, 106; Twitter versus,
    111, 112; unique features of,
    99–103; user statistics, 30, 80, 98;
    virtual demos posted on, 173
Listening posts, establishing, 163
Loyalty, 11, 56
Luft, Joseph, 46, 50
Lurking, 61
Lutz, Bob, 47

Mackay, Harvey, 45
MacLeod, Hugh, 138–39
Made to Stick (Heath and
    Heath), 120

Managing Sticky Situations at Work (Curtis), 17
Marketing, 3, 70–71
Marketing Profs, 131
Marshall, Elizabeth, 8, 9, 10–11, 67
Mason, David, 84
McAfee, Andrew, 127, 138
McCain, John, xi
Micro-blogging, 111, 113.
   See also Twitter
Microsoft, 48
Miller, Arthur, 64
Monitoring online reputations, 70
Monty, Scott, 146
MySpace, 18, 91

Naked Conversations (Scoble and Israel), ix, 48, 129–31
National Cash Register Company (NCR), 5–6, 12
Negative press. *See* Customer complaints
Netiquette, 141–54, 178–79; case examples, 151–54; described, 142–44; how to toe the netiquette line, 148–51; online networking, 145–48; self-monitoring, 145
The New Handshake blog, 139f, 185
Newsletters, 83
The New Solution Selling (Eades), 38
New York Times, 64, 70
The Nielsen Company, 56
Ning, 50

Obama, Barack, xi–xii, 15, 36
Objective setting, 159–60
Ochman, B. L., 180
On Human Interaction (Luft and Ingham), 46
Online article marketing, 82

Openness, 47, 50, 95, 121–22
Opinion Research Corporation online survey, 64
OracleDirect, 24–27, 34–35, 36, 41, 46, 78, 178, 184
O'Reilly, Tim, 7, 23

P&G (Procter & Gamble), 33–34, 83, 132–33
Paternot, Stephan, 21, 22
Patience, 36–37
Patterson, John Henry, 5–6, 12
PDQ Shelving case study, 158–80; buyer assessment, 163–64; continuing to grow the network, 174; creating a company blog, 162–63; engaging the sales team and setting objectives, 159–60; establishing a listening post, 163; establishing an online presence, 162; evaluating the social media sales strategy, 177–78; expand and access, 167–68; Facebook, 172; fan pages on Facebook, 166–67; getting started, 158–59; getting upper management support, 160; increasing followings on social media sites, 165–66; individual brand assessment and sales strengths, 177; joining social media sites, 164–65; keeping up with the technology, 173–74; key steps taken by, 171; lead generation from social media, 176; LinkedIn, 167; listening and responding, 168–69; organizing Tweets and blog posts, 171–72; reevaluating and reassessing goals, 175–76, 179; research and benchmarking, 160–62; staff training, 177; tagging information through the social media, 176;

time management, 179; trade
shows, 172–73; updating profiles,
174–75; virtual demos, 173;
YouTube, 173
Pelosi, Emily, 71
People, Purpose, Plan, and
Technology (PPPT), 33–36, 44
People (3Ps: Purpose, plan, people),
78–84
Perramond, Marc, 16, 99–100, 104,
110, 111–12
Peters, Tom, 143
Phone Works, 184
Photographs, 85, 92, 94–95, 97, 105,
114, 115, 137
Ping.fm, 126
Pink, Daniel, 10, 133
Planning, 5
Plan (3Ps: Purpose, plan, people),
76–78
Plouffe, David, xii
Pollard, David, 137–38
Polls, 59, 102, 117, 138, 151
Port, Michael, 8, 9, 10–11, 67
Postman, Joel, 37, 38
Powell, Julie, 127, 128
PowerPoint SlideShare
shows, 173
PPPT (People, Purpose, Plan,
and Technology), 33–36, 44
Prager, Dr. Iris, 33
Prance, Jason, 33
Pricing information, 65
Privacy issues, 95, 97–98
Private versus public messaging
options, 149, 150
Proactive versus reactive sales, xiii,
30, 67
Procter & Gamble (P&G), 33–34, 83,
132–33
Profiles, 92, 95–96, 105–7, 114–16,
174–75

Publicly thanking others, 150
Public versus private messaging,
149, 150
Publishable blogs, 130
Purpose, plan, people (3Ps), 73–85;
Domino's Pizza example, 84–85;
people, 78–84; plan, 76–78;
purpose, 74–76
The Pursuit of WOW (Peters), 143

Quality-plus-quantity-equals-access
phenomenon, 18, 80–81

Rating social media readiness, 69
Ray, Augie, 148
Razorfish Social Influence
Marketing Survey, 12, 16,
18, 19
Reactive versus proactive sales, xiii,
30, 67
Reciprocity, 143
Referral networks, 56–57, 65
Relationships, x, 45, 46, 67, 107
Repetition, xii
Research and benchmarking,
160–62
Resistance to using social media
tools, 30–32, 36, 64, 84
Return on investment (ROI),
38–41, 160
Re-tweets (RT), 114
Reviews by customers, 14, 16, 54,
64, 70, 124
Richardson, Linda, 9, 43–44
Robert Wisdom Web site, 128
ROI (return on investment),
38–41, 160
Rose, Kevin, 60
Rowse, Darren, 132
RSS feeds, 131
RT (re-tweets), 114, 115
Russell, Karen, 110

Sales (overview): cycles, 114; defined, 3; early history of transactional sales, 3; marketing versus sales, 70–71; Sales 2.0, described, ix–xv, 6, 7–8

Salespeople: active employee involvement in customer acquisition, retention, and loyalty strategies, 56–57; branding by, 11, 16, 177; employee accountability, 32; monitoring sales teams' posts, 82; opportunities lost in current accounts, 79–85; as potential customers and referral partners, 56–57; selecting sales teams, 5; Social Media Sales Plan executed by, 78–84; staff training, 78–79, 159–60, 177

Sales 2.0 (company), 184–85

Sales 2.0 (Seley and Holloway), 7–8, 17–18, 24, 34–35, 36, 44, 46, 134. *See also* Seley, Anneke

Schmidt, Warren, 57

Schultze, Axel, ix, 3, 10, 31, 66–67

Scoble, Robert, ix, 48, 129–31

Seagate, 138

Search engines, 122, 136. *See also* Google

Seesmic Desktops, 125

Selecting sales teams, 5

Seley, Anneke: on employee accountability, 32; on essence of Sales 2.0, 7–8; on the evolution in buying, x, 9–10, 12, 13, 17–18, 36; on face-to-face interactions, 134; OracleDirect story, 24–27, 34–35, 36, 46; on proactive salespeople, 67; on revenue from Sales 2.0 strategies, 41, 66; three-prong social media approach, 44; "Transforming a Sales Organization," 31

Self-promotion, 142–43, 151–52

Shih, Clara, 15, 18, 45, 46, 50, 56–57, 91

Shirky, Clay, xi, 17, 41

Sicinski, Alan, 113

SlideShare, 106

Small businesses, 40–41, 70

Smarketing, x, 110

Smashmouth Marketing, 117

Social bookmarking sites, 119–26; dashboard tools, 125–26; Delicious, 122–23, 124f, 168, 181; Digg, 60, 122, 123f, 181; overview, 119–21; PDQ Shelving case study, 168, 176; StumbleUpon, 123–25

SocialCorp (Postman), 37

Social Media Sales Challenge, 157–80; blogs, 162–63; buyer assessment, 163–64; expand and access, 167–68, 174; Facebook, 166–67, 172; getting started, 158–60, 162, 164–65; increasing followings on social media sites, 165–66; individual brand assessment and sales strengths, 177; keeping up with the technology, 173–74; lead generation from social media, 176; LinkedIn, 167; listening and responding, 163, 168–69; overall analysis of the 30-day challenge, 178–79; profiles, 174–75; reevaluating and reassessing goals, 175–76, 177–78, 179; research and benchmarking, 160–62; staff training, 159–60, 177; tagging information through the social media, 176; time management, 179; trade shows, 172–73; Twitter, 171–72; virtual demos, 173; YouTube, 173

Social selling, described, x, 10, 67
Social Technographics® profile tool, 54–55, 61
Solution selling, 6
Spam, 151
Staff training, 78–79, 159–60, 177
Status updates, 92–93, 150
Stephens, Guy, 49
StopAutoDM.com, 149
StumbleUpon, 123–25
Swartz, Jonathan, 128
Syndicatable blogs, 131
Synergy, 60–61

T&S (Tannenbaum and Schmidt) Leadership Model, 57–61
Tagging information, 176
Tannenbaum and Schmidt (T&S) Leadership Model, 57–61
Target audiences, 75–76, 80
Taylor Guitars, 180
Technorati, 128, 130
Telephone calls, 8, 17, 36, 176
30-Day Challenge. *See* Social Media Sales Challenge
Thrive America, 33
Time spent on social sites, 19, 32, 119–20, 124, 134, 148, 179
Tipping Point (Gladwell), 19–20
Tito, Kathy, 15, 16, 26, 30, 90, 95, 129
Trade shows, 172–73
Training staff, 78–79, 159–60, 177
TrainingTime blog, 85
"Transforming a Sales Organization" (Seley), 31
Transparency, 16, 133
Trust, 12, 46, 100
Trust Agents (Brogan), 137
Twain, Mark, 4–5
TweetDeck, 125, 166
TweetLater, 148

Twitter, 109–18; #followfriday, 150; accessibility and customer service, 181–82; advantages of using, 109–10; automatic Tweets, 149–50, 151; blogging and, 109, 129, 131; continuing to grow the network, 174; creation and evolution of, 111; dashboard tools, 125–26; direct messages (DM), 114; establishing expertise on, 110; Facebook and LinkedIn versus, 111, 112, 114; Green Leads example, 116–17; InsideView example, 104; links, 149, 150; monitoring sales teams' posts, 82; as most time-sensitive social media tool, 113–14; organizing Tweets, 171–72; PDQ Shelving case study, 165–66; polls, 151; private versus public messaging options, 149, 150; profiles, 114–16, 174–75; reevaluating and reassessing goals, 175; responding to negative Tweets, 168–69; re-tweets (RT), 114, 115; spam, 151; Technorati, 130; TweetDeck, 125, 166; Tweeting during trade shows, 172–73; unique features of, 111–14; user reputations, 66; user statistics, 30, 111
"Twitter for Hire. More Businesses Hire Tweeters" (Lalley), 143, 146
Twitter Karma, 112
Twitter Power (Comm), 146
"The 2008 Social Technographics Data Reveal Rapid Adoption" (blog post), 55

Underwood, Dale, 39–40, 41, 61, 65
"United Breaks Guitars" (Carroll), 180

The Unknown Area, 50–51
Upper management, 160

van Hoften, Kyle, 67, 68, 93, 96, 149
Video blogs, 134, 137
Viral nature of social media, 65, 131.
  See also Word-of-mouth
Visibility, 59, 161

Wales, Jimmy, 60
Wall Street Journal, 109–10
WebEx, 41
Weblogs, 127. *See also* Blogs and
  bloggers
Webster, Charles, 4–5
Web 2.0, 7, 23–24
Web 2.0 and Beyond (Funk), 7
Weil, Debbie, 128, 129, 133, 134, 136
"What Is Social Selling" (Schultze), x
A Whole New Mind (Pink), 10

Wibbels, Andy, 130
Wikipedia, 60–61, 145
Wikis, 56
Wilson, Woodrow, 4
Winfrey, Oprah, 50
Woods, Tiger, 67
Word-of-mouth: customer com-
  plaints spread via, 11; marketing
  by best-in-class companies, 65–66;
  social media tools versus, xi; viral
  nature of social media, 65, 131
Wordpress.com, 135
World Salesmanship Congress
  (1916), 4, 6
Wortham, Jenna, 128

Xeequa, 185
XeeSM, 125

YouTube, 84–85, 134, 173

About the Authors

JOAN C. CURTIS is chief executive officer of Total Communications Coaching, where she is an ICF-certified coach and nationally known speaker. Dr. Curtis is the author of *Managing Sticky Situations at Work* and *Strategic Interviewing*. She has won numerous awards for her writing and speaking abilities.

BARBARA GIAMANCO is chief executive officer of Talent Builders and an experienced sales strategist, consultant, and speaker who has a proven track record for generating sales. She capped a corporate career at Microsoft, where she led sales teams and coached executives. She has received numerous leadership and sales awards.